The Lion
of St Mark

The Lion of St Mark

Aubrey Feist

Venice: The Story of a City from Attila to Napoleon

The Bobbs-Merrill Company, Inc.
Indianapolis / New York

The Bobbs-Merrill Company, Inc.
A Subsidiary of Howard W. Sams & Co., Inc.
Publishers: Indianapolis / Kansas City / New York

For Kay

Contents

She was a maiden City, bright and free;
No guile seduced, no force could violate;
And, when she took unto herself a mate,
She must espouse the everlasting Sea.

William Wordsworth

The Lion
of St Mark

1. The Forerunners

Flight to the Islands
The Imperial City
Rialto
The Return of St Mark

The story of Venice really begins with the eruption of the Tartar hordes from the steppes and deserts of Central Asia. What strange forces motivated that mass-migration we shall never know; but, like slow streams of devouring lava, wave after wave of flat-faced savages with sallow skins and slanting eyes began riding towards the west. Squat, shapeless bundles in filthy sheepskin caps, they were mounted on shaggy little ponies—stirrupless, hunched over the saddle, their bridles decked with scalps and on their hips the short Tartar bow. The Hi-ung-nu were on the move again, that branch of the Mongol race now known as the Huns. Their ancestors had wasted their strength against the Great Wall of China. But now an irresistible impulse drove them towards the setting sun; and, like some sacred ark, they carried with them their god, a naked sword—a magic blade which they believed gave them power over the spirit of Death.

As it had been with the Children of Israel during their wanderings in the wilderness, that march of myriads of nomads with their families, their wagons, their flocks and herds took many years. Skirting the Caspian, the hordes slowly surged across southern Russia; the plains of modern Poland and Hungary were black with their circular yurts, or tents, and with the immense herds which provided them with their meat and fermented mare's-milk. Led by their khan Attila, the Scourge of God, whose boast it was that no grass grew where his horse's hoofs had fallen, they crossed the Danube and the Rhine, leaving behind them a scorched and blackened land where the nights were red with fire and where the only crops were lines of crosses hung with meals for kites and crows. For the sword-god lusted for slaughter and tribute was paid to him in blood and pyramids of skulls.

On they drove in their teeming thousands, absorbing or driving before them those barbarian tribes which time was to mould into the nations of Europe: Goths, Vandals, Franks, Herulians, Avars, Lombards and others. It may well be that this steady, unceasing pressure from east to west across a whole continent was one of the factors that made the Saxons and Jutes of the far west decide that the time had come to cross the sea into Britain.

The Roman Empire, in its death-throes, roused itself for one final feat of arms. In A.D. 451 on the plain of Champagne, about five miles from Chalons, Attila's way was barred by the legions of Aetius and his allies, the Christian Visigoths. It was a desperate stand. But the Huns were defeated in one of the bloodiest battles in history and Europe was saved from domination by the hordes of Tartary.

Slowly and sullenly the Huns fell back, but that one effort had exhausted the dying Empire's power of resistance. For some reason Aetius did not follow up his advantage; and next year the Huns, turned back from Rome itself by the faith and courage of St Leo, swept like a plague along the northern shores of the Adriatic. Soon the once-prosperous province of Venetia lay desolate—a blackened waste where wild beasts prowled among the ruins. On the coast of what is now the Gulf of Venice, cities like Padua, Aquileia and Altinum were sacked. But not all the inhabitants died on the walls or in the inferno of the streets. At first sight of the distant line of fires which was the herald of the Hun, many had sought temporary refuge on the islands of the lagoons which fringe the northwest corner of the Adriatic. It was better to live like sea birds among the mudbanks and marshes of those huge saltwater lakes than trust to the mercy of Attila, whose delight was to destroy.

This was only one of many flights from the mainland, and when the Huns finally withdrew into the wilds of Pannonia there were other barbarians to take their place—fierce tribes of Teutons driven from their homes and almost as ruthless. As each new tide of invasion ebbed, the emigrants returned to their ruined cities. But this could not go on forever; and when, in 568, the Langobards (Longbeards), or Lombards, came rampaging into Venetia, many of its harassed inhabitants decided to make their permanent home on the islands, protected on the seaward side by the long sand reefs of the Lido and only accessible by secret channels through the shallow water.

Those troubled centuries of the Dark Ages were a time for saints, martyrs and miracles. Things appeared larger than life, as in a vision of the Apocalypse. A strangely shaped cloud could be interpreted as a warning or an omen; horns blowing in the mist became the voices of angels or demons. Heaven seemed very near in those days and Hell could be seen in any town which had suffered the horrors of the sack. Men were more credulous. But although their religion sometimes lapsed into superstition, it was their comfort and their shield. We may call this the Age of Darkness, but it was also the Age of Faith.

The story was told and believed that to the ancient town of Altinum was vouchsafed a sign from God. It was said that, as warning that there must be an exodus, all the birds in the towers took flight, carrying their young in their beaks. Terrified by this portent, some of the townspeople fled to Ravenna and some to Istria and elsewhere. But Bishop Paulus was by no means certain that this was the Divine Will. He waited for further instructions and before long he received them.

In our modern wisdom we may smile at the idea of fledglings being carried in their mothers' beaks like kittens. But there is another kind of miracle when something quite ordinary happens at the very moment when its influence will be most potent. Surely it may have been an Act of God which one night induced Bishop Paulus to climb to the top of the highest tower and suddenly realize that the stars in the sky looked just like the islands in the lagoon.

Now, at last, the good Bishop knew what had been ordained; so after public prayer and fasting, he led his people across the water to the island of Torcello, carrying with them not only their goods and chattels, but the sacred relics from their churches and some of the very stones of Altinum. There, in that strange enchanted region of mist and light and opal distances, where the salt wind blows from the Adriatic and the distant northern horizon is the jagged blue line of the Alps, they built a town which has almost disappeared, a noble cathedral and a church which can be seen to this day. The modern Torcello is a pathetic place with hardly a sign of its past grandeur. It is a ghost town, lost in the lagoon. But it has been called the Mother of Venice.

In all, there were twelve of these lagoon townships and islands: Grado, where the Bishop of Aquileia was installed, Bibone, Caorle, Jesolo, Heraclea, Torcello, Murano, Rivo Alto, Malamocco, Poveglia, Chioggia and Sottomarina. In fifteen hundred years they have lost their importance. Some have been deserted. One, at least, was swallowed up by the sea. But in those dawn years the little communities of refugees soon developed great skill as sailors and fishermen, learning the lore of the sea from descendants of the earlier fugitives and from such of the aboriginal islanders as had not been dispossessed. They became traders too, for they had one commodity at hand in almost unlimited quantities—salt. This, with salt fish, they bartered up and down the coast and along the estuaries. These forerunners of the Venetians were nothing if not enterprising. Using the rivers and canals, they penetrated into the heart of Italy, no doubt driving those hard bargains for which their descendants were to become notorious.

They began to make longer voyages in larger ships; and gradually those shrewd, forceful islanders with their plain stone churches and thatched houses among the reeds, acquired a certain importance beyond the sandbanks and still waters. Torcello was their commercial capital—when commerce became possible—and first Heraclea and then Malamocco became the centre of such government as existed among them. But all this was not to be for many years. Federation was a slow process. To all intents and purposes the twelve settlements were separate republics which found nothing more difficult than to combine for their mutual benefit. But deep down in the grass roots something was stirring. The first patron of maritime Venetia was St Theodore and, invoking his aid and blessing, a few wise and ambitious men began to dream of something better—even, perhaps, of a vague future as an independent community. But they needed a strong friend to protect them while they were still weak and undeveloped. And as St Theodore of Pontus was one of the three soldier saints of the East, it was only to be expected that help would come from that direction.

In those Dark Ages, when the western world was a jungle of warring tribes and embryo nations, slowly emerging from chaos and struggling for survival, there was one great city which was still the heart and core of a mighty empire. Constantinople. The ancient Byzantium. When the Roman Empire was finally divided into East and West, Rome itself was doomed to be overwhelmed by the Goths and the Vandals; but the Eastern, Greek, or Byzantine Empire became the wonder of the world. Even the Huns had retired, baffled by the colossal walls of its capital. Within their twelve-mile circuit, art, learning and medicine still flourished; in fourteen churches priests still practised the offices of religion; and its Roman laws, later codified by the Emperor Justinian, became the basis of all European legal systems except the English.

In the streets of Constantinople a man could walk unarmed and unmolested; and to its magnificent harbour, the Golden Horn, came all the trade of the Levant. But—and more important for our purpose—the key to the history of Venice is to be found in that city on the Bosphorus. Together their names come echoing down the centuries like a recurring theme. First they were patron and dependent, then equals, then rivals, then bitter enemies. The threads of their destinies crossed and recrossed, entwining, straining apart, till in the end they snapped. Then the downfall of Byzantium was the proximate cause of the downfall of the Venetian Republic two and a half centuries later. There are few sequences of events which fit so neatly into a pattern. So if one would follow the fortunes of Venice— it is necessary first to consider Constantinople.

That glorious city of white and gold, with its palaces, domes, porticos, and gardens, its statues, obelisks, and cypress groves, rose tier upon tier—on seven hills, like Rome—above the deep blue of the Sea of Marmora. It was the link between Europe and Asia, an island in an ocean of savagery, where the flame of civilisation was kept burning behind strong ramparts.

The Byzantine Greeks were not warlike but they were formidable antagonists, for they relied for success on clever tactics and a close study of the art of war. Scientifically minded, on a campaign they had only one object: to win (as they usually did) with the least possible loss to themselves. For the musclebound heroes of western folklore they had no use at all. To them, war was a contest of wits, not a glorious but dangerous game. At the peak of their efficiency, their highly disciplined and uniformed armies, consisting mainly of mercenaries, were accompanied in the field by supply wagons, engineers, and medical units, though not for another hundred years were they to discover the weapon on which for a long time they held the monopoly, the terrible Greek Fire. This was an inflammable mixture discharged through tubes or hurled by hand or catapult in earthenware containers. The secret of this liquid fire has been lost, but it could wrap ships or scaling-ladders in sheets of flame, and water would not put it out. "To spread like wildfire" is no mere figure of speech.

The imperial armies were victorious because, in a world of warriors, they could produce trained soldiers. Later these people degenerated and paid the inevitable penalty. But although their name became a synonym for cowardice and treachery, it should be remembered that they held the gates of Christendom for a thousand years. Nor should it be forgotten that they held out the hand of friendship to an obscure little group of islanders off the shore of the Adriatic—fishermen, salt-gatherers and traders. The rulers of Constantinople, taking their ease in the Bucoleon Palace or watching the chariots race in the Hippodrome, were not to know that they had taken the first step towards the destruction of their empire.

In Justinian's reign, Belisarius made use of the islanders' ships in his victorious war against the Goths; and Narses, an aged eunuch but a brilliant commander, sought the aid of the lagoon townships in transporting his army from Grado to the siege of Ravenna which, governed by exarchs appointed by the Emperor in Constantinople, was soon to become the centre of imperial rule in Italy.

As a reward for their services, the people of the islands received signal marks of the general's favour. Angered by their high-handed assertion that the islands and river-mouths belonged to those who put them to the best use, the Paduans asked Narses to restore their own rights over the estuary of the Brents. But he refused to intervene, and thus the islanders established their independence of the mainland. It was an important step forward. In due course, in return for quite substantial trading rights and privileges, they made a formal act of submission to the Emperor, though they took very good care that it should not be upon oath.

The years passed—terrible years of suffering and violence, which must have seemed like an endless nightmare to those who had the misfortune to live through them. But, for all the horror and confusion, something very great was being born in that cluster of insignificant townships which as yet had nothing in common except a legacy of hatred and fear, and a growing but unconscious urge to carve out their own future, free from the trammels of both Pope and Emperor.

These early centuries of faction and bloodshed are, and will remain, a mystery. Nobody really knows what happened. Authorities even differ about quite important dates. One can only conjecture, basing one's reasoning on legends and on such scanty chronicles as have survived. The truth is hidden in the mists of the past, just as, in winter, the sea-fogs veil the islands of the lagoons.

Of the sixth-century island townships, Cassiodorus, monk, statesman, and historian, in the service of Theodoric, King of the Ostrogoths, wrote: "They have a soil which is always abundant—the waters, namely, which are full of fish. The poor and the rich there live on equal terms; the same soil and the same humble habitations serving for all. No one can therefore envy another; by avoiding this vice they avoid all the causes of discord which disturb the world."

Unfortunately this was not true. If ever there had been equality among the settlers it had not lasted for long, while discord had become the normal state of their existence. In the lonely expanse of those quiet waters, life was short and life was cheap. Feuds begun years before on the mainland flared up and were fought out by new generations of amphibious warriors, and many a savage skirmish took place among the osier-beds and the shallows. There had been some attempt to bring law and order and to curb this internecine warfare. Soon after the flight from the Huns, twelve Tribunes had been elected—one from each settlement. But this only led to further jealousy and dissension. Therefore, at the time of Alboin's Lombard invasion, an inner circle was formed of twelve other Senior Tribunes:

Tribuni Maiores. Theoretically, election of the tribunes was subject to the Emperor's veto, but Constantinople was far away and the imperial yoke hung lightly on the men of the lagoons.

The turmoil and the strife continued. Towards the end of the seventh century there was a major crisis. In 697, the Patriarch of Grado called a meeting in Heraclea. He proposed that the Tribunes should be abolished and that all the separate republics of maritime Venetia should be united under one leader or Doge. His proposal was agreed to: a momentous decision. The first Doge to be elected was Pauluccio Anafesto and his *Dogado* consisted of the twelve townships. In due course, his election was ratified by the Emperor; and the very use of the word Doge proclaims his allegiance, for this was the title borne by the governors of the Italian provinces of the Empire.

In days to come, the Doge's powers became so circumscribed and curtailed that he was little more than a puppet in the hands of his councillors. But in the beginning, within their limited sphere, the Doges' authority was absolute. They possessed great influence in ecclesiastical affairs, and serving under them were Masters of the Forces who controlled the armed levies. Small wonder then that they tried to make the Dogeship hereditary, an issue which was to be the cause of civil strife for centuries.

The history of the earliest Doges is obscure, an unedifying welter of bloodshed about which little is certain except the sheer horror of the times. From out of that distant dawn comes the faint echo of names—Marcello, Deodato, Galla Gaulo: Doges who lived and sinned and died and have been all but forgotten. Three successive Doges were deposed and blinded, another was murdered, and again and again the little townships of thatched houses among the reeds were the scene of ferocious street fights. Rome, in her decadence, had much to answer for when she forgot her skill at arms and allowed the Pax Romana to lapse into barbarism.

But a new Europe was germinating, even in the lonely lagoons. With the growing importance of the twelve towns and their increase in wealth and trade, it became clear that the islanders would have to make a choice. On the one hand lay Constantinople and the Eastern Empire; on the other, new competitors for power—the Frankish kingdoms of the West. Broadly speaking, the Doge and the aristocracy (descendants of the ancient noble families of Venetia) favoured the Byzantine connection, while the democratic party supported the Church of Rome and the Franks, who were the champions of that Church. In the end, their old desire for freedom became their dominating purpose and they were bold enough to stand alone, independent of both East and West.

It was during this confusing period between the election of the first Doge and war with the Franks that another important step forward was taken. Dimly it was beginning to be realized that in unity lay strength and that, out of all the townships, one should become the capital of a single community. This led to fresh quarrels, with various factions arguing the rival claims of Heraclea, favoured by the aristocratic party, and Jessolo, which was the choice of the Church and the democrats. At last a compromise was reached. Neither was chosen. Instead, the seat of government was fixed at Malamocco—not the present little fishing town but an island which long ago disappeared beneath the sea and the exact location of which the experts are still arguing.

The growing-pains of the young Venetian Republic continued. Old wrongs gave place to new ones; friends became enemies; and enmity became even more savage as yet another schism came near to destroying the community. Matters came to a head when Emperor Leo the Isurian quarrelled bitterly with the Pope about the question of images, and a theological dispute between two Christian leaders ended in an appeal to arms. The Pope asked Luitbrand, King of the Lombards, for help. Luitbrand promptly attacked Ravenna and expelled the Exarch, who fled for safety to the lagoons and remained there until he was restored to power by a Byzantine army and a force of islanders led by Doge Orso Ipato.

But soon the Pope realized that his new allies were becoming dangerous, for the Lombard horsemen had begun to occupy Papal territory. Was this the thin end of the wedge? The Pontiff thought it wiser to play for safety by appealing to another branch of the Teutonic race which had just risen to power in the West. Ever since his resounding victory over the Saracens (the name given in early times to all Moslems—in this case, the Arabs) at Tours, all Christendom had rung with the name of Charles Martel—Charles the Hammer. It was to the Franks then that the Pope called for help, and they did not fail him. After being crowned King of Italy, Pepin the Short, son of Charles Martel, marched into the country with his mail-clad horsemen and captured Ravenna, which he presented to the Pope—retaining, however, the feudal suzerainty. A few years later, Deside-rius, last King of the Lombards, tried to regain the city, but Pepin's son Charlemagne invaded Italy and destroyed the kingdom of the Lombards once and for all.

On Christmas Day, in the year 800, Charlemagne was crowned in Rome and founded the Holy Roman Empire in an unsuccessful attempt to revive the temporal power of the Caesars. Charlemagne confirmed his father's gift of Ravenna to the Pope, and in revenge for help given by the islanders to the Exarch, he demanded that Papal forces should drive them from the Pentapolis* while his son—another Pepin, now crowned King of Italy—began shipbuilding in preparation for an attack on the lagoons.

On the whole, the reaction in the lagoon townships was a swing towards Byzantium, led by the Doge of the time, Giovanni Galbaio, who, as was often the case in those early years, had taken his son Maurizio to be associated with him in the Dogeship. But the Pope and King Pepin had a strong following too. The Patriarch of Grado, knowing that Pepin was building a great fleet at Ravenna, proposed an alliance with the all-conquering Franks. This was bitterly resented by the two Doges, who went to the length of sending ships to attack Grado. There was severe street fighting in which the Patriarch was wounded and captured. Regardless of his sacred office—for these were times of blood and iron—the Patriarch was dragged to the top of the highest tower and hurled to his death. So the die was cast. That Pepin the Frank would try to avenge his martyrdom was inevitable.

It was now, threatened by King Pepin's fleet, that the islanders found their seat of government at Malamocco too vulnerable. When the fugitives from Roman Venetia first emigrated to the islands, it had been to escape enemies who were advancing on them by land. Now, however, the danger came from the sea; from Grado in the north to Chioggia in the south, townships on the long string of sand-banks were open to assault. After long discussion, therefore, it was

---

* The five Italian cities ruled by the Exarch or Governor of Ravenna: Rimini, Pesaro, Fano, Sinigaglia, and Ancona.

decided to concentrate on Rivo Alto (Rialto)—a cluster of islands and islets in the very heart of the lagoon, midway between the mainland and the long low line of the *lidi*. From that final retreat in 809 dates the real foundation of the Republic of Venice—a little republic which was to rise to greatness, become a world power, decline and fall.

So, with wisdom and foresight, the islanders fell back to an almost impregnable position, where two and a half miles of dangerously shallow water and dark, tangled shoals of seaweed separated them from the land, and where hostile ships would have to negotiate the narrow channels between the sand-banks. The *bricole* or stakes which marked those deep-water channels had, of course, been removed.

It was during the attack by the Franks that there occurred the curious incident of the Old Woman. Among several versions of the legend, which doubtless has some basis of truth, the simplest seems the least likely to have been embroidered.

This version has it that Pepin's men captured Chioggia; then, their numbers already decreased by malaria, they advanced northwards along the Lido. After overcoming stubborn resistance, clearing channels blocked by the yards of ships, and fighting off archers who greeted them with a hail of arrows, the Franks swarmed ashore at Malamocco—heavy yellow-haired men in mail or scale-armour, carrying javelins, shields, and huge clumsy broadswords. They stormed through the capital of maritime Venetia to find the place virtually deserted. Just one old woman had been left behind—the *poverina* of heroic legend. Quietly she awaited the fierce northern warriors. It may have been that she was too frail or too ill to flee with her friends. It may have been that she was a heroine who sacrificed herself to deceive the enemy. No one will ever know.

We may be sure that the Franks had their own methods of extracting information, but on this occasion they seemed not to have found it necessary to use them. The old lady "talked." From her they learned that the Venetians had retreated to Rialto. They asked directions for bringing their ships across the treacherous lagoon. The tide was out but there were channels, she told them. Where? *"Sempre diritto!"* she replied.

So King Pepin's ships set sail from Malamocco, only to founder and run aground on hidden sandbanks and odorous mud flats. And there, while they lay helpless, the Venetians counterattacked, secure in their knowledge of the shoals and waterways. Above the mew of the sea birds and the quiet splash of oars, angry cries were heard as the first Frankish craft ran aground in the mud and seaweed. Then came the whine and swish of arrows shot by bowmen hidden among the reeds—confusion—screaming—the shouting of contradictory orders, followed by the lowing of war horns as, looming slowly out of the mist, the coloured sails of Venetian ships came bearing down through the deep channels. The Franks were slaughtered: thousands were cut down, shot full of arrows, drowned or suffocated in the mud. There is still a Canale Orfano or Canal of the Orphans to mark the spot where many of them died.

What happened to the old woman, history does not record.

The first Doge to rule in Rialto was Agnello Partecipazio. He had two sons, Guistinian and Giovanni. As we have seen, in those early days it was not unusual for a brother or a son to be associated with the Dogeship, and Giovanni found himself sharing the throne with his father. Unfortunately, he was the younger brother and this may have caused the trouble. At the time of his elevation, Guistinian was far away at the imperial court and there is some reason to suspect that he was jealous of Giovanni. This may have been why, when he returned to Venice, he retired to live a semi-cloistered life in a religious community attached to the church of San Servolo. His retirement may have been a prudent precaution. Jealous aspirants to power and honours had been known to receive short shrift, and he knew that in the care of Holy Church he would be safe.

At the same time, it may well be true that he was right to suspect his brother Giovanni's loyalty to the Emperor, and it is more than a possibility that in the peaceful cloisters on the island of San Servolo were born those rumours which were to topple the Doge's younger son from the throne. When it came to light that Giovanni's sympathies were with the West, he was deposed and banished to Zara, in Dalmatia. Then, after he had escaped to the court of King Louis I, pressure was brought to bear and he was expelled from France and despatched to Constantinople, where the very efficient imperial spies could keep this francophile under observation. Meanwhile, the saintly

Guistinian, meek but triumphant, came forth from his cloister to share the Dogeship with his father and to succeed him when Agnello died in 827.

Guistinian was not an outstanding personality and his reign made little impact on history, but in 829 occurred the one event for which it will always be remembered. Inspired perhaps by memories of conversations at San Servolo, the Doge had an idea for which he could hardly have taken credit publicly. Perhaps he did no more than drop a hint or talk vaguely of rewards. But it is difficult to avoid the suspicion that Guistinian Partecipazio, Doge of Venice, was the power behind a very audacious and successful theft.

This was the heyday of the Saracens. It is true that nearly a century had passed since Charles Martel routed them at Tours and saved Western Europe from Islam. But the great Caliph of Bagdad, Haroun al-Raschid, had been dead for only twenty years and the Arab tide was still in flood in the Levant and all along the coast of North Africa. Christian traders in the Mediterranean were increasingly menaced by Moslem corsairs, and in Spain the Emirs of Cordova were battling for the Peninsula.

In conquered cities the Arab rule was just and tolerant, but Christian churches were being robbed of their treasures. And there was one relic which the Venetians held in special veneration. In Alexandria, the church of St Mark, rich in gold and gems and precious marble ripe for the looting, enshrined the mummified body of St Mark the Evangelist, who is said to have been martyred there in the reign of the Emperor Trajan. According to legend, it was St Mark who founded the church of Aquileia and who, on these very islands of Rialto, had once talked with an angel. "Peace be to thee, Mark," the heavenly visitant had said. "Here shall thy body rest."

Clearly there was very real danger of the relic being destroyed by the infidels, whereas if it was safe in Venice it would be honoured by all men and bring everlasting glory to the Republic which had given it shelter. Such thoughts, bred of monkish gossip and travellers' tales, must have occurred many times to the devout Guistinian. It seemed an opportunity too good to be missed. So not long afterwards there arrived in Alexandria two Venetian travellers, Rustico of Torcello and Buono of Malamocco. They must have possessed most eloquent tongues or an ample supply of "palm oil," for they persuaded a monk named Staurizius and one Theodore, a priest, to aid and abet them in stealing the body of the Evangelist. All that is known for certain is that, with the help of these accomplices, St Mark's body was smuggled out of his church in a barrel of pickled pork, which is abhorrent to all good followers of the Prophet. There were horrified cries of *"Khanzir!"* from the Arabs at the sight of this unclean swine's flesh but not one of them lingered long enough to discover what was hidden beneath it. The precious cargo was carried on board their ship by Rustico and Buono and, after a rough passage, was brought safely to the new capital of the Republic. On the thirty-first of January, 829, they cast anchor at Rialto. Men and women prayed, priests chanted, and acolytes swung their censers, as the ancient prophecy was fulfilled and the Evangelist came to rest at last in the heart of the lagoon. Adjoining the palace begun by Doge Agnello Partecipazio, the foundations of the church which was to become famous throughout the world were laid by his son. It was built to receive the saint's body, which had lain in a small wooden chapel dedicated to St Theodore, but which was now to be entombed before the High Altar; and although St Theodore would always be honoured, the Venetians had found a new patron. From now on, they fought and traded under the Winged Lion of St Mark.

2. The Young Republic

The next two hundred years of Venetian history show a great increase in trade, wealth and importance, while internal politics were dominated by the struggle for power between three great families—Partecipazio, Candiano and Orseolo. Fifteen members of the three clans were Doges in almost unbroken succession; and this gave rise to an ever-increasing resentment among the people, who rightly suspected that attempts were being made to establish an hereditary Dogeship.

The scene on which the drama was played out was continually changing, as buildings of wattle, wood and thatch gradually gave place to brick, stone and tiles, and as footpaths of trodden mud were slowly transformed into the twisting alleys which were to follow the course of the canals between high banks of houses. Where once there was only marshland—a wilderness of reeds and saltwater grasses—piles were being driven to carry noble churches, while the little fields which were the original *campi* had become squares where markets could be held. One day they, like many of the streets, would be paved with flagstones of Istrian marble, artificially roughened so that the foot would not slip.

From the first days of the settlement in Rialto, officials had been appointed to superintend the reclamation of land and the alteration, where necessary, of the course of the waterways. It was a tremendous undertaking which occupied many years; but slowly, steadily, earth was embanked and land won back from the sea. Once reclaimed, it was consolidated with piles and palisades; later the numerous islands and islets of Rialto were strung together by rough wooden bridges. Modern Venice is a solid mass of courts, alleys and houses through which the canals weave like silver threads, half-hidden by the buildings. But in those early days the houses were spaced far apart round the edges of the islands, except where they clustered at centres like Rivo Alto (Ruskin's *Deep Stream*) or in the neighbourhood of St Mark's, even then the heart of the city.

At first, many of the humbler buildings rose no higher than a single storey, but most of the better sort were built round a court-yard from which an outside stair led to upper floors. The principal entrance was usually on the water side of the house, opening either straight on to a canal or on to a *fondamenta* or quay which, as the name suggests, was simply a continuation of the foundations. Most of the wealthier Venetians, however noble, were traders, so here too were stores for their merchandise and covered spaces for the gondolas which, in those days when there were few bridges, were more essential than they are now. The gondola, which has become the symbol of Venice, dates from the earliest days of the Republic, though at first, both in appearance and purpose, it was more like a ship's longboat and was taken to sea in tow. Broad and sturdy and painted all colours, it was very different from the sleek little black craft of today.

At the top of the larger houses there was often an *altana*, an open gallery or loggia used for domestic purposes and also as a retiring room where the ladies delighted to dry their long hair in the sun. These ladies looked down on a city which was still little more than a large village—a village in which, with the possible exception of the Grand Canal, there was nothing which we would recognize today. No Rialto Bridge. No Salute. No columns on the Piazzetta. No St Mark's —or, rather, only a small private chapel adjoining the Doge's Palace. Even the word palace is a misnomer. At that time it was only a rough stone fortress of which nothing remains but one angle-tower, now the Treasury of the Basilica. The great Campanile had not yet been thought of and the Piazza was a green meadow. It is said that trees grew there and that it was divided in two by a stream called the Rivo Battario.

This then was the Venice of the ninth century, constantly growing, changing all the time, but, it is safe to say, already beautiful. The churches of San Giorgio and San Pietro shone white through the black cypresses and grey olive orchards which covered their islands. And although winter in Venice has always been a season of sea mist and drenching rain, when spring and summer came, then, as now, the Adriatic sunshine, reflected from the glittering water, made every shape sharp and clear-cut, every colour unbelievably vivid. A Venetian crowd, dressed in the hard, gem-like colours of those early days— violet, blue, green, crimson—must have dazzled the eye as it moved and shifted in that marvellous light, with here and there, perhaps, the cold sheen of mail, the startlingly white robes of priests, or the gleaming gold of the winged lion on the scarlet banner of St Mark.

So the chronicle continues, but, tragically, it is still a chronicle of blood. The last centuries of the Dark Ages were as grim in Venice as elsewhere, for Europe was in the melting-pot and all through those terrible years she was boiling over, spurting violence.

The Venetians were fast learning to be cool and cunning merchants and traders, master players in the game of bluff and always ready to drive a hard bargain. Slowly, too, they were evolving an ideology of their own, a deep and passionate love of freedom which yet insisted on complete subservience of the individual to the State. It was a doctrine which to us may smack of Fascism. But, if so, it was Fascism with a difference. For many years, until they lost their long fight with the aristocracy, the adulation of the people was not given to any ruler or rulers but to Venice herself—that future queen among cities for whom they were ready to make any sacrifice, dare any danger. Venice was everything; the individual citizen—rich, poor, noble or simple—nothing. The glory of the Republic and the beauty of the city were set high above personal gain or ambition, even by men who otherwise might be proud, grasping and quite unscrupulous.

As we shall see later, laws were passed to ensure that this should be so; but during the period with which we are now dealing, the taming of those fierce islanders had hardly begun. They had always been a turbulent breed; and now, at each new sign of a dynastic tendency among their rulers or any attempt at oppression, they would swarm into the grass-grown square with weapons in their hands and shouts of *"Viva San Marco!"* on their lips, ready to kill or be killed, but never to be enslaved, to tolerate tyrant or traitor, or to allow their freely elected Doge to fancy himself a king.

Before Guistinian Partecipazio died in 829, he had recalled his brother Giovanni from Constantinople, forgiven him freely for any real or fancied disloyalty, and made him coadjutor in the Dogeship. Giovanni was a gambler who had played for high stakes and lost, only to find unexpectedly that the game was not yet over. When at last he came to power in Venice he had achieved his ambition, but the prize which he had coveted for so long brought him little happiness. It is true that during his troubled reign the first Basilica of St. Mark, which had been begun by his brother, was consecrated, but the rest of his story—a very short one—only tells of his desperate efforts to maintain law and order.

He found himself faced with two insurrections. The first was led by an ex-Doge, Obelerio, a strong supporter of the Franks, who had been deposed while the seat of government was still at Malamocco. Giovanni acted promptly and firmly. The rising was suppressed, and in the barbarous fashion of those days, Obelerio's head was cut off and exhibited on a pole. But if this was meant to discourage other conspirators, it failed in its purpose.

The second rebellion was more dangerous and came within an ace of succeeding. Giovanni was forced to flee from Venice and for six months a usurper named Pietro Caroso occupied the throne. The rising failed, Caroso was deposed and blinded, and Giovanni returned to power; but that dangerous rivalry still smouldered. The ancient feuds had not been forgotten. Giovanni must have known in his heart that Venice was tired of the Partecipazii: there had been too many of them. His very name was a weapon in the hands of those enemies who dreaded above all things the founding of a dynasty.

Without warning the blow fell. Seized as he was coming out of church on the island of Olivolo, he was forced to enter a convent and spent the short time that remained to him in the monastery of Grado. But he was lucky. He escaped with his life and his eyesight, which, for an unpopular ninth-century Doge, was something of an achievement.

In choosing their next Doge, the Venetians settled, at any rate for the time being, the vexing question of an hereditary Dogeship. The Partecipazii were a noble Heraclean family, so it was decided that the new ruler should be a native of the rival township of Jesolo.

Their choice was a wise one: Pietro Tradonico, a man of energy and drive and a clever statesman who in less troubled times might have lived to make an even greater mark in the world. He was a warrior, too, who led many expeditions against the Slavonian pirates.

These freebooters—Schiavoni from the rocky coasts of Dalmatia and Croatia—were a continual menace, as were the armies and fleets of the Saracens, still riding high on the wave of conquest and offering their terrible choice: the Koran or the edge of the scimitar. When the Moslem hordes invaded Calabria, the Byzantine Emperor Theodosius asked Doge Tradonico for help—a sign of the more important part which the Venetian Republic was beginning to play in world affairs. The Doge despatched a fleet of sixty dromonds—big heavy ships suitable for either war or trading—and by a clever stroke of policy he entrusted the command to a certain Pietro Partecipazio who, bearing the name he did, might well have fancied himself as the next Doge. He was safer at sea.

The expedition deserved success, but fortune was not with the Venetians. Another, smaller flotilla was overwhelmed by a Saracen fleet in the Adriatic; and, with Partecipazio and his dromonds far away, the Slavonians seized their chance to penetrate into the lagoon almost unopposed. They got as far as the town of Caorle, which they sacked at their leisure, and in Venice itself the people thought their city was doomed. But these were pirate craft, not a warfleet, and the expected invasion failed to materialize. The Slavs sailed away with their loot and with captives for the slave markets of the East.

In peace Tradonico was more fortunate than in war. At Pavia, in 840, the terms of a treaty between him and the German Emperor Lothair not only guaranteed him five years of peace but put the seal on an agreement clarifying trading rights and defining the areas in which German and Venetian merchants were to be permitted to ply their trade. In advance of his time, Pietro Tradonico planned a league for mutual protection and cooperation between all the Italian ports on the Adriatic; other clauses confirmed earlier trading rights and agreements. This treaty is of interest, for it is still in existence— the earliest written record of Venetian diplomacy.

The Republic was growing up. A few years later, Lothair's successor visited Venice in state and was entertained for three days with a pomp and magnificence which would have been unthinkable at Malamocco. It is clear, too, that the descendants of the little community of fishermen and salt-gatherers were at last being taken seriously, not only by the Byzantines but by the new kings and princes of the Holy Roman Empire. Acting as a fulcrum by means of which either East or West could bring pressure to bear on the other, Venice, guided by Tradonico, remained on good terms with both. A born leader, great things were hoped of him. But this was ninth-century Italy.

Just after Easter in 861, the Doge was attacked and stabbed to death as he was leaving the church of San Zaccaria after Vespers. Women screamed; there were shouting and the clash of steel as the people turned out and the rival factions flew at each others' throats. During the riot that followed, Tradonico's body was trampled on as the fight surged over him. Later it was taken up by the monks and laid to rest in the church which he had so generously endowed.

Why was this good man murdered? Ambition? Jealousy? Fear that he might become a tyrant? Who knows on what specious pretext the assassins armed themselves against him? One can only hazard a guess. There is just one clue. We know that two powerful families, the Polani and the Barbolani, were at feud and that Tradonico had favoured the former, to whom he was related. For a time the Barbolani had been banished. Could the motive, then, have been vengeance? Was this senseless crime an incident in one of those vendettas which, even at this early date, were beginning to stain the pages of Italian history?

And now the Partecipazii were in power again. The new ruler, Orso, the first of that family, ranks as one of the great Doges, a strong man, wise in council, unyielding to threats, and a bold leader in war. When the Slav pirates attacked Grado, he commanded in person the small fleet which repulsed them; and on several expeditions, with varying success but on the whole victoriously, he carried the fighting into their own home waters along the jagged Dalmatian coast.

Yet his hardest conflict was fought in Venice itself, and it was a very different conflict—a struggle for men's hearts and minds. For years the Doges and the Popes had quarrelled about the see of Grado. Now it all flared up again over the bishopric of Torcello. A new bishop was to be appointed and there were two candidates. One of them, favoured by Doge Orso, was Domenico Caloprino, but the Patriarch of Grado considered him unfit for the post. The matter was referred to Pope John VIII, who pronounced in favour of the Metropolitan and summoned all Venetian bishops to a council at Ravenna. But the Doge considered himself, to some extent, ruler of Venice in spiritual as well as in temporal matters. The word was passed round and the Venetian bishops stayed away. It was a momentous step which required all Orso's courage and self-confidence, for it amounted virtually to open defiance of the Papacy. But it showed the world that this new republic, although it considered itself loyal to the Church, was not prepared to tolerate interference from either Pope or Emperor. Domenico Caloprino became Bishop of Grado.

At Constantinople Orso was in high favour with the Emperor Basil, whose daughter he married; and at home he did good work, building palaces and houses, and reclaiming still more land from the Republic's old ally, the sea.

The next few Doges can be dealt with very briefly, which, as no fewer than five of them were named Pietro, is perhaps just as well. Another Giovanni Partecipazio, the son and associate of Orso, found the cares of the ducal office too heavy and retired into private life. His successor, whom he himself appointed, Pietro Candiano I, a member of the rival family of Candiano, was killed fighting the Slav pirates.

Next came Pietro Tribuno, a man related to the Candiani on his mother's side. The Venetian nobility is said to be the oldest in Europe and the House of Tribuno (variously Trono or Tron) is one of its most illustrious families, for its members can claim descent from the Tribunes of Imperial Rome. Doge Pietro Tribuno led his men in battle against invading Hungarians. The enemy penetrated into the Venetian lagoon, and once again precautions had to be taken against an attack on the city. As in the days of the Frankish threat, the *bricole* which marked the deep-water channels were removed; at night a chain was stretched across the Grand Canal; and fortifications were built, including a wall along what is now the Riva degli Schiavoni and forts the memory of which lingers in names like Castello and Castleforte. The danger only receded when the Hungarians were routed in a sea fight off Albiolo, a port between Venice and Chioggia.

But there was one event which was remembered long after the din of battle had faded, for it was at the end of Pietro Tribuno's reign that the great Campanile or belfry of St Mark's was begun. They began driving the piles in A.D. 912 and the tall, rose-red tower, which took nearly two centuries to complete, stood firm and four-square on its timber foundations for nearly a thousand years—a worthy monument to a worthy man.

The next Doge was a Partecipazio, Orso II. In history, as in journalism, there is little to record in the quiet, uneventful years: it is war and rebellion, murder and misery which make the headlines. So of the long reign of Orso II there is little to be said except that, before he retired into a monastery, he gave the Republic twenty years of peace and prosperity, a welcome interlude in the monotonous saga of blood-feud and battle. And of the next two Doges in the long line there is even less to be said. Another Candiano and another Partecipazio. They were born. They lived. They reigned. They died. But then came Pietro Candiano III and it would seem to have been in his time, although the exact year is uncertain, that the famous Rape of the Brides took place.

In those days it was customary for many Venetian marriages to be contracted by a simple promise and an exchange of rings, a cere-mony not unlike the hand-fasting of our Scottish and Norse ancestors. Such unions, however, although legally binding, still lacked the bless-ing of the Church. So on the second of February, the Feast of the Puri-fication of the Blessed Virgin, it had become the custom for the Doge to grace with his presence a mass wedding held in what was still the cathedral church of Venice: San Pietro di Castello, on the island of Olivolo which lies on the eastern edge of the city.

Although it had been going on for years, in 943 or thereabouts the charming little ceremony did not proceed according to plan, for in the darkness of the night a crew of Slavonian pirates had landed and were lying hidden among the reeds and bushes which at that time covered the island. Under the eye of the Doge himself, the girls advanced in solemn procession, each carrying her dowry before her in a casket, while the expectant bridegrooms, unarmed on this happy occasion, lined up to receive them. The priest appeared in the doorway of the church. Then suddenly things went wrong. There must have been some signal—a whistle or the blast of a horn—for all at once the place was alive with swarthy, half-naked ruffians, bristling with weapons.

The startled brides were quite literally swept off their feet, as the corsairs dashed in among them and carried them off, together with the dowries which they had brought with them. All was noise and confusion: shouting, screaming, and perhaps the sound of blows as some desperate young Venetian tried to rescue his bride. Then the Slavs were gone, crashing through the undergrowth. There was the creak of oars; the crying of the captives became fainter and fainter; the pointed lateen sails were hoisted; and the corsair craft faded into the mist and winter grey of the Adriatic.

Some say that it was the Doge himself who urged the frantic bridegrooms to action, but they were brave men and it is unlikely that they needed any urging. They dashed away to arm themselves, then out went the boats, up went the sails, and they were scudding in pursuit. It was a long chase but they overhauled the marauders and brought them to bay in the port of Caorle which, in memory of those damsels in distress, was later renamed Porto delle Donzelle. It was there they fought—a savage business, with quarter neither asked nor given. The Venetians, half mad with rage, took their revenge; and when at last they rested on their arms, not one of the pirates was alive. So the bridegrooms hoisted their sails again and carried home their brides in triumph, married them, asked no questions, and lived happily ever after.

Thus ended the Rape of the Brides. Foremost among the rescuers had been the cabinetmakers who had made the caskets in which the girls carried their dowries. The Doge felt that their gallantry should be rewarded; and when he asked how this might best be done, they begged that he would visit them once a year in their own church of

Sta Maria Formosa. In a waggish mood Pietro Candiano asked the deputation what would happen if he were to be overcome by the heat. A quick-wit immediately replied that he would be offered refreshment. "And what if it rains?" went on the Doge. Out came the snap answer: "We will give you a hat." No doubt this sally was greeted with the laughter reserved throughout the ages for the great personage who makes a little joke. But nevertheless a new yearly festival had been instituted. The Doge was presented with wine to cool him and a straw hat to keep off the sun, and it was agreed that on the occasion of his annual visit to the cabinetmakers' quarter, twelve poor girls who hoped to be married should each receive a dowry from the State.

Venice now had its Festival of the Marys, but it was not long before what had started as a simple little ceremony had become a procession of decorated boats in which local beauties represented the stolen brides for the delectation of the rabble. It is probable that they were scantily clad. It is quite certain that the exhibition caused grave scandal. Tongues wagged; clerical eyebrows were raised; the jokes became bawdier until at last—though not until the end of the fourteenth century—someone conceived the idea of substituting wooden dummies for the real flesh-and-blood which went on display annually.

But this innovation was not at all well received. The Wooden Marys, as they were called, did not meet with the approval of connoisseurs of beauty. Turnips were thrown, we are told, and onions and bad eggs. Yet it was only at the end of the long and exhausting war with Genoa in the fourteenth century that the procession of boats was discontinued. The Doge continued to visit Sta Maria Formosa until, in 1797, Bonaparte put an end to everything; and within living memory any dowdy or unattractive woman in Venice ran the risk of being called a *Maria di legno*—a wooden Mary.

And now we must darken the stage again for black tragedy. Doge Pietro Candiano III had a son—still another Pietro—whom he rashly associated with himself in the Dogeship. The most ardent apologist must admit that Pietro was so completely and so flagrantly bad that even the broadminded men of his own time were appalled by his wickedness. They knew him to be arrogant, treacherous and cruel; but when he was also found guilty of treason, conspiracy and warlike action against the Republic itself, it must have been obvious to everyone that he could expect no mercy. Yet when he was condemned to death, his aged father pleaded so hard for his life that the sentence was commuted to prepetual exile. One wise precaution was taken, however: an action unprecedented and unparalleled. It was solemnly decreed by all the leaders of the community—bishops, priests and the representatives of the people—that this evil man should be forever debarred from the Dogeship. Oaths were taken to this effect. Nothing could have been more binding.

So Pietro departed; and almost immediately came the plague, an outbreak of a pestilence so terrible that thousands died and trade was brought almost to a standstill. What could have caused it but the wrath of God? This awful visitation was thought by many to be the vengeance of Heaven on a sinful city which had allowed an evildoer to escape his just punishment. The Doge himself was condemned for his pleading: it broke the old man's heart and he died.

Then followed one of those historical mysteries which are so difficult to explain: concerted action by rational people which seems to contravene commonsense. After the death of Candiano III, Venice was given over to disorder and misrule. Lacking a strong hand at the helm, she seemed to be foundering into anarchy. There was no suitable candidate for the Dogeship and, incredibly, thoughts turned to the man in exile who, perhaps for revenge, perhaps merely for the devilment of it, had "shark'd up a list of lawless resolutes" and was harrying the Gulf of Venice as a common corsair. Could perfidy go further? Yet the City Fathers had other thoughts. Where were they going to find their new Doge? Was there a better man than this gallant rover, even though he did prey on their shipping? Had they been too hasty? Was that solemn oath so irrevocable after all? How the about-face began nobody knows; but we do know how it ended. The prodigal son was invited to return as Pietro Candiano IV, and an escort was sent to bring him triumphantly home from Ravenna.

For a time all went well. There were even hopes that his responsibilities might reform the new Doge. But Pietro was no Prince Hal. Soon things were worse than they had ever been. He divorced his wife to marry Waldrada, daughter of Ugo of Tuscany, and she brought with her not only a rich dowry but a choice collection of

Tuscan thugs whom Pietro was pleased to call his bodyguard. They filled his palace and overflowed into the streets and taverns of the city, terrorizing the populace and imitating their new master's excesses. There was no holding the Doge. He was pitiless and unscrupulous. He had forced his first wife to enter a nunnery; now he decided that her son would be better out of the way. So, whether he liked it or not, the young man was made a priest. Later he became Bishop of Grado.

Like the Gadarene swine, Candiano IV hurtled to his own destruction. He was a Venetian. He should have known his own people well enough to realize that they would allow him to go thus far and no farther. But he could not read the danger signals. He assumed the airs of a king, while no man's life and no woman's honour were safe from his band of Tuscan bullies who ranged the city at will.

Then in August 976, some say at the instigation of one of the Orseolo clan, the people rose against the tyrant and set fire to the Doge's Palace. The conflagration spread until not only St Mark's was in flames, but all the houses along the Grand Canal as far as Sta. Maria Zobenigo. The Dogaressa escaped in time but her husband was trapped. Terrified by the blaze and the terrible baying of the crowd, he tried to make his way out through the church, followed by a nurse carrying his infant son. Somehow they struggled through the crackling flames and suffocating smoke, but the doorway was barred by angry men and women with swords, knives and axes.

Facing what must have appeared like an inferno of flushed faces, open mouths and flame reflected in glaring eyeballs, Pietro Candiano frantically appealed to his people. He would yield to all their demands. He would do anything they wished. In desperation he snatched the baby and held it up for them to see. But they were no longer men and women: they had become one monster—a mob. They howled with one voice. They struck with one arm. They thought with one brain—the brain of a beast lusting for slaughter. There were oaths and screams and execrations and swift flashes of firestreaked steel, as Doge and baby were hacked to pieces and dragged away to be fed to the dogs. That they were spared this final indignity was due to the charity of one good man, a certain Giovanni Gradenigo, who gathered up the pitiful remains and gave them Christian burial in the Abbey of Sant' Ilario at Fusina on the mainland.

Slowly the flames died down, leaving the charred wreckage of a church, a palace, and three hundred houses. And slowly that monster the mob resolved itself into its component parts: merchants, tradesmen, sailors, young boys, pretty girls, and kindly old people who would not have crushed a spider if they had seen one in their way. Their crime was savage, brutal murder, but something evil had been removed. Venice—all that was left of it—was a cleaner place. But that baby had done no harm.

The Tuscan bodyguard died as the fire swept through the Doge's Palace, or as, one by one, they made a dash for it, smoked out by the people whom they had wronged. Some of them may have made a stand and so given their mistress time to escape. But the behaviour of the Dogaressa was, to say the least, peculiar. All the evidence points to the fact that she abandoned the Doge and their infant son; and when next we hear of Waldrada, she was a fugitive at the court of the German Emperor, Otto II. After that time, the accounts vary. Some historians paint a pathetic picture of her as the tragic widow, pleading with the Emperor for vengeance on the murderers of her husband and her baby. Others declare that she was completely satisfied by the return of her personal property and that she wrote to the Venetians, assuring them that she was quite prepared to let the matter drop and promising never to seek revenge. Which is the truth? After a thousand years, the answer is unlikely to be discovered.

Before August was over a new Doge had been elected: that same Orseolo who was suspected of having incited the people to riot. Seemingly a most unfortunate coincidence, but again, it would be unwise to jump to conclusions.

Two rulers more unlike each other than Pietro Candiano IV and Pietro Orseolo I would be difficult to imagine. Candiano was cruel, arrogant and selfish. Orseolo the Pious was a kindly man, humble and given to good works. He did his duty as he saw it, but he was always happier in his oratory than in the council chamber. A man of God. But selfish too? That is a matter of opinion.

The public emergency was exploited to the full by the Candiani, the old rivals of the Orseolo family. But Orseolo was fortified by prayer and mortified by fasting, so hurtful rumours and even civil tumults seldom disturbed his serenity. One of his first acts as Doge was to restore the fortune of the widowed Waldrada; then, with the energy of a man inspired, he set to work to rebuild the ruined city. The first St Mark's had been destroyed and with it, many believe, the body of the Evangelist; the Doge's Palace was uninhabitable, and three hundred houses had been gutted. Orseolo instituted a system of tithes on all property, the proceeds to be devoted to the erection of churches and civic buildings; the homeless were housed and fed; and somehow, in spite of the adverse circumstances, law and order were maintained.

So began this strange man's short reign of two years and one month. Tireless in the performance of his many tasks, in the eyes of the world his private life was irreproachable. But Orseolo was unhappy. Secretly he longed for the cloisters. He was ascetic to the point of excess, and by inclination a celibate. He had had one son by his wife Felicia; but deciding that further marital intercourse between them would be sinful, he separated from her and devoted himself to his public duties and his private quest for holiness.

Now, whether by accident or design, it happened that the Doge received a visit from a French monk, a man named Carinus or Guerino, Abbot of the monastery of St Michael de Cusano in Aquitaine. Doge and Abbot talked together; they had much in common; but Orseolo cannot have helped contrasting his dangerous throne in this turbulent republic with the peaceful life of a monk—the tranquil round from Matins to Compline, the never ending prayer and praise.

In due course, the Abbot gave the Doge his farewell blessing and returned to Aquitaine. But even then there must have been some secret understanding between them, for a year later the Abbot was in Venice again, ostensibly as a pilgrim on his way to the Holy Land. This time, however, he brought three monks with him. Once more Carinus was the guest of the Doge, and we can well imagine that the two friends talked deep into the night, for a decision had been reached and there were arrangements to be made.

Only after long hours of prayer and soul-searching had Orseolo made up his mind, but now at last he was ready to take the irrevocable step. On the night of September 1, 978, without any message of farewell to his wife, his son or his most trusted councillors, the Doge of Venice slipped past his guards and left his own house forever. A gondola was waiting, which carried him swiftly across the dark lagoon, accompanied only by his son-in-law and by that same Giovanni Gradenigo who had given the murdered Candiani burial. Again Gradenigo was bound for Fusina. At the Abbey of Sant' Ilario horses were already saddled; and soon the Doge, with the three French monks as escort, was galloping through the night towards Aquitaine.

In the monastery of St Michael, Orseolo took the lifelong vows of poverty, chastity and obedience. We are told that he was happy in the cloisters despite the strict discipline to which he was subjected until he died after nearly twenty years as a simple monk. We are told, too, that among the Venetians he was revered as a saint—this leader who had deserted his post and put his own salvation before the welfare of his people. Saintly or selfish? Perhaps there is no single answer.

To end a chapter which reeks of blood it is a relief to turn into the golden cavern of St Mark's, where stiff saints with dark-rimmed, mournful eyes stare out of the mosaics as if they were dreaming of a Byzantine heaven. A noble church, enriched by the spoils of Italy and the Levant, a church to which merchants returning from the East were later required by law to bring back materials for its adornment. Nowadays, the whole building is a treasury of precious things: alabaster, malachite, deep-green serpentine, porphyry, calcedony, jasper, agate and cipollino marble. Clouds of incense drift by; silver lamps glow in the gilded twilight; choristers' voices soar into the domes; the Patriarch in his mitre moves beneath a golden canopy. A dim, mysterious church lit by sudden glints of gold, with nothing of the friendly charm of the grey cathedrals of England. But it is a link with the gorgeous East. St Mark's is an open door to Asia.

And like the rest of the city, it was begun again by the first Orseolo, the Doge who deserted his people. It was thanks to him that from the ruin and desolation of that disastrous fire of 976 there gradually arose the Venice that we know today. He laid the foundations; that is all. But he laid them truly and well, and the project nearest to his heart was the creation of a new St Mark's, to rise like a phoenix from the ashes. The present Basilica is the third which has stood on the site, and Orseolo's task was to begin the rebuilding of Giustinian's ruined church. He was not a rich man but he poured out money freely for the great work. It was he who sent to Constantinople for the reredos of the High Altar which is the glory of St Mark's—that magnificent Pala d'Oro, enlarged and enriched throughout the centuries, sometimes by the munificence of the devout, sometimes by the loot of conquerors. With its gold and silver, its rare enamels, and its thousands of precious stones, it ranks as one of the most exquisite pieces of craftsmanship in the world.

From the Imperial City, too, Orseolo at his own expense brought the sculptors, masons and mosaicists who were to carry out the work. According to legend, the master builder was an elderly cripple—a hunchback whose hideousness was equalled only by his vanity. Boastfully he promised to build a church unrivalled in beauty and magnificence, provided—and here was the snag—that when the work was finished, his own statue should occupy a place of honour in the most conspicuous part of the building.

The Doge agreed. He knew his man—his conceit and his great ability. So the bargain was struck. But one day—it cannot have been long before he fled from Venice—Orseolo was strolling among the rising walls of his church, inspecting the progress of the work and dreaming perhaps of a quiet cloister in Aquitaine, when suddenly he overheard the voice of the master builder. The cripple had lost his temper. He was complaining bitterly that so many obstacles had been put in his way that he could not and would not keep his part of the bargain.

"In that case," said the Doge quietly, disclosing himself, "I cannot keep mine." So instead of a statue in the place of honour, the twisted figure of the old cripple with his crutches was carved on one of the archivolts. Hunched and repulsive, with his finger to his lips as if to warn future generations against speaking out of turn, he is to be seen there to this day.

3. Orseolo The Great

The Office of Doge
The Rocca of Lagosta
An Emperor in Disguise
The Normans

Orseolo the Pious was followed by two Doges of little note. When Orseolo so abruptly abandoned his post, the Candiano clan seized their chance to have their own candidate elected. He was Vitale Candiano, brother of the Doge who had been lynched by the mob. He reigned for exactly fourteen months; then, finding the pace too strenuous, he abdicated and took the vows in the Abbey of Sant' Ilario. Four days later he died.

Vitale's successor was another member of the Candiano faction: Tribuno Memo, whose short reign was disgraced by the bloody feud between two great families, the Morosini and the Caloprini. The peace of Venice was shattered by some of the worst riots she had ever known. Street brawls and murders continued intermittently until three of the Caloprini were cut down as they left the Doge's Palace to step into their gondola. It was the last straw. "A plague o' both your houses!" was the judgement of the Venetians; and the whisper went round that Tribuno Memo, if not directly implicated, might have prevented this latest outrage if he had wished to do so.

Only a few years before, a Doge who could not or would not maintain order could hardly have expected to keep his own head on his shoulders. But times were changing. Tribuno Memo was deposed but he escaped with his life—at any rate, for the time being. With shaven head and dressed in a monk's habit, he was forced to enter the monastery of San Zaccaria. Mysteriously, six days later, he too died.

If the Venetians from time to time rose in rebellion against their ruler they could hardly be blamed. The time was to come when the Doge of Venice, lapped in pomp and ceremony but stripped of all real power, would be little more than a puppet in the hands of his ministers. But that time was not yet. His power was absolute; and if, by ill fortune, he was a wicked man or a weakling, the people could do nothing but turn out with weapons in their hands and depose him. He was still elected by the whole community, who acknowledged the leader of their choice by a triumphant shout—the *arengo*. It was a sign of that democracy which struggled for survival in Venice until it was crushed by the ever growing power of the patricians.

In the great days of the Serenissima, as the proud Republic chose to call herself, the Doge was supposed to be, and usually was, a dedicated man, for although the trappings of his office reflected the gorgeousness of Byzantium, the life that he led was often a model of hard work and austerity. He rose at dawn to hear Mass, and for the rest of the day devoted himself to his manifold and arduous duties. There was little time for leisure. As Chief Magistrate of the Republic he was obliged to sit in judgement and listen to legal arguments and quibbles—always in public. Tortuously he had to weave his way through intricate affairs of State, weighing every word, assessing every risk, as he held the ambassadors of the Pope and two Emperors in play. With a voice in Church affairs, he had to spend much time on such important matters as the appointment of bishops, a ticklish business which often meant difficult negotiations with Rome. And when the red banner of St Mark was unfurled against an enemy, it was his task, with the aid of his commanders, to organize the expedition and sometimes to direct operations from the poop of the foremost galley.

Statesman, judge, religious leader, soldier, sailor: it is a wonder that His Serenity ever found time for his own business. But somehow he did. Many a Doge had his private argosies plying in the Mediterranean or anchored in the sweltering white ports of the Levant, and out of the profits of their trading those great men made generous donations towards the building of churches and the endowment of charities as monuments to their piety. As the years went by they poured out their gold without stint, that they might leave their beloved Venice a little more beautiful than they had found her.

When, with trumpeters and banners and guards, the Doge showed himself to his people under his great swaying *baldachino* or umbrella of State, he was a gorgeously exotic, almost an Oriental figure in his heavy mantle of silk or cloth of gold, his red shoes and his red hose. His throne was of ivory; he carried a sceptre; and he had the right to wear a sword—a right which, as men became more civilised, was granted in Venice to very few. His horned Phrygian-cap, sparkling with gems, known till the sixteenth century as the *birettum* and after that as the *corno ducale,* was always worn over another close-fitting cap of white linen so that if for some reason the Doge had to remove his jewelled bonnet, he might not suffer the indignity of appearing uncovered, as though he were in the presence of a superior.

A story is told of the fourteenth-century Doge, Lorenzo Celsi, whose aged father refused to bend the knee to his own son. Matters seemed to have reached an impasse when the difficulty was solved by the tact of the Doge himself, who ordered a small jewelled cross to be sewn in the front of his *birettum.* Thus he received his due obeisance without breach of etiquette; the old gentleman made his reverence to the Cross; and everybody was happy.

Legend has it that while the saintly Orseolo was a monk in Aquitaine he was visited by his son, and that there, in the sunlit cloisters, they talked of many things. The elder, they say, foretold honour and renown for the Republic and for his son, and if this was so, events proved him to be a true prophet.

When one is studying the history of Venice and remembering what one has seen there, it is strange to find this supremely beautiful Italian city referred to as a world power. Yet for centuries Venice stood in the front rank of Christendom and bargained on equal terms with England, France and the Holy Roman Empire. And the beginning of her glory can be traced to the young man who talked for hours with his father in the cloisters of St Michael's. For he was to become Orseolo II, one of the great Doges, for whom all the trumpets of history sound.

He was elected in 991 and one of his first acts was to bridle the mob who for some time past had been getting out of control. There had been grave wrongs to be righted and the people had had no choice but to rebel. They could hardly be blamed. But once the rabble had been roused and had come pouring out of the growing maze of *campi* and alleys, there was no knowing where or when the looting and the killing would stop. The fire of 976 was still burning in people's memories.

With a strong hand the new Doge imposed law and order, and troublemakers realized that they had met their master. Then, having made sure of security at home, Orseolo turned his attention to foreign affairs. Skillfully he negotiated with the potentates of East and West, wisely treating their rulers as friends rather than as rivals. And his diplomacy reaped a rich harvest of privileges and concessions. With Otto, the Holy Roman Emperor, he ironed out differences which over the years had risen from their conflicting interests. A line of communication was opened between Venice and Central Europe, and the Republic was granted new trading rights on the Piave and Sile rivers.

The brothers Basil and Constantine, who shared the imperial throne of the East, and whose reign Gibbon described as "the longest and most obscure of the Byzantine history," rewarded Orseolo's negotiations by the Chrysobol or Golden Bull, an edict which confirmed valuable concessions to the merchants of the Republic and gave them a firm foothold in the bazaars of the Levant. Having successfully wooed Christendom, Orseolo now turned to her enemies and—the first western ruler to do so—concluded treaties with the Saracens, from whom most Christians shrank in horror as being the followers of Mahound. This unorthodox stroke caused a major scandal, but Orseolo knew very well what he was doing. The others fought them. He would use them.

Gradually, under their Doge's leadership, Venetians were finding their own strength; their wealth and importance were increasing. The men of the lagoons had become not an industrial nation—the Venetians were never that—but the proprietors of an international exchange and mart, a magnet which, except for unavoidable losses to Constantinople, was increasingly drawing the commerce of East and West to the quays of Rialto. Those bronzed hardy men, bred to salt water, knew how to build and sail ships for either peace or war.

And as they always had one eye on the main chance, those ships were at anyone's disposal. If principalities and powers needed transport, they could find it in Venice, provided they were prepared to pay the price, which was usually a stiff one.

And now the Lion of St Mark had to spread his wings and bare his teeth for battle. Those old enemies, the Dalmation pirates, were plundering ships and terrorizing towns all along the coast of Illyria. This time they were Narentines or Narentani, fierce tribes from the estuary of the Narente river. They have also been called Slavs and Croats; but whatever their origin, their chief stronghold was on the island of Lagosta (now Lastovo). Between two tall pinnacles of rock, visible far out at sea, lay the harbour of the corsairs, while high above the town, on the topmost crag, the sea hawks had their eyrie, the ill-famed castle or Rocca of Lagosta.

The business of the Narentines, apart from piracy and rapine, was blackmail in the old sense. They ran a primitive protection racket, exacting tribute from their victims, among whom were included the citizens of the Republic. And in order to overcome any natural reluctance to pay up, it was the custom of the corsairs to mount an occasional raid—a sample of what might be expected to happen if the tribute was not forthcoming.

In the year 997 several of the Lido townships had been harried, and these outrages were followed by the usual demand for payment. But the Narentines did not reckon with the vigor and the vision of the Doge. Orseolo had received a deputation carrying piteous appeals for help from the people of Zara, Justinople and other cities of Dalmatia whose land had been repeatedly ravaged by their renegade fellow-countrymen. Being both resolute and far-sighted, Orseolo knew that the only way of dealing with this problem was to take firm action, while as a statesman he saw very clearly that Venice could never attain her full stature until she controlled the Adriatic. The pirates had pushed their luck too far. They were no longer dealing with an unworldly saint or some nervous weakling. Orseolo II was a man and he sent them a man's answer. There would be no more messengers, no more money. He would visit Dalmatia himself. He did.

To distract the Narentines' attention, he sent six galleys across the Adriatic and tempted the enemy to an attack which was easily repelled. Meanwhile, under cover of these operations, Orseolo was fitting out a fleet. He took his time. But on Ascension Day, in the spring of 998, there sailed from Venice what was, for those days, a formidable armada of two hundred ships, and the young Doge in his glimmering mail was there to lead his men.

They carried with them a consecrated banner and the blessing of the Church, pronounced by the Bishop of Castello. At Grado they received the sacred standards of SS. Hermagora and Fortunato; and again at Parenzo and at Pola there were enthusiastic receptions, with more benedictions and cheering. For were not these warriors pledged to rid the seas of a scourge? And was it not time that they held dominion over the Adriatic?

The Doge met with fierce resistance before he was able to subdue Curzola (the modern Korčula), one of the haunts of the Narentines; but on other islands of the archipelago and on the mainland he was welcomed as a deliverer. Many Dalmatian cities, including Zara and Spalato (now Zadar and Split), placed themselves under his protection, while from the mountain strongholds of the interior wild chieftains with their half-savage retainers came hurrying to acknowledge the suzerainty of the Venetian Republic and to offer their swords and their lives to the cause which they had made their own. So Orseolo found his ranks swollen by many a band of picturesque warriors, but those ancestors of the Jugoslavs were born fighting men and their help was very welcome.

There remained Lagosta—a hard fortress to break. After a long and bitter battle, the Venetians and their allies cleared the town; but the Narentines made a fighting retreat to their almost impregnable refuge and there was no choice but to attempt to carry the Rocca by storm.

One can imagine the scene. Covered by crossbowmen and archers, the assault party began the ascent. Sweltering in their mail hauberks and heavy pointed helmets, they fought their way up the narrow path, holding their long kite-shaped shields before them to ward off the arrows, crossbow bolts and sling-stones which harassed them without ceasing. Meanwhile, other troops, more lightly armed, were scaling the almost perpendicular precipice to take the enemy in flank. Men were falling all the time, either from wounds or exhaustion, for a mail-shirt was necessarily worn over thick leather, and on such a steep ascent, one of the worst hazards was heatstroke. But the attackers struggled on under the merciless hail of missiles. On and on—up the walls of that fortress which had seen so much bloodshed and cruelty. One final effort; the gates were forced; and with hoarse shouts of *"Viva San Marco!"* the Venetians staggered and hacked their way into courtyard and keep where, with such an enemy to bring to justice, there can have been no question or quarter. But in the end all was quiet. The last Narentines had been slain or sent hurtling over the precipice; the tired and sweating men leaned on their reeking swords; and the banner of the Winged Lion flew over the Rocca of Lagosta.

This notable feat of arms was the first great victory of the Republic. The Doge and his successors were granted the additional title of Duke of Dalmatia; and that country, including the small independent republic of Ragusa (Dubrovnik), became a tributary of Venice. There is no evidence that the inhabitants resented the change. They were well governed; Dalmatia was allowed to retain her own laws; and the new taxation was not oppressive. But the conquest was of immense value to Venetian commerce. The harbours of the coast and archipelago were stepping-stones to the Morea and the rich lands of the East, while the Dalmatians' inexhaustible supply of timber was a priceless acquisition to a nation of shipbuilders with no forests of their own.

It was Orseolo who laid the foundations of the Venetian navy. In his time, too, in honour of his victory, there was instituted that strange maritime ceremony which, later, was to become the famous *Sposalizio del Mare* or Marriage of the Sea. In its earlier and simpler form, however, *La Sensa,* as it was called, was a beautiful ritual of libation and prayer for peace upon the waters.

On Ascension Day, the anniversary of the departure of Orseolo's fleet, a barge hung with rich materials set sail from the cathedral church of San Pietro di Castello, carrying clergy and choristers in all the glory of full canonicals. At the sea gate of the Lido they met the Doge and his court in an even more magnificently decorated barge, and the Bishop prayed that the ocean might be tranquil for all peaceful seafarers. Then, while the choristers intoned a litany, he sprinkled the Doge and his courtiers with holy water, pouring the rest into the sea. That was all. An impressive rite, the more moving for its simplicity, but a gentle reminder to the rest of Europe that the Adriatic was Venetian. And simple it remained for nearly two hundred years.

Not long after the first celebration of *La Sensa* there occurred an intriguing mystery which has never really been solved. When Orseolo came home from the wars, all Italy resounded with his fame; and the young German Emperor, impressed by accounts of his statesmanship and valour, had a great desire to meet this ruler of the Maritime Republic. As it happened, the Emperor Otto had been on pilgrimage to Ravenna, and before returning home he let it be known that he was going into retreat on the island of Pomposa, which was conveniently close to Venetian territorial waters. His messengers had already made the necessary arrangements, so one night, dressed in black and muffled to the eyes, the Emperor and five or six companions embarked on a small craft and were carried across the lagoon to the island monastery of San Servolo which since the eighth century had been a famous house of the Benedictines.

There Orseolo awaited him; and the two young rulers, who seem to have been on the best of terms from the beginning, talked long and earnestly on this and subsequent occasions. Most of the details of the Emperor's visit are still shrouded in mystery, but it is certain that Orseolo obtained commercial concessions from these private discussions, free from the quibbling of councillors. Unknown to the people of Venice, Otto visited the Palace, stood sponsor at the christening of the Doge's baby daughter and, after a show of reluctance, accepted gifts from his new friend: some say an ivory chair, a vase and a chalice. There are other stories, too, not so well authenticated, of the Emperor disguised as an abbot and wandering through the streets of the city at night, like Haroun al-Raschid.

That strange visit lasted three days; then the Emperor Otto III left Venice as secretly as he had come, to return to his own country and die at the age of twenty-two. The story of his adventures is the first recorded example of those tales of romantic intrigue for which Venice was to become notorious. All the ingredients were there: the muffled men, the anonymity, the midnight flight across the lagoon. But the question remains—why? Why all the secrecy and playacting?

Perhaps the answer may be found in the fact that Emperor and Doge were both young. Men matured early in those days, but there must have been exceptions—dreamers who remained boys at heart and welcomed a mystery for its own sake. Was this the case? Was the tedium of statecraft relieved by the thrill of secrecy? We shall never know.

Three days after Otto had gone home, the news of his visit was disclosed to the citizens of Venice. Venetians have always loved a show, and at first there was bitter disappointment that they should have been deprived of the pageantry which usually accompanies a royal visit. But Orseolo was a shrewd man and he knew his people. He ordered three days of military games and contests to be held in the grass-grown Piazza, where the walls of the Campanile were rising and scaffolding still veiled the growing beauty of St Mark's. He also allowed the people to see clearly what they had gained from Otto's visit; and when the full story was told, scowls turned to smiles and the cheering crowd shouted *"Viva!"* for this best of Doges, who understood so well the needs of a commercial people.

Other triumphs were to follow. In 1004, the Byzantine Emperors appealed for help against a Saracen army which was besieging the town of Bari. Orseolo sailed for Apulia at once with a strong force and raised the siege, a victory which earned him the sincere gratitude of Basil and Constantine. The Doge's son, Giovanni, became their honoured guest at Constantinople, and when he returned to Venice he brought with him a bride, the Emperor's niece Maria.

And so the years went by until Orseolo the Great was in middle age. Then appeared a comet in the sky, a monstrous portent which the wise men and the astrologers interpreted as an evil omen. And for once they were right. With returning argosies from the East there came that dreaded visitant, the plague. It claimed thousands of victims in Venice, among them the Doge's son Giovanni, his Byzantine bride, and their infant son Basil. They were buried in one grave in the church of San Zaccaria.

When at last the pestilence subsided, Orseolo was a broken man. Apparently he was happily married; but by some strange kink of mind, either he or his wife must have come to believe that their union was sinful and contrary to the will of God and that they themselves were to blame for the misfortunes which had befallen them.

Both took vows of chastity; intercourse between them ceased; and they retired to the solitude of separate rooms in the Doge's Palace—rooms so small and bare that they were cells in their austerity. Thus, by withdrawal from the world, this tragic pair signified their atonement. It was meant to be a lifelong penance, but Orseolo died two years later. He was only forty-eight years of age.

Orseolo The Great was succeeded by his son and associate, Ottone, whose name had been changed from Pietro in honour of the Emperor's visit. Another son, Orso, became Bishop of Torcello and later Patriarch of Grado; and when he was elevated to the patriarchate, yet another son was promptly presented with the vacant bishopric. It is not surprising that there were accusations of nepotism, with dissatisfaction culminating in open revolt. Complicated quarrels and intrigues involving the House of Orseolo and the Patriarch of Aquileia ended in the expulsion of the Orseoli from Venice and the downfall of yet another Doge. In the fashion of those more enlightened times, Ottone's sentence was not death but simply exile to Constantinople—a not unenviable fate.

There followed the short and ineffective reign of Pietro Centranico who in four years contrived to undo much of Orseolo II's good work by offending the new German Emperor Conrad. Those hard-won and valuable concessions granted by Otto were withdrawn; and the Venetians, who had a short way with fools, tumbled the Doge from his throne. He too was banished to Constantinople and Ottone was invited to return. But the summons came too late. When the messenger reached the Imperial City, Ottone was dead.

The vacant throne was seized by an adventurer, one of the exiled Orseoli, but he was soon driven out. Feeble Doge succeeded feeble Doge—their names not worth recording—while the Dalmatian cities, no longer intimidated by the Narentine pirates and lacking the strong hand of Orseolo on the reigns, tried unsuccessfully to throw off what they now regarded as the yoke of Venice. But it was during those troubled times that changes were made which in the next hundred years or so were to alter the whole course of Venetian history. One was a law abolishing forever the right of a Doge to nominate an associate to share his office, for it was believed, not without reason, that the Partecipazii, Candiani and Orseoli had each tried to make use of a consort as a means of founding a dynasty. So firm measures were taken. Nominal advisers were appointed to guide the Doge, and it now became obligatory for him to consult the wisest of his nobles on all matters of importance. Out of these reforms there gradually emerged the Privy Council (*Consiglieri Ducale*) and the Senate (the *Pregadi* or *Invited*) which together did so much to reduce the all-powerful Doge to a mere figure-head.

Other steps were taken which it is not so easy for us to approve. But we live in a different age and are inclined to forget that circumstances change and that an eleventh-century Venetian noble did not pay even lip service to democracy. Already he and his fellow patricians saw quite clearly that their first task was to curb the commonality, a task which had already been begun by the great Orseolo. Gradually they would squeeze all plebeians out of the government. In the *concione* or general assembly the people still had a voice, but it was a voice which would be silenced forever when the nobles achieved their ambition and took all authority into their own hands. The seizure of power by a privileged minority would take many years to complete. The balance was tilting very slowly. But it would come down on their side.

In 1042 a Doge named Contarini died after twenty-eight years of harmless inactivity broken only by the recapture of Zara, which had revolted once more against Venetian rule. But during his obsequies in the church of San Nicolo del Lido, there was an extraordinary scene when the crowd, unanimously and spontaneously, called on one Domenico Selvo to become their next ruler.

Doge by popular acclaim, Selvo was a cultured man and a good soldier, but his career proved disappointing. It is chiefly remarkable for the fact that during his reign St Mark's was completed and consecrated. He was a great admirer of Byzantine art and it was in his time that the law was passed which made it illegal for any ship to return to Venice from the Levant without gold, marble or precious stones for the decoration of the Basilica. He loved the church and ransacked the Empire for riches with which to adorn and embellish it so that one day the whole interior would be inlaid with mosaic and worshippers would walk on onyx, agate and lapis lazuli. Thanks to Doge Selvo, St Mark's is said to be the finest Byzantine church in Western Europe.

The Empire also gave Doge Selvo a wife, the beautiful Princess Theodora from Constantinople, who is remembered for her voluptuousness, her inordinate love of perfumes, and for her curious habit of eating her food with a two-pronged golden fork after it had been cut up by eunuch slaves whom she had brought with her from Byzantium. There were rumours of gross immorality—probably slander spread by disapproving clerics who frowned upon her clothes, her scents and her sensuous habits.

It was in Domenico Selvo's time that Venice first came to grips with the Normans, that remarkable race of saints and soldiers which blazed briefly like a comet across Europe and the fringe of Asia, carrying in its wake the splendid concept of chivalry. Out of the mists of the North they had sailed as Vikings with Rolf the Ganger who was to end his days as Duke Rollo. Ceded land by Charles the Simple on condition that they were baptized, they had settled in France—or Frankland, as they called it—and embraced in all sincerity the faith which they had received so lightly. In a very short time Thor and Odin had yielded to the Cross of Christ and the sons of the sea rovers had adopted the language and customs of the French. They left their mark in the rounded, dog-toothed arches of many a church and castle and in a tradition of stern austerity both in their buildings and in their lives. But although they had abandoned their dragon-ships for knightly destriers, and the Viking *"Ahoy!"* for the Norman *"Haro!"* which was to ring across the known world from Hastings to Jerusalem, their nature had not changed. Nor had their love of war and conquest. On Senlac Hill their stark Duke William had just carved himself a kingdom; by 1081 Roger Tancred's son had wrested Sicily from the Saracens, while Robert Guiscard had made himself lord of Calabria and Apulia. It was these Italian adventures which brought them into conflict with Venice.

Robert Guiscard was an ambitious man. Provinces filched from the Byzantines did not satisfy him; his eyes were on Constantinople itself. As a stepping stone, the next conquest had to be Dalmatia, where a Norman army duly landed and besieged the port of Durazzo. Again the Dalmatians turned to Venice for help; and in view of their recent rebellions, there is a certain irony in the fact that their plea was addressed to the Doge as Duke of Dalmatia.

The Emperor Alexius Comnenus added his most urgent entreaty for help, for the great days of the Empire were over and the Byzantines, stripped of their provinces and under constant pressure from the Saracens, saw very clearly the significance of this new move. To the fury of the Normans, Venice was prompt to respond. A powerful fleet, commanded by Doge Selvo in person, crossed the Adriatic. But in an engagement on the landward side of Durazzo, the combined Venetian and Byzantine forces were routed by the invaders.

In 1085 the Republic suffered another severe defeat. This time, urged on by Vitale Falier,* one of Selvo's most jealous enemies, the Venetians rebelled and the unfortunate Doge, like several of his predecessors, heard monastery gates close firmly behind him. It is hardly surprising that his successor was Vitale Falier, for that is how the political game was played in eleventh-century Venice. To be fair, Falier ruled wisely and well and won the love of his people. But if he was to make good his position, his first task must be to redeem the honour of the Republic in the field. So when another appeal came from the Emperor Alexius, he equipped a strong fleet and army and set sail for Corfu. He was a fine leader and he was lucky, for this time the allies were victorious in their encounter with the Normans, and shortly afterwards Robert Guiscard died of the plague.

Alexius Comnenus showed his gratitude to Venice by issuing a second Golden Bull which granted his allies special rights and privileges. The Republic became a favoured nation with free entrance and exit for her ships in all Byzantine ports; and in Constantinople and other cities, whole streets of shops and warehouses were reserved for the exclusive use of Venetian merchants and traders.

Fortune was smiling on Venice and, as if this were not enough, a miracle was vouchsafed her. Since the disastrous fire of 976 nothing had been seen of the body of St Mark. There were doubters who whispered that it had perished in the flames, while others, more pious or more gullible, accepted the official story that it had been lost. This was a serious state of affairs, for pilgrims would flock to the shrine of a saint, and pilgrims were good spenders. No one would deny the

---

* "The concluding vowel is cut off according to familiar use in many Venetian names—Cornaro being pronounced Cornar; Loredano, Loredan; and so forth." *Makers of Venice*, Mrs. Oliphant, Macmillan (London, 1889), p. 40.

Venetians' sincerity in religious matters, but equally no one would deny that they had a sharp eye for business.

It is not known who had the inspiration; but one day it was announced with becoming gravity that, after a fast of three days and various religious processions, a solemn service of Intercession would be held in the Basilica in the hope that the city's most sacred relic might be restored to her.

On July 25, 1094, the service took place, attended by the Doge, by Henry the Holy Roman Emperor, and by all the chief representatives of Church and State. The priests were intoning, the choristers were chanting, when suddenly with a grinding noise two stones in a pillar supporting the altar of St James slowly opened and the whole great church was filled with a strange, delicious perfume.

As to what happened next, nobody seems to be quite clear. Some would have it that the Evangelist was revealed in his coffin. According to others, there was no casket, but from an opening in the pillar there emerged, first a hand, then an arm, and finally the whole body. Who would presume to say which is the correct version? But there can be no doubt that it was a most impressive miracle, of inestimable value to all faithful souls—and to the offertory.

Today, the actual point of emergence is marked by an elaborate mosaic tablet.

4. The Sign of The Cross

The Clearing House
The Call to Arms
The Siege of Tyre
The Rivals

The Republic of St Mark was now a force to be reckoned with. Placed as she was between East and West, she had hopes of becoming the clearing house for all the merchandise of the Mediterranean. The cream of the trade was still skimmed by her great rival, Constantinople; but in the Doge's Palace and on the Rialto Exchange her leaders were dreaming dreams; and always at the heart of them was Venice. Her ships and convoys carried her goods along the rivers and roads of Italy. Her fleets of merchantmen plied their trade in the Adriatic and the Aegean, and ranged the Mediterranean—the hub and centre of the known world. The Golden Bulls had given her the freedom of the Levantine ports. But that was not enough. She had competitors, and Venice must reign alone. That was the Venetians' ambition; and in their bold, unscrupulous way they set to work to achieve it.

Already, given one stroke of good fortune, they had the means to do so. For they had built ships which in their turn could build them a mighty maritime empire. And they were breeding a strong race of merchant adventurers: traders, sailors, soldiers if need be, who soon would be at home in London, Rouen and the towns of the Rhineland, in the markets of Trebizond and the bazaars of Beirut and Aleppo.

Their ships, and their ships only, would bring silk and jade and carved ivory from China, gems and spices from Hindustan, and carpets from Balkh, Bokhara and Samarkand, carried to the Levantine ports by the slow-plodding Arab caravans, to be bartered in Venice for Baltic amber, English wool and the fine cloth of Flanders. A dream that was destined to come true. But not yet. There were too many rivals in the field. The republics of Pisa and Genoa also produced fine ships and brave seamen; and most formidable of all as a trading competitor was her old ally and benefactor on the shores of the Sea of Marmora.

In Contantinople the long decline had begun. Byzantine territory had been overrun by Avars, Russians and Saracens, while the Emperor Constantine Ducas had tried to economize by making drastic cuts in the army just as a new and even more dangerous enemy loomed out of the East. Erupting from the plateaux of Turkestan, the Seljuk Turks had captured Khorassan, swept through Persia, and taken over the Abbasid Caliphate of Bagdad. Then their hordes of mounted archers from the banks of the Oxus had come pouring into Asia Minor; and in 1071, at Manzikert, Alp Arslan had won a victory over the imperial army which has been described by the historian Sir C. W. Oman as "the turning-point of the whole course of Byzantine history." With that marvellous resilience that enabled her to defy the infidel for a thousand years, Constantinople survived. Her army had been shattered, her Emperor taken by the Turks, and the pitiful remains of her empire reduced to impotence and anarchy. But the Imperial City was still guarded by the great Wall of Theodosius; and the Greek Fire, the secret of which had not yet been stolen from her by the Arabs, still enabled her to wage defensive war by land and sea. Shipping crowded the quays of the Golden Horn. Trade was slowly recovering. Constantinople, not Venice, was still the clearing house of the world. The Venetians were always scheming to usurp her position, but it was not until 1096 that things began to go their way, though the wisest among them could not have foreseen the change that was coming—or dreamed that the downfall of Constantinople would one day recoil on Venice herself.

It all began when a half-crazy priest from Amiens, whom the crowds called Peter the Hermit, rode through Western Europe on an ass, bearing a wooden cross and calling on all men to arm and march against the enemies of God. Jerusalem and the Holy Places had long been in the hands of the Moslems; but Omar, who had captured the city in 637, had treated all Christians, including pilgrims, with tolerance and clemency, and his example had been followed by other rulers. Indeed, Haroun al-Raschid, with typical Saracen chivalry, had symbolically ceded the Church of the Holy Sepulchre to the Emperor Charlemagne. But now things were different. The Turks were in possession—the terrible Seljuks who, like the Huns before them, were said to kill for the sheer love and lust of it, laying waste whole provinces.

There are signs that when they reached the Holy Land the Turks had had their fill of blood, but pilgrims were hampered and abused, and there was danger that Christ's Sepulchre might be desecrated or destroyed. It is possible that Peter the Hermit may have been ill-treated while on pilgrimage. Whether he was the victim of physical violence or whether the Turks prevented him from reaching the Holy Places is not known: all that is certain is that Moslems—all Moslems—had made a dangerous enemy. This fanatic possessed a fiery eloquence and he was a born rabble-rouser. Whole cities and provinces hung on his words as if he had been inspired; and as he travelled like an avenging angel through the kingdoms of the West, men sobbed and prayed and openly adored the beast that bore him.

Never was there such a religious revival as that begun by the priest from Amiens. Coming as it did not long after an impassioned sermon on the same theme by Pope Urban at Clermont, it was the direct cause of the First Crusade—if not of all seven. The Pope had reaffirmed the Truce of God, ending all private feuds and calling on all Christians to recover the Tomb of Christ. The summons spread like flame. All over Europe men flew to arms and took the cross with shouts of "God wills it!" Princes and commoners dedicated their lives to the Holy War, while the maritime republics of Italy vied with each other in supplying transport for the armies which were being raised. All, that is, except Venice.

That the powers of Christendom should thus be united was a good thing. Singly, they would have been overwhelmed by the tidal wave of Islam. And that so many men should have answered the call is one of the wonders of history. Of course men's motives were mixed. Even though we read with horror of the excesses of the crusaders, it would be wrong to belittle the genuine religious fervour which drew many thousands, perhaps the majority, from their homes to venture into the unknown on what they sincerely believed to be a divinely inspired mission. There were many of godly life and unblemished honour: men like St Louis of France, and Godfrey de Bouillon who led the First Crusade and who, when offered the throne of Jerusalem, would accept only the title of Defender of the Holy Sepulchre; he was not worthy, he said, to wear a crown of gold where his Saviour had worn a Crown of Thorns. Others of coarser fibre were out for plunder, or, like Richard Lion-Heart, simply because they liked fighting. And there must have been many who saw in a crusade a heaven-sent way of escape. Palestine was a long way off. It meant freedom and change for years and years.

One must always remember that one of the worst trials of life in the Middle Ages was sheer, unmitigated boredom, especially for those unfortunates who spent their lives cooped up in castles. They were bored to death by inactivity and by the sight of the same faces day after day, bored by the eternal salt beef and herrings of the long winter months, by the minstrels' extremely limited repertoire and the jester's bewhiskered wisecracks, even perhaps by a nagging wife—who was just as bored by her husband. And now an escape was offered by this glorious enterprise: travel, adventure, knightly deeds to be done, merit acquired by the mere fact of setting foot in the Holy Land, the voluptuous houris of the East, Saracens to be slain, and—most important of all—forgiveness of sins (*peccaminum remissio*, as the priests called it), even if one's past peccadillos included such trifles as rape and murder.

The call to the crusades roused the highest and lowest instincts in man. All honour to those who drew their swords for the love of God, for the love of chivalry: we must not underestimate their number. But the mediaeval baron and man-at-arms was a fighting animal; and this was one of the few occasions in history when a man could gratify his blood lust in the confident hope that by doing so he was ensuring his own salvation. He could—and did, quite literally—splash through blood up to his ankles in the streets of Jerusalem and then raise his reeking hands in prayer, with tears of joy running down his cheeks. What is so strange and so horrible is that in many cases he was quite sincere.

The crusaders' record of atrocities was appalling, even for those days. When they set up their ramshackle little realm of Outremer, with its Kingdom of Jerusalem, its principalities and counties—Edessa, Tripoli and Antioch—they combined the luxury of the Orient with the morals of robber barons. And all this where Christ had lived and died and taught men to love their neighbours.

Among those who took part in the First Crusade was the Army of the Poor, recruited from a brutalized peasantry and the rabble of the cities. It followed Peter the Hermit in a huge struggling column through Central Europe and the Balkans, plundering, killing and being killed, and leaving behind it a trail of devastation and misery. The others too—the Armies of the Princes—mostly travelled overland to the muster at Constantinople, though some crossed the Adriatic in Italian transports. Yet still the Venetians held back, and this is surprising. Shrewd though they were, it seems to have escaped them that they were failing to take advantage of a very profitable undertaking.

The first crusaders to reach the Bosphorus were Peter the Hermit's Poor. The Byzantines received them kindly and were repaid by looting and outrage. The armed rabble then crossed into Asia, where the Turkish archers mowed them down and made a great pyramid of their corpses. Peter himself was one of the very few who escaped the carnage.

The better organized contingents of the nobles were more fortunate. But when that conglomerate force from all over Europe prepared to march through Byzantine territory, the Emperor began to make difficulties. In many ways His Magnificence, the Emperor Alexius Comnenus, was an admirable ruler. He did not lack courage, he was merciful to his enemies, and he did much to save the remains of the Empire from complete disintegration. But even by Byzantine standards the man was a consummate liar who regarded prevarication as a legitimate weapon of diplomacy. Subtle and devious, he now brought all his cunning into play to reap what advantage he could from this very tricky situation. Realizing that the Army of the Cross would be operating in his own lost provinces, he persuaded the leaders to pay him homage, for thus, he reasoned, they became his vassals. Any conquests they made would be in his name, and the territory would be returned to him as part of his lost empire. It was very clever; it cost him some veiled threats, a lot of tact, and a lot of money. But His Magnificence did not understand the men with whom he was dealing.

Soon the Venetians would have to choose between the smooth, cultured Greeks and the iron warriors from the West. They represented two different and potentially hostile civilizations, and with the crusaders in Constantinople the situation was explosive. For the time being, an open breach was avoided. But it must have been with profound relief that in the spring of 1097 the Byzantines watched the crusading host—the Latins, as they called them—cross the Bosphorus, to be greeted by a huge mound of bleached bones. Peter's Army of the Poor. For the Crusaders it was not an encouraging omen.

Still the Venetians hung back, unwilling to commit themselves. At last, however, after the storming of Jerusalem in which, it has been estimated, 70,000 Saracens were slaughtered, a fresh appeal from the Pope roused them to action. The new Doge, Vitale Michiel I, convened a general assembly at which he pointed out, rather belatedly, the Republic's religious duty. So, after a service at St Mark's where new banners were consecrated, a fleet of two hundred ships sailed from the Lido, commanded by the Doge's son Giovanni and the Bishop of Costello—doubtless one of those warrior-prelates who wore mail under their robes and fought with a mace lest, as priests, they should be guilty of the effusion of blood.

One can imagine their splendid departure, with silken standards and sails making great splashes of vivid colour against the dull shimmer of mail, for the decks were crowded with a brave company bearing on shield and shoulder the azure cross of Italian crusaders. Brass trumpets sparkled in the sunlight as the armada got under way—stately galleys and dromonds, sails billowing and banks of wet oars glistening as slowly they rose and fell. On the sandy shore the people cheered, priests prayed, and the white-robed choristers sang, as gradually the shrill of the trumpets and the throbbing drums faded and died. The singing stopped. The spectators on the Lido strained their eyes till, growing smaller and smaller, like bright toys, those two hundred ships melted into the deep blue of the Adriatic.

The Venetians wintered at Rhodes and almost at once there was trouble, for the Pisans were there, and Pisa and Venice were enemies of long standing. There was a quarrel—some say about the owner-ship of the sacred relic—and, not for the last time, crusaders pledged to a holy cause turned their swords against each other. In the fight that followed, which almost amounted to a pitched battle, the Venetians were victorious. But the harm had been done. They may well have had their tongues in their cheeks when, in the presence chamber of the Blaquernal Palace at Constantinople, they made their reverence to the Emperor; but the fight at Rhodes must have encouraged Alexius in his efforts to drive a wedge between his old allies and their fellow crusaders. In this he failed, and his failure was certainly one of the reasons for the steadily worsening relations between Venice and Constantinople.

In their first campaign in Palestine the Venetians acquitted themselves well. Having rendered good service at the siege of Jaffa, they returned to Venice; but in 1102 a second expedition sailed to the help of Baldwin, King of Jerusalem. On his behalf they captured the city of Sidon and were richly rewarded by the gift of a church, a street and a marketplace, with the right to use their own weights and measures and to legislate in their own courts.

Meanwhile, at home in Italy, things were not going too well for the Republic. There had been some fighting: in Tuscany, in support of the Pope, and as the ally of Caloman, King of Hungary, against Normans who had been harrying the coast of Dalmatia. The reward of victory had been the usual trading rights, for Venice had no use for laurels: she much preferred sound commercial treaties to crown her feats of arms.

These gains were great but they were soon offset by the disasters which ravaged the lagoon towns. The islands were swept by storms and hurricanes of almost tropical fury, and it was at this time that the old Malamocco was submerged beneath the sea. Following the tempests came two of the worst fires that the city had experienced. The Doge's Palace and the Basilica were both damaged and many other churches were burned, including San Zaccaria, where over a hundred nuns died of suffocation.

To add to these troubles, Caloman of Hungary chose this moment to turn against his former ally. Marching into Croatia, he invited the Slavs of the Dalmatian coast to rise against their Venetian overlords, and a powerful fleet had to be sent to quell the insurrection. Two years later the trouble flared up again; and this time, at the edge of Zara, the Venetians were defeated and their Doge killed in an engagement outside the walls of the city. This grievous loss, following so closely on their other misfortunes, so disheartened the Venetians that they sank their pride and sent envoys to sue for peace with the Hungarians.

The Doge who was killed at Zara was the first of the Falieri, an able and active man who, if he had lived, might well have become one of the great Doges. It was he who began to build the enormous Arsenal of Venice which, until the fall of the Republic, was one of the sights of Europe. He was succeeded by another of the Michieli, Domenico, one of whose first acts was to conclude a five-year peace with Stephen, the new King of Hungary. Like his predecessor, he was a man of integrity, combining courage and caution with sound judgement.

Bad news was coming out of Palestine, and King Baldwin of Jerusalem had appealed to the Pope for help. Since the War of the Investiture between the Papacy and the German Emperor had just come to an end, Calixtus II forwarded Baldwin's letter to the Doge, at the same time urging the Venetians to take up arms and go to the aid of their hard-pressed brethren in the Holy Land.

Michiel's response was immediate and typical of the man. A leader in more than name, he had resolved to take command of an expedition in person. But first his people must be roused to action. In an eloquent address in St Mark's, he called for volunteers to take the cross. With reverence he stressed the religious nature of the expedition, but—and here spoke the true Venetian—he did not forget to mention the glory to be won for the Republic or the financial advantages which would follow a successful campaign in the East.

A strong fleet set sail from the Lido and besieged Corfu where, having gained command of the harbour, the crusaders wintered. Then, in the spring of 1123, they weighed anchor and continued on their leisurely way to Palestine, breaking their journey—apparently for no good reason—to ravage the Greek islands. Still full of crusading zeal and considerably richer than when they left Venice, they were met by the disturbing news that the Saracens were blockading Jaffa.

The Doge was equal to the occasion. Dividing his fleet into two squadrons, he ordered one to head straight for Jaffa and the other to change course, in the hope that its ships might be mistaken for merchantmen carrying pilgrims from Cyprus. The ruse succeeded. The Saracens, sighting what appeared to be easy prey, sailed out to intercept the smaller squadron; but the Venetians had cunningly timed their movements so that the enemy could not come to grips before nightfall. Then, as arranged, during the hours of darkness the two squadrons joined forces and when dawn broke the Saracens found themselves facing the whole Venetian fleet. There are sickening accounts of the slaughter—and of the sea itself stained red— sickening even to the men of those cruel times. But it was a great victory for the crusaders, and Michiel and his men cast anchor safely in the port of Jaffa.

Without delay the Venetian army pushed on to Jerusalem. By this time King Baldwin was a prisoner of the Saracen chieftain Balak of Mardin. But Eustace Graverius was acting as Regent, and he, the Doge, and other lords of the Latins held a council of war to decide where to strike. After many setbacks, it was essential that they should take the offensive; but should their attack be launched on Tyre or on that comparatively easy objective, the city of Ascalon? It was a difficult question, and their method of finding an answer would be unthinkable today. One hardly dares to imagine the reaction to such a suggestion in Whitehall or the Pentagon. But, after all, this was the Age of Faith; and to those hardbitten warriors, fighting in God's quarrel, it seemed only logical to leave the judgement to God. They decided to cast lots.

There does not seem to have been a single dissentient voice. But before he committed himself and his men, the wily Doge Michiel dictated his terms. He set a high price on Venetian cooperation and he did not mince his words. One whole street in every city of the Kingdom of Jerusalem was to become the property of the Republic, with its own church, market and bakehouse: in other words, a Venetian quarter. The Venetians were to be exempt from taxes; they were to enjoy certain legal rights; all imports were to be free of duty; and every year the Kingdom would pay the Republic three hundred golden bezants. And finally, as if this were not enough, the Doge added that to Venice must be ceded one-third of Tyre, Ascalon and their dependent fiefs when, as everyone hoped and believed, those cities fell to the crusaders.

No doubt he expressed himself most courteously, but it was a question of take it or leave it. The Regent accepted: he had no alternative. And only then, business satisfactorily settled, did the Venetians throw themselves wholeheartedly into the enterprise, proving themselves loyal and valiant allies in an arduous campaign. But first the lots were cast—a matter of life and death for many men, Christian and Moslem. In church, after Mass had been celebrated, two slips of parchment were placed in a pyx on the altar. On one was written the word "Ascalon"; on the other, "Tyre." A child was led forward. He drew one slip. "Tyre." They had received their marching orders.

So the city of Tyre was invested, and it proved even harder to subdue than had been expected. Giant catapults, mangonels, movable siege-towers and all the engines of mediaeval warfare were employed, but the garrison held out resolutely and the crusaders began to lose heart. In their lines morale was low, for their spies had brought them news, true or false, of an army from Damascus and an Egyptian fleet which would soon be on their way to relieve the beleaguered city. Then ugly rumours began to circulate that the Venetians were not to be trusted. There were many who hated them—outside as well as inside the walls of Tyre; and it was those secret enemies who whispered that if the siege went on much longer, the Venetians would slip away in their ships, leaving their allies to face the onset of the infidels alone.

When this canard reached the ears of Doge Michiel, his answer was prompt and characteristic of the man. He had certain planks removed from each of his ships, thus rendering them unseaworthy; then, with these planks and a number of rudders and oars carried behind him, he strode into the Council of War and had them flung down, smelling as they did of pitch and sea salt, under the noses of the assembled nobles and dignitaries of the Church. And then he spoke his mind. In blistering words he made them understand that although Venetians drove a hard bargain they did not shirk the consequences.

Another two months passed before the siege of Tyre was brought to an end by the capture of a carrier pigeon. How the bird was taken is uncertain; but soon it was on its way again into the city, carrying, not the message of hope and encouragement sent by the Sultan of Damascus, but another message, also in Arabic, which was calculated to spread alarm and despondency among the garrison.

That simple stratagem was decisive. Not knowing that an army from Damascus was being sent to relieve them, the defenders of Tyre laid down their arms; and on the towers of the ancient Phoenician stronghold there flew the royal standard of Jerusalem, the banner of the Count of Tripoli, and the Lion of St Mark. A short time afterwards, Ascalon fell; and all arrangements having been made for the handing over and administration of their new territories, the Venetians decided that their work was done. Once more they sailed for home. In the holds of their ships were much goldsmiths' work, fine cloth of the famous Tyrian purple, and another trophy of war, of infinitely greater value. Outside the gates of Tyre the crusaders had seen and wondered at a certain great stone. According to tradition, Jesus Himself had rested on it after a journey; it was even said that He had used it as a pulpit from which to address the crowd. It is now in the Baptistry of St Mark's.

Venetian gains in the Holy Land were difficult for the Byzantines to accept. Their one-time dependents and humble allies, now acting with all the energy and drive which they themselves had lost, were winning too large a proportion of the trade which until now had passed through the great clearing house of Constantinople. And certainly the Venetian traders were arrogant and aggressive. At one time there were 200,000 of them in the imperial capital itself; and in the maze of quays, alleys and warehouses, down by the Golden Horn, their riotous behavior and frequent brawls had become a public nuisance. So the Emperor and his advisers decided to take firm action. They gave instructions that Venetian trading should be hampered and that all Venetian shipping in Byzantine waters should be impounded.

It is not difficult to guess what the reaction was on the Rialto. Those effete Byzantines must be taught a lesson. His Magnificence on his tottering throne must learn to give way to the men of tomorrow. The call to arms was immediate; and the Doge himself sailed with an avenging fleet to cut a swathe of destruction through the archipelago and the Morea, proving to that gilded idol in his palace on the Bosphorus that the Lion of St Mark had not only wings but also teeth and claws. His mission accomplished, he went home by way of the Dalmatian coast, stopping to teach yet another lesson to Zara and other Slavonian cities which, as usual, were in revolt. Then, back in his beloved Venice, amid the plaudits of his people, Domenico Michiel sheathed his sword forever. Wiser than many in his high office who outlived their good luck, the "Terror of the Greeks," as they called him on his monument, retired to the peaceful island monastery of San Giorgio Maggiore—whether as monk or honoured guest, we do not know—and there, among the olive groves, he died in 1130.

The next two Doges, Michiel's son-in-law, Pietro Polani, and Domenico Morosini, are treated somewhat cavalierly in the history books because their reigns were, for those days, comparatively free from battle, murder and sudden death. Between them, they gave the Republic over a quarter of a century of strong, peaceful government. It was a period of consolidation from which Venice emerged well on her way to becoming a great nation. Trade and, consequently, wealth and power increased. Treaties were negotiated with neighbouring Italian states, with Antioch and other cities of Syria, and with the Norman rulers of Apulia and Sicily, all of which was gall and wormwood to the Byzantines. It has been estimated that in the fifty years following the First Crusade, Constantinople lost between a third and a half of her trade, mostly to Venice and Genoa. What particularly shocked the Emperor and other Christian rulers was that the Venetians, although they would go crusading if it suited them, were still quite unrepentant about retaining commercial relations with the hated Saracens. The Republic, as ever, had an eye to the main chance.

That there were minor military operations goes without saying. It was in Pietro Polani's time, in a campaign against Padua, that Venice first employed mercenaries on the mainland of Italy; there was some fighting with the Pisans; and later, in 1147, the Doge led an expedition against the Normans, who were again menacing the eastern coast of the Adriatic. Surprisingly, this action was in response to an appeal from the Emperor Manuel. By this time, there was no love lost between the Republic and the Empire; but the Venetians were realists, and the bold and efficient Normans, striking out from their kingdoms in Sicily and in the toe and heel of Italy, were as grave a menace to the Republic as they were to Constantinople. Surely it was more intelligent to fight with allies than without? Moreover, Manuel had made a campaign worth while by promising to renew the privilege granted to the Venetians by his grandfather Alexius. So the drums rolled, the trumpets brayed, and another fleet sailed from the Lido with the Doge in command. But at Corfu Pietro Polani was taken ill, and soon afterwards he died.

Morosini's short reign of seven years saw the end of the patched-up peace between the Venetians and the Byzantines. In the fighting that followed, the Venetians had the worst of it. They were beaten in several engagements and vented spleen in an insult which was to have grave consequences. Having captured an imperial galley, they decked it with cloth of gold and other rich hangings; and in this splendid setting, they posed a particularly hideous slave, dressed in a dalmatic of stiff brocade which was a recognizable parody of the imperial robe of state. On his head was an imitation diadem and in his hand they placed some object to represent the orb. Then, as he went the round of the fleet, they bowed low, cheering and hailing him as Emperor of the East.

It was an ill-natured joke which they were bitterly to regret. It has been generally admitted that Manuel Comnenus was not handsome; but, to his own subjects, he was a semi-sacred personage before whom lesser beings prostrated themselves in the Oriental fashion. Such a jest, therefore, was almost blasphemy and quite unforgivable. But Manuel was a true Byzantine. At the time he was too closely engaged even to dream of vengeance. So he held his peace and waited. But he did not forget.

The next Doge, Vitale, was another of the Michieli. He mounted the throne in 1156 and the early years of his unhappy reign were occupied by the struggle which was rending Italy in two—between the Guelphs, adherents of the Pope, and the Ghibellines, who supported the Holy Roman Emperor. Then, in 1171, after waiting for over twenty years for his revenge, Manuel Comnenus struck. On the twelfth of March, suddenly and without warning, every Venetian throughout the Byzantine dominions was to be thrown into a dungeon and his property confiscated. The secret was well kept until the time came for action; but it so happened that in Constantinople there was a certain Venetian shipbuilder who was high in the Emperor's favour. In his yard was a fast little ship which had just been fitted out. Somehow he heard of the plot and disclosed it to two of his fellow countrymen, Sebastiano Ziani and Orio Malipiero, both then serving as plenipotentiaries and both future Doges of Venice. Just before the arrests were made, he smuggled them and a few other Venetians down to his shipyard on the Golden Horn; and before it was even suspected that an escape had been made, his ship was away and out through the Dardanelles, to carry home to the Rialto this story of Byzantine treachery.

There could be only one answer to this outrage. The citizens of the Republic demanded vengeance. Vitale Michiel II set to work to equip an expedition; but even while obeying the overwhelming demand of his people, it was this unhappy man's misfortune to incur their animosity. After several decades of sporadic warfare, the coffers were empty; and the Doge resorted to the unpopular expedient of levying a loan at an interest of four percent, payable twice yearly, on the six *sestieri* or districts into which the city was, and still is, divided. Eventually this led to the formation of the Banco Giro, which also paid four percent interest semi-annually to the holders of its bonds, which could be sold, bequeathed or mortgaged. Thus to Venice belongs the honour of founding the first State bank in Europe, while at the same time she was responsible for the first national debt.

In September of that same year, 1171, a fleet was ready and sailed for the East, with the Doge in command. In leading his men in person he was only following the example of his predecessors; but he was not blessed with their good fortune. It can hardly be denied that he was partly to blame for the troubles which were to follow. As a rule, the Venetians could not be accused of lacking craft and guile. But Vitale Michiel was completely outwitted by the wily Greeks and played into their hands from the first.

The Venetian fleet sailed southwards along the coast of Dalmatia, fighting several minor actions; then set a course for the Aegean and the unhappy Greek islands, which had suffered greatly in the turmoil of those warlike days. Perhaps the Doge expected to meet an enemy squadron. If so, he was disappointed. The Emperor Manuel was playing a deeper and more subtle game than open war. As the Venetians were nearing the great island of Negropont (now Euboea) they were met by Byzantines, not in mail but in the silken robes of peace. They were ambassadors from Manuel and they blandly suggested that the present dispute could best be settled in a civilized manner at a conference.

It sounded reasonable enough. But one had to be very wary of those smiling courtiers from Constantinople. Vitale Michiel was no match for them and he fell into the trap. He ordered his fleet to anchor at Scio; and then for weeks and months there were negotiations. All through the winter the talks dragged on, sapping the fighting spirit of the Venetians and breeding discord in their camp. Boredom proved a more dangerous enemy than the Greek Emperor's Varangian Guards. Then came that even deadlier foe, the pestilence, which swept through the Venetian lines and decimated their forces. There were rumours, probably unfounded, that the Byzantines had poisoned the wells; but whatever the cause, little could be done in those days against the infection. The Venetians' courage and weapons were useless, and their rout was absolute. There was no need for the Emperor Manuel to order his fleet into action. All that was left of Michiel's expedition straggled back to the Lido in a few ships; and, as if this were not enough, they took the pestilence with them. It raged through all the quarters of the city, taking toll of men, women and children, and fanning public anger against the Doge who had allowed himself to be fooled.

A pathetic story is told of the Guistiani, one of the oldest and noblest families in Venice. Like most other families, gentle and simple, they had responded at once to the call to arms. One son had entered the monastery of San Nicolo; but with that one exception, every male Guistiani of military age had volunteered for service, and every one of them had died. The ancient family faced extinction; but when news of this tragedy reached the Pope, His Holiness gave his consent and the ex-novice was married to Anna Michiel, the daughter of the Doge. They had several sons and then parted forever, he to take his vows at San Nicolo del Lido, and she to enter a nunnery where, we are told, she led such a holy life that she was honoured after death with the title of *beata* or blessed.

And now Doge Vitale Michiel reaped the fruits of his folly. The appalling death roll of the plague, the loss of their fleet, and the humiliating knowledge that they had been outwitted, so infuriated the people that when the Doge tried to explain himself before an angry crowd in St Mark's, weapons were brandished and his voice was drowned in the uproar. He faced them bravely, calm and dignified until, realizing that words were useless—and perhaps guessing what was coming—he quietly left the Basilica and set off alone through narrow ways to the church of San Zaccario to seek in private prayer divine help and guidance in his trouble. A tragic, lonely figure, he did not quite reach the end of his journey, for he had been followed by an enemy—some say a man of good family. In that lane which is now called the Calle delle Rasse, this man came softly up behind the Doge, reached over his shoulder, and struck downwards with his dagger. Vitale Michiel had just enough strength left to stagger to the church and into the arms of the priest, who heard his whispered confession and gave him absolution before he died.

5. Barbarossa

For all the increase in trade, 1171 was a black year for Venice, and there must have been many who wondered whether her attempt to gain more power at the expense of her great rival had failed ignominiously. The city was seething with unrest, and, discredited abroad, the Venetians' longing for revenge on the Byzantines remained unsatisfied. It is true that Constantinople was no longer the sole clearing house for the Mediterranean, but Venice was not the only competitor in the race. Both Genoa and Pisa were running her close, and the Republic had temporarily lost heart and strength for the contest.

Desperate needs require desperate remedies, and there were strong men, nobles of the ancient families, who kept their heads in the crisis and took matters into their own hands. They decided that before they elected another Doge, the very basis of their government would have to be remodelled. No one, high or low, had any desire for a dictator. Therefore, it must no longer be possible for a Doge, acting on his own initiative, to do irreparable harm to the State by some irresponsible or ill-timed move for which he could not be called to account. On the other hand, these nobles were equally determined that all power should be taken out of the hands of the common people, that unpredictable crowd of men and women, fickle and dangerous, who came swarming out of the alleys at the first sign of trouble. Both must be barred: the tyranny of an autocrat and the tyranny of the mob. What the patricians of Venice wanted and eventually achieved was all power in their own hands: an aristocratic oligarchy.

Their first step was to lay the foundations of the Great Council (*Maggior Consiglio*). Twelve electors, two from each of the six *sestieri*, were each to choose forty reliable men, making 480 councillors in all. From now on, this council was to be paramount in all matters affecting the safety and well-being of the Republic.

As for the Doge, his power was supposed to have been curbed by the appointment of two nominal advisers, but he had usually managed to twist these pliant gentlemen round his finger. Now this was to end. The number of his "advisers" was to be increased to six and they would have real authority. In no matter of importance would the Doge be free to act without their advice—or, perhaps it would be more correct to say, their consent. But to compensate the Doge for this brake upon his actions, he was to be allowed an extra measure of quite meaningless pomp. Whenever he deigned to leave the palace he was to be escorted by nobles; and, in addition to the trumpets and banners and *baldachino*, beloved by the monarchs of the East, he was to be carried in a magnificent chair, scattering money to the cheering crowd.

And lastly, the people. Here the nobles struck a snag. They had determined that a new Doge must be chosen by eleven councillors and that he must win at least nine of their votes before he was elected. Then in St Mark's, merely as a formality, he would be presented to the people, who would be asked to ratify the decision that had been made for them. It was hardly subtle and the astute Venetians saw at once that their freedom of choice was becoming a mockery. There was an uproar within the precincts of the Basilica until to the proclamation were added these words: "This is your Doge, if it please you"—meaning that no election would be valid without the approval of the people. That satisfied them and they raised a triumphant *arengo*.

The first Doge to be elected under the new rule was the aged Sebastiano Ziani. It is said that Orio Malipiero, who had been his companion during that hazardous escape from Constantinople, was the electors' first choice but that generously he gave way to his friend, insisting that Ziani was the better man. Be that as it may, the new Doge, who was seventy when he took office in 1172, was one of the greatest rulers of Venice and his short reign of six years was crowded with strange and stirring events.

His first act was to punish the murderer of his predecessor; then, being a man of peace, he devoted all his powers to the difficult task of pacifying the enemies of the Republic. With the Norman rulers of Sicily and Southern Italy he was successful and a peace of twenty years was agreed on. But there was no placating the outraged Emperor of the Byzantines. That insulting impersonation of Manuel had not been forgotten or forgiven. Ziani tried to effect a reconciliation but there was no response. In the end he became tired of negotiating with those vengeful Greeks, and when the Holy Roman Emperor asked for help against them, the Venetians sent a fleet to take part in the siege of Ancona. Their action was not entirely disinterested, for this promontory town on the Adriatic was one of the few remaining Byzantine possessions in Italy, and as such, the Venetians would have been only too ready to eliminate it. By its gallant defence, however, the garrison resisted all their efforts, and the German Emperor and his allies were forced to withdraw.

This Emperor, Frederick Barbarossa, or Redbeard, not to be confused with the Barbarossa brothers, Khair-ed-Din and Baba-Aroudj, notorious Algerine corsairs of the sixteenth century, was one of the most remarkable characters of the Middle Ages. He has been described as a magnificent failure, but the story of his deeds furnished many a minstrel with song and story; and, like Arthur of Britain, he became a legendary figure to his own subjects. For years they cherished the belief that Barbarossa did not die but slept in a cavern under the Kyffhäuser mountain in Thuringia, and that he would rouse himself to save Germany in the hour of her greatest need.

When one studies these mediaeval people one finds nothing more amazing than the good and evil, the god and devil, which could coexist in the same person. A man might be a devout Christian, just to his neighbour and kind to the poor, yet be capable of pitiless ferocity. Such a man was Barbarossa. Everything about this heroic redbeard was larger than life: he bestrode the turbulent Europe of his time like a colossus. In his own land he was revered as an enlightened and benevolent ruler; beyond the Alps his very name struck terror as being that of a ruthless aggressor and an enemy of God. He could be brutally cruel, for he lived in an age when cruelty was customary; but he was also magnanimous and wise, and his reign was enriched by other arts besides the ancient art of war. It was in his time that those knightly poets, the minnesingers, first flourished in Germany and that ancient myths were woven into that great epic, the *Niebelungenlied*.

Already the titular ruler of Germany and Italy, Barbarossa's life-long ambition was to revive the fading glories of the Holy Roman Empire, with himself as a second Charlemagne and the Pontiff as his complaisant partner. And this was the rock on which he foundered. In 1159, long before Ziani became Doge, a new Pope had been elected—Alexander III. But the Emperor had arranged for a nominee of his own to be chosen by a minority of the cardinals. When he set up this candidate, Victor IV, as an anti-pope, Alexander had no alternative but to resort to arms, and it became a struggle for supremacy between the spiritual and temporal lords of western Christendom.

Six times during those years of war between Guelphs and Ghibellines, Barbarossa had invaded Italy. But he had met his match in Alexander—his equal in courage, his superior in perseverance and tenacity. Twice this great Pope had been driven from Rome; but even in exile, the man who could force Henry II of England to do penance for the murder of Becket refused to bow before the armed might of this fiery redbeard from the black forests of Swabia.

In 1162 Barbarossa had taken Milan, and for the time being the city-states of the North had submitted to his rule. But five years later, after he had stormed his way into Rome itself, the plague decimated his army and the cities of the Plain of Lombardy seized their chance to rise against him. There followed years of warfare between this Lombard League and the Imperialists. The Pope was a fugitive and it looked as if Barbarossa would crush all opposition. Then, in 1176, at the battle of Legnano, in the Ticino Valley, the German invaders were routed by the Milanese and their allies. In those days Milan, like most city-states, arrayed her army round the *carroccio,* a high car drawn by oxen and carrying banners, trumpeters, and an altar at which a priest prayed for victory. This moving shrine was their ark, their rallying point, just as, in years to come, the colours were the rallying point of a regiment. Men were ready to die in its defence, and Barbarossa knew that the psychological effect of the capture of the *carroccio* could be decisive. He drove straight at the sacred car with his heavy mailed cavalry, but before the Germans could reach it, they were repulsed and driven from the field in disorder by a company of Milanese youths who wore the badge of the skull and crossbones and called themselves the Band of Death. Barbarossa, his horse killed under him, was buried under a heap of dead and wounded. The loss of their leader disheartened his men, who broke and fled, hotly pursued, many of them drowning in the river. When the first fugitives reached Como, the Empress put on mourning for him. But Barbarossa was not dead. He had managed to free himself; under cover of darkness he had escaped from the field, and three days later he was safe in Pavia.

It was then that Venice intervened. All this time she had tried to keep aloof from the strife of Guelph and Ghilbelline which was rending Italy in two. In the city there had been a certain amount of brawling between adherents of the rival factions; but officially the Republic preferred not to declare herself openly, for she was determined not to find herself on the losing side. Safe on her islands, she had affected neutrality while secretly supporting the Lombard League. But after Legnano she hastened to acknowledge Alexander as Sovereign Pontiff, thus earning the gratitude of the Pope and incurring the anger of Barbarossa.

And now we come to one of the strangest episodes in the history of Venice—if, indeed, it is fact and not fiction. Opinion is divided. Some modern historians are inclined to dismiss the story as a myth; but Sanudo, Sabellico and other old chroniclers believed it implicitly. And as if to defy all doubt, the whole tale is told in pictures in the Hall of the Great Council. This legend has it that Pope Alexander, while a fugitive, visited Venice in the disguise of a pilgrim and lived secretly, some say for as long as six months, in the monastery of Santa Maria della Carita, the remains of which now form part of the Accademia di Belle Arti. As usual in these cases, there are several versions of the story. According to one, the Pope spent his first night in Venice in the porch of San Salvatore, not far from St Mark's, and his second wandering through the dark winding alleys of the city till, just as dawn broke, he knocked at the door of a building which looked like a religious house. It was, in fact, Carita, where he was accepted as a guest, earning his keep by working as a scullion. In the end he was recognized, either by a monk who had seen him in exile, or by a pilgrim who had been in Rome during the short period which preceded Alexander's flight from the city.

At all events, sometime during the summer of 1177 the aged Doge Ziani was told the amazing news that the Pope had sought sanctuary in Venice. When the story had been confirmed he gave orders for a ship to be made ready to convey His Holiness to the palace of the Bishop of Grado. Then Doge and Bishop and all the chief clergy and officers of state went in solemn procession to the door of the monastery which had received this signal honour. One can imagine that summer day so long ago: the line of boats slowly gliding down the sunlit Grand Canal, the gleams and flecks of light on jewelled vestments, the almost blinding white of surplices, the glitter of the water, the banner of St Mark—scarlet and gold against a cobalt sky—and over all, the haze of incense rising from the swinging censers, as the Vicar of Christ was led from the kitchen to the palace of the Patriarch.

Is this story true? One would like to think so. When we recall the visit of Otto, 176 years before, and the atmosphere of melodrama which permeates all Venetian history, it is easy to believe that the chroniclers may have been telling the truth. Certainly the fugitive Pope was a clever man, and until Legnano had been fought and won he cannot have been sure of his welcome. The sensible course was to go into hiding and see how the Venetians would react. Or did he, as some authorities maintain, visit Venice quite openly? It would have been dangerous. Perhaps the truth lies somewhere between the two. Perhaps Alexander did arrive secretly and stay incognito at a monastery until such time as it was safe for him to make his presence known in the right quarter; and later the chroniclers may have added colourful details, pandering to the Venetian taste for intrigue. It is a fascinating question but it is unlikely that there will ever be a satisfactory answer.

Only one thing is certain: the Pope was in Venice, and Ziani the peacemaker hastened to take advantage of this unexpected good fortune. When one considers the character of this truly great Doge one cannot believe that his desire for peace was anything but disinterested. Nevertheless, the fact remains that if Pope and Emperor were reconciled the Republic would benefit, for trade does not flourish in time of war and Venice had acquired useful markets in both papal and imperial territory.

So Doge Ziani sent his ambassadors to Barbarossa, informing him that the Pope was his guest and begging that there might be peace between them. He received an insolent answer. The Emperor, thundering like some Wagnerian god of the Rhineland, demanded the instant surrender of Alexander, failing which, he said, the Venetian Republic would incur his mortal enmity and he would plant his victorious eagles before the Basilica of St Mark.

It was magnificent. The herald who declaimed that message must have rolled out his words with relish. But it was not just an empty rhodomontade. An imperial fleet, reinforced by Genoese and Pisan galleys, was being made ready for action and had been placed under the command of Barbarossa's son Otto.

The good Ziani was a man of peace but he was not a fool. He knew that some men love war and that the only argument they understand is the sword. He knew also that if there was to be a sea fight, it would be better if it did not take place in Venetian waters. So although only thirty galleys could be mustered—less than half the number of the enemy's ships—they were hurriedly fitted out; and the Doge himself, in spite of his age, announced that he would take command. With the papal blessing to uphold him and his men, he sailed away with his little fleet to meet this new threat from Barbarossa. The action took place in the Adriatic and, although he was fighting against heavy odds, Ziani was victorious.

The Pope was waiting at the Molo to greet him on his return to Venice and presented the Doge with a consecrated ring with which symbolically to wed the Adriatic. It was then, as mentioned earlier, that the simple libation ceremony, *La Sensa,* which had been instituted by Orseolo after he had defeated the Narentine corsairs, began to change into that more elaborate *Sposalizio del Mare* or Espousal of the Sea which in the course of the centuries was to degenerate into a meaningless pageant. First, holy water was poured over the waves. Then, standing in his state barge—a forerunner of that ornate floating palace, the *Bucintoro*—the Doge cast the ring into the ocean, declaiming in a loud voice: "O sea, we wed thee in token of our true and everlasting dominion."* This rite took place every year on Ascension Day, in memory of Orseolo's victory; and in the Treasury of St Mark's one of the rings, which had been found inside a fish, can still be seen.

When Doge Ziani came home in triumph, he brought with him as his prisoner the Emperor's son; but, with characteristic generosity, he released young Otto without ransom and sent him back to his father with Venetian envoys to renew his peace proposals. Whether this magnanimous gesture appealed to that same trait in Barbarossa or whether, at last, he realized that the game had gone against him, we are not told; but it is only just to remember that all three protagonists in this drama—Pope, Emperor and Doge—were men incapable of pettiness. Whatever the Emperor's motive, he agreed to accept Alexander as his spiritual overlord, to make submission to the Holy See, and to ask pardon for having waged war against the Sovereign Pontiff. And, after much deliberation, Venice was chosen as the most suitable neutral ground on which the ceremony of reconciliation could take place.

In the atrium of St Mark's there is a slab of red Verona marble inlaid with a white marble lozenge. This marks the spot where, in July 1177, Frederic Barbarossa abased himself before his old enemy. Taking off his royal robe and laying aside his crown and sceptre, he knelt to kiss Alexander's foot; but there was a moment of tension when he was heard to growl: "Not to thee but to St Peter." And the Pope, it is said, placed his other foot on the neck of the prostrate Emperor, muttering tersely: "Both to me *and* to St Peter!"

If this sounds malicious, it was not. Alexander knew that whatever was said that day would be repeated all over Europe. Barbarossa was a man of honour but his word must be irrevocably committed: there must be no opportunity for mental reservations or ambiguity. So those few curt words, audible only to those near at hand, and that one firm, decisive gesture gave the Emperor no choice but to rebel at once if he was to rebel at all. Those who heard and saw it must have

---

* There are several versions of the Doge's words. This translation from the Latin is taken from *The World of Venice* by James Morris (London: Faber & Faber, 1960), p. 309.

held their breath. But the moment passed. The fiery Barbarossa controlled himself. Alexander raised him to his feet, the kiss of reconciliation was given, and the long conflict was at an end.

The Peace of Venice was a six-year truce, at the end of which time a treaty was signed at Constance between the Emperor and the Lombard League. Of the rest of Barbarossa's stormy reign, it is enough to say that in his old age he marched to join Philip of France and Richard of England in the Third Crusade. As an ally, Richard Lion-Heart was not an easy man to deal with, but he might well have understood and admired the indomitable old firebrand. Unfortunately they never met, for Barbarossa was drowned while swimming in the River Salef in Asia Minor. Of his place of burial there is no record, and thousands of Germans refused to believe the news of his death. It may well have been this which gave rise to the legend that the great Emperor did not die but still sleeps in his enchanted cavern beneath the Kyffhäuser, with his silent knights ranged round him in their ranks like statues of stone, his long beard grown through the table before him and twining round his feet.

After the reconciliation in the Basilica the Emperor had expressed his gratitude to the Doge by granting new commercial treaties and renewing old ones, while Alexander did Sebastiano Ziani the great honour of presenting him with the Golden Rose, that exquisite specimen of the goldsmith's art which is a special mark of the Pope's favour. And when the Pontiff returned to Rome, the old Doge accompanied him, to be lodged and entertained as sumptuously as His Holiness had been in Venice.

The remaining months of Ziani's glorious reign were spent in beautifying the city which he had loved and served so well. Then, in April 1178, he abdicated and retired to the monastery of San Giorgio Maggiore, where he died at the age of seventy-six. He is remembered as a wise ruler in peace and a brave warrior in war; but above all as a peacemaker, and for his innumerable acts of charity and kindness. Strolling in the garden of the island monastery, the old man must often have gazed across the Basin of St Mark towards the city which he had done so much to embellish. There was the Doge's Palace, enlarged and restored—not the Gothic building of today, with its white colonnade and pink diapered facade, but the earlier Byzantine palace which had arisen after the fires of 976 and 1106. The Piazza and Piazzetta were paved now and the Rio Batterio which once divided the square had been filled in. And towering above all was the great Campanile of rosy brick, which was to stand there for nearly a thousand years. Its spire was not yet crowned by its glittering revolving angel, a weather vane and guide to mariners: that belongs to the seventeenth century. But the ex-Doge, who had shown so much compassion for prisoners in the dungeons, can hardly have failed to disapprove of one addition to the bell tower. Attached to the brickwork at a giddy height from the ground was a small cage lined with wood. This was for the imprisonment of clergy who had committed some grave offence and had been condemned to this torture chamber, where cramped, exposed to sun, rain and cold, and fed through a tube, a priest might remain for months, years, even for life. *La Gabbia* or The Cage was not abolished until 1518.

An atmosphere of execution has always hung over that otherwise loveliest of cities, and the compassionate Ziani may well have averted his eyes from *la Gabbia* to look at the two columns with which he had adorned the Piazzetta. Yet even there he was reminded of executions. The columns had been brought from Tyre by Domenico Michiel in 1126; but it was Ziani who had caused them to be erected. On one, in 1329, would be placed the statue of St Theodore, first patron of the Republic. The other was already surmounted by the bronze Lion of St Mark, with pale agate eyes, his outstretched paws resting on an open book. Some say that this famous winged lion was brought from the East: some that Ziani himself had it cast by Venetian craftsmen. On other representations of the national emblem the pages of the book are visible and one can read: *Pax tibi, Marce, Evangelista Meus.*

The erection of the two columns had been a major problem but it had been solved by a Lombard named Barattieri, who had made ingenious use of wet ropes. Asked to name his own reward, he had claimed the right to run gaming tables between the two columns, knowing very well that public gambling was forbidden in the Republic. The idea was preposterous, unthinkable, yet it was equally impossible for the rulers of Venice to go back on their word. They were in a dilemma until someone had suggested slyly that it might put the gamblers off their game if the space between the two columns were also to become the scene of all future executions. Eventually this had been decreed. And it had worked. As the columns became more and more closely associated with the scaffold and the block, the gamblers took their forbidden games elsewhere or abandoned them altogether.

The clever Lombard was a rascal but he had had his uses. Ziani could not have seen it, for it was out of sight from San Giorgio, round the great S-bend of water, but at Rialto, Barattieri had built the first bridge across the Grand Canal. It was a strong wooden structure, replacing the ramshackle pontoon of boats which alone had spanned the canal since time immemorial. The townspeople called it Ponte della Moneta or Ponte del Quaterol, after that small coin they had to pay for the privilege of crossing it. Sebastiano Ziani was not to know that his Rialto Bridge and its successors would be the only link between the two sides of the city for seven hundred years, until the iron bridges (now replaced) were built by the Austrians near the Railway Station and the Accademia di Belle Arti.

6. The Fourth Crusade

"Blind Old Dandolo"
The Muster
Byzantine Tragedy
The Sack

Ziani's successor was his friend Orio Malipiero, the man who, six years before, had stood down in his favour. Malipiero's reign was uneventful, but it was in his time that the Procurators of St Mark were increased from one to three, in order that they might more efficiently administer the large sums of money which the late Doge had bequeathed to the poor. These Procurators who, in their flowing robes of crimson damask, figure so frequently in the paintings of later generations were usually elderly men whose outstanding services to the State had earned them the honour of ranking next to the Doge. They were responsible for the safety of members of the Great Council when in session, and also for the security of St Mark's and its treasures.

With the peaceful retirement of Malipiero and the elevation of his successor, we come to one of the most outstanding personalities in Venetian history: Enrico Dandolo. "Blind old Dandolo," as Byron called him. He was eighty-four when he became Doge and he had been blind, or nearly blind, for years. There is a persistent but hardly credible story that while he was serving as Venetian Ambassador at Constantinople, the Emperor Manuel had, with his own hands, held red-hot irons to his eyes. But Venice would hardly have

allowed such an outrage to go unpunished, and there is another tradition, more likely to be true, that Dandolo lost his sight as the
result of a blow on the head in battle. He was a strange mixture of
good and evil: clever, selfish, utterly fearless, inspired by devotion
to his country and by an implacable hatred of the Byzantines. But
when we think of this aged man, it is of his indomitable will, of his
cunning, and of the courage with which he triumphed over his dis-
abilities. He might be old and he might be blind, but by sheer strength
of character he could still dominate some of the most masterful men
in Europe and force them to become the slaves of his adamantine
will.

Dandolo was waiting for his hour, and it struck in 1199, when
Innocent III preached the Fourth Crusade. It is not easy to draw a
line between the different crusades: small expeditions were always
leaving for the Holy Land. But this was different. The distant guard-
ians of Outremer were struggling desperately for survival, with all
but Antioch, Tripoli and a strip of coast in the hands of the Saracens.
In response to their call for help the Pope declared another Holy
War, and down the old Roman roads went his messengers calling all
Christendom to arms.

From every pulpit and in every market place the summons was
sounded. Cardinal Peter of Capua was empowered to promise that
all those who took the cross would be pardoned for their sins; and at
the château of Ecri in Champagne, a company of noblemen and
knights who had assembled for a tournament were won for the Cause
by the eloquence of a village priest, Fulk of Neuilly. They came to
joust: they ended by offering their swords to God, led by their host,
that high-souled gentleman and mirror of chivalry, Thibaut, Count of
Champagne. With him were Count Louis of Blois and Boniface,
Marquis of Montferret, while among those who followed Count
Thibaut was his own Marshal, Geoffroi de Villehardouin, who was to
become the chronicler of that tragic Fourth Crusade.

Thibaut himself died at Troyes in 1201; and in view of the in-
famous outcome of the adventure, this may well have been the fate
he would have chosen. At a great council held at Soissons, de Villehardouin formally proposed that Montferrat should now become the
new leader of the expedition, and he was elected. But although the
Marquis was a brave soldier and the patron of poets and trouba-

dours, morally he was of coarser fibre than the late Count of Champagne.

Owing to the severe losses in wealth and prosperity which the Byzantine Empire—or what was left of it—had incurred as a result of the first three crusades, Constantinople was no longer in a position to help great armies make the overland journey across Europe. Therefore the leaders of the crusaders decided that the most sensible course would be to travel by sea to Venice, and envoys, of whom de Villehardouin was one, were sent to negotiate with the blind Doge. To Dandolo their arrival was welcome, for he had problems of his own which they might well help to solve. It would be unfair to say that, in this age of crusades, the old man had no religious enthusiasm, though undoubtedly the thoughts which were uppermost in his mind were how he could turn this new enterprise to the advantage of the Republic and, by doing so, gratify his own private desire for revenge on the Byzantines. But Dandolo was subtle; he could dissemble. He put up quite a show of resistance before he gave way to the envoys' request for transport.

The crusaders' plan was to launch their first attack, not on the Holy Land itself but on Egypt, which Malik-al-Adil, Sultan of Egypt and Syria and brother of the redoubtable Saladin, had made the centre of Moslem power. Unlike other Christian kingdoms and republics, Venice was trading freely with Malik; but the Doge let it be known that subject, of course, to the will of his people, not only would he supply all the transport, but he would send fifty of his own galleys with the expedition. Then he stated his price and it was a stiff one: 85,000 silver marks (about £300,000 or $840,000) with one-half of all conquests in land or treasure to be ceded to Venice.

The crusaders accepted these terms: they had no choice. Now all that remained was for the agreement to be ratified by the people. This was vitally important, for the Venetians must still be allowed the illusion of power. The Mass of the Holy Ghost was duly celebrated in St Mark's in the presence of a crowd which overflowed into the Piazza. Then, with plaudits and with tears, the citizens of the Republic gave their noisy consent to yet another *fait accompli*.

In the summer of 1202 the crusaders began to reach Venice. There were fewer than had been expected, for some, impatient of the long delay, had made their way to other seaports. But before autumn, 30,000 men were encamped on one of the islands of the Lido, well away from the Rialto and the vulnerable heart of the city. At San Nicolo there were good quarters for the knights and men-at-arms, where the Fleet could keep an eye on them. Crusaders could be dangerous guests.

And now a new difficulty arose. The wily old Doge demanded cash in advance before he would transport all those men and horses to Constantinople. But 85,000 marks was a large sum of money, and with their diminished numbers, the crusaders could not pay. In vain, individuals sacrificed their gold and silver plate. Between them they could raise no more than 51,000 marks. And they were dealing with Venetians —no money, no ships.

Dandolo was in no hurry. Bland and affable, he allowed them plenty of rope. Then, when finally it became apparent that they could never find the sum required, he made what appeared to be a generous gesture. He would transport the army as arranged if, before sailing to Egypt and Palestine, they would lend their strength to help him reduce his rebellious city of Zara. When some of the crusaders protested that they were in arms against the infidel and not against their fellow Christians, he reminded them that Zara, held by an enemy, would be an ever present danger in their rear. He could be very persuasive, that old man. As for the debt, he told them that payment could be postponed, but not cancelled, until they were all enriched by the spoils of the expedition.

Reluctantly the crusaders agreed to this proposal and Dandolo had won the first round. In a second great service in the Basilica he delivered an impassioned harangue from the pulpit, winning all hearts by his declaration that, in spite of his age and infirmities, he would lead the Venetians himself. Then, abasing himself before the High Altar, the old warrior, in tears, fixed a cross in his bonnet and rose from his knees a dedicated crusader!

There followed a protest from the Pope, who was justifiably incensed by this misuse of his crusade. When protests failed, excommunication and anathemas were pronounced against the Venetians. Dandolo was completely unmoved, though some of the other leaders were so shaken that they sent messages to the Pope in an attempt to excuse themselves. They explained that they were in the Doge's hands: without his ships they would have no chance of ever reaching Palestine. This must have been galling for Innocent, who had set his heart on the venture; and something of his bitterness shows in his reply to the French barons, in which he told them to take advantage of the Venetians' transport, but once on the soil of the Holy Land to have no further dealings with them.

On the tenth of November, 1202, with pomp and pageantry and fanfaronade, the fleet sailed from Venice: 50 fighting galleys, 240 troopships, 70 supply vessels, and 120 flat-bottom palanders for the transport of horses. In his *Chronicle of the Fourth Crusade and the Conquest of Constantinople*, de Villehardouin tells us: "On the eve of St Martin they came before Zara in Sclavonia, and beheld the city enclosed by high walls and high towers; and vainly would you have sought for a fairer city or one of greater strength, or a richer. And when the pilgrims saw it they marvelled greatly and said to one another, 'How could such a city be taken by force, save by the help of God himself?' " But he also tells us that "the vessels carried more than three hundred petraries and mangonels, and all such engines as are needed for the taking of cities, in great plenty."

The crusading host—de Villehardouin's "pilgrims"—came ashore in their strength at Zara. The mailed knights must have looked like some grim array of faceless automata in their flat-topped, cylindrical helms, with their shields slung from their necks and their long lances held bolt upright as they rode. They ringed the city with their siege lines, their silken pavilions and their banners; the ponderous stone-slinging engines creaked into position and began their bombardment; and sappers, protected by mobile shed roofs, prepared to breach the walls.

The garrison held out for exactly five days and then surrendered at discretion. For those brutal times, the city escaped lightly. The lives of the inhabitants were spared, although their houses were pillaged and their fortifications demolished. Then the crusaders settled down to pass the winter on the scene of their triumph, and Doge Dandolo prepared to carry out the second part of his plan. Luck favoured him. Montferrat, who had stayed behind in Venice, now arrived at Zara with his friend Alexius, exiled heir to the throne of Constantinople. This runaway prince was an inexperienced, feckless young man, but his story is tragic enough and throws a lurid light on Byzantine politics in those days of decadence and corruption. His father, the former Emperor Isaac Angelus, had been deposed and blinded by the Prince's uncle, who had assumed the scarlet buskins and now reigned as Alexius III. The unfortunate Isaac was a despicable creature and himself a usurper; but that he should have been deprived of sight and thrown into a dungeon by his own brother was something which outraged even a mediaeval baron, and it gave rise to a wave of sympathy for Isaac's equally worthless son.

The advent of young Alexius exactly suited Dandolo's plan, which was to divert the crusade from the Holy Land altogether and use this powerful army which he virtually controlled for an all-out attack on the ancient friend and foe, the Great Rival, Constantinople. The Doge's hatred had recently been fanned by the Usurper's refusal to conclude a trade agreement with Venice; and, after sounding out the men who mattered, he found that he could count on the support of Montferrat, Count Baldwin of Flanders, and other influential leaders. One can lose oneself in a maze of speculation wondering how the history of Europe and the Levant might have been changed if that good knight Thibaut, Count of Champagne, had still been alive and in command.

But now the alluring prospect of plundering the richest city in Europe drove every other thought from the minds of those rapacious men who had just pledged their knightly honour to rescue the Sepulchre of Christ. As for the Young Alexius, he was swayed by no lofty ideals. His motive was purely selfish—to drive the Usurper from the throne. Though lacking both gold and an army, he was ready to promise both, if only the warriors of the West would make his cause their own. He swore to furnish them with the handsome sum of 200,000 silver marks, together with 10,000 men for an Egyptian expedition and another 500 always ready to embark for Palestine. As a final inducement, he promised to do his utmost to bring about a reconciliation between the Churches of Rome and Constantinople. Thus, and not for the first time, religion and cupidity marched arm in arm.

In the summer of 1203 the crusaders sailed for Constantinople under the leadership of Montferrat and Baldwin of Flanders, with Doge Dandolo in command of the Venetian contingent. They went by way of Corfu, where they renewed their pledge to restore young Alexius, and reached the Dardanelles without encountering opposition. Why? The answer is almost incredible. The so-called Emperor of Byzantium had sold the Imperial Fleet! Only a few years before, it had been a powerful force of 1,600 vessels. But now masts, rigging and oars had been disposed of, and it was impossible to refit because the imperial forests—those that remained—were reserved for the Emperor's hunting.

Under the cypress trees in the gardens overlooking the Sea of Marmora, or in the halls of the Bucoleon and the Blaquernal—his favourite palace—His Magnificence lounged with his courtiers and eunuchs, revelling in the lustrous silken robes which were his principal joy in life, just as the pleasures of the table had been the delight of his blinded brother. Like too many of his subjects, he had given up the struggle to resuscitate the dying empire, preferring to live for luxury and to close eyes and ears to the harsh realities of a warlike world.

Sure sign of decadence, the military spirit was now entirely lacking in this ghost of a great power. John Ruskin once said, "No great art ever yet rose on earth, but among a nation of soldiers." And it would seem that what is true of art is equally true of a people's virtue, for much as any right-minded man must deplore wars of aggression, history proves again and again that when the will for self-defence is lacking, other qualities vanish with it, leaving only the husk of a nation to be trampled underfoot. In Constantinople, as in the British Raj of later centuries, there were army families which produced generations of officers. But discipline had slackened and there were few reliable rank and file. Gone were the great days of Belisarius and Leo the Isaurian. For too long it had been the mistaken policy of the rulers of Byzantium to maintain an insurmountable barrier between soldier and civilian, and to exclude the peaceful citizen from practise in the use of arms. Instead, lapped in good living, they had learned to rely for their defence on their magnificent fortifications, on their Greek Fire, on the Varangian Guard and other mercenaries, and on the warriors of subject people like the fierce mountaineers of Greece and Anatolia.

But now the Empire did not extend far beyond the walls of Constantinople; those levies of wild highlanders were no longer available; and even the secret of the Greek Fire had been acquired by the Saracens, who had used it with great effect against the crusaders in Palestine. There remained the loyal Varangians and certain other troops, but comparatively few. As for the soft Byzantines of the capital—effete, untrained, and taught to despise the fighting-man —they were about to pay the penalty for the neglect of their defences and for a policy of pacifism carried beyond the limits of safety. They were to learn what seems to be one of the laws of life in this dangerous world: for the strong in arms there is some hope of peace; for the weak there is none.

Skilled in every trick of diplomacy, the Greeks might have talked themselves out of this crisis if only they could have brought their enemies to the conference table. But the Venetians had not forgotten how the Emperor Manuel had tricked the unhappy Vitale Michiel. As for those stern warriors from the West, most of them French or French feudatories, they preferred to fight with swords rather than words. They gave His Magnificence no time to parley but drove straight for their objective and on Midsummer Day the Bosphorus was brilliant with their sails.

Gleaming white behind walls twelve miles in circumference and strengthened by four hundred towers, the Imperial City lay before them: golden cupolas, pinnacles, banks of houses clear-cut against the summer sky and distant snow-peaks of the Bithynian Alps, and crowned by that glory of Eastern Christendom, the great church of Sancta Sophia. A wonderful sight; but did those hardbitten men in their rusty mail appreciate its exotic beauty? A few perhaps, like de Villehardouin, but to the majority it was just a plum ripe for the picking.

The entrance to the Golden Horn was blocked by an enormous chain just under the surface of the water. One end issued from the city wall; the other, on the opposite side of the harbour, was secured to a strong tower in the suburb of Galata. This tower was the crusaders' immediate objective. First, however, they sailed close under the walls and showed young Alexius to his people. Then a few days later, in their attack on the port, they met their first serious opposition. Without haste the main body of the army disembarked, heard Mass, and held a conference. Then they formed their ranks, put on their helms, and mounted their heavy destriers. A trumpet rang out; and slowly, silently save for the clink of mail and the soft jingle of harness, those faceless men began to move forward, their lances with their fluttering pennons still upright in their rests. Another trumpet blast and they couched their spears; the walk became a trot, the trot, a gallop. Crouching behind their shields, they charged. Their advance was not unopposed; but that steady, inexorable onset had its effect on the volatile Byzantines. "The Greeks made a goodly show of resistance," de Villehardouin tells us in his *Chronicle*, "but when it came to the lowering of lances, they turned their backs, and went away flying, and abandoned the shore."

The crusaders took the tower and cut the chain, but not without a hard fight. A fortnight later the whole harbour was in their hands and they were ready to launch an all-out attack on the city. The French knights and men-at-arms assaulted the land-walls, which were valiantly defended by the famous Varangians—members of the Emperor's bodyguard who were originally Russians but who were now recruited almost exclusively from Englishmen and Norsemen. At the same time, as de Villehardouin describes it:

"The Venetians were firmly minded that the scaling ladders ought to be planted on the ships, and all the attack made from the side by the sea. The French, on the other hand, said that they did not know so well how to defend themselves on sea as on land, but that when they had their horses and arms they could help themselves on land right well. So in the end it was devised that the Venetians should attack by sea, and the barons and those of the host by land.

"They adjourned thus for four days. On the fifth day the whole host were armed, and the divisions advanced on horseback, each in the order appointed, along the harbour, till they came to the palace of Blachernae (Blaquernal); and the ships drew inside the harbour till they came over against the self-same place, and this was near to the end of the harbour.

"They planted two ladders at a barbican near the sea; and the wall was well defended by Englishmen and Danes; and the attack was stiff and good and fierce. By main strength certain knights and two sergeants got up the ladders and made themselves masters of the wall; and at least fifteen got upon the wall and fought there, hand to hand, with axes and swords, and those within redoubled their efforts. . . .

"Meanwhile the Doge of Venice had not forgotten to do his part, but had ranged his ships and transports and vessels in line, and that line was well three crossbow-shots in length; and the Venetians began to draw near to the part of the shore that lay under the walls and the towers. Then might you have seen the mangonels shooting from the ships and transports, and the crossbow bolts flying, and the bows letting fly their arrows deftly and well; and those within defending the walls and towers very fiercely; and the ladders on the ships coming so near that in many places swords and lances crossed; and the tumult and noise were so great that it seemed as if the very earth and sea were melting together. . . .

"Now you may hear a strange deed of prowess; for the Doge of Venice, who was an old man and saw naught (seeing he was blind) stood, fully armed, on the prow of his galley, and had the standard of St Mark before him; and he cried to his people to put him on land, or else he would do justice on their bodies with his hands. And so they did, for the galley was run aground, and they leapt therefrom and bore the standard of St Mark before him on to the land.

"And when the Venetians saw the standard of St Mark on land, and the galley of their lord touching ground before them, each held himself for shamed, and they all gat to the land; and those in the transports leapt forth and landed; and those in the big ships got into barges, and made for the shore, each and all as best they could. Then might you have seen an assault, great and marvellous; and to this bears witness Geoffroi de Villehardouin, who makes this book, that more than forty people told him for sooth that they saw the standard of St Mark of Venice at the top of one of the towers, and no man knew who bore it thither."

It is an unforgettable picture. There was much in Enrico Dandolo's manipulation of events which, even judged by the standard of his own time, was deplorable. But one must admire that lion-hearted old hero of eighty-eight as he stood on the prow of his foremost galley, with the banner of St Mark in his hand, and his white beard flowing down over his steel hauberk, shouting in his cracked voice, taunting, threatening, urging on his men till they had set the Winged Lion, which he could not see, on the ramparts of Constantinople.

And where was His Magnificence? Where was the Usurper? Armed and on the walls? When twenty-five towers had been taken and fire had broken out in the city, he did make a sortie from one of the gates far removed from the main scene of the battle. He had with him a force which de Villehardouin described as overwhelming. But Alexius Angelus, that blinder of brothers, had no taste for cold steel. He withdrew without striking a blow and seized the first opportunity to escape with his daughter Irene and as much gold as he could carry. Spurring away from his capital, he sought refuge in Thrace, leaving his wife and the rest of his family to the mercy of the enemy.

Deserted by their leader, the Byzantines called for a parley. They opened their gates and invited the Young Alexius to enter the city and be reunited with his father. So the fighting ceased; and the Prince with two Venetians and two Frenchmen, of whom de Ville-hardouin was one, rode into Constantinople and made their way to the Blaquernal Palace, just inside the northwest angle of the walls. Lining the route were the Varangian Vikings with their battle-axes. They were no longer enemies but a guard of honour.

The envoys were conducted to the presence chamber, where a macabre sight awaited them. By order of the Greek officers, blind old Isaac, half-dazed and dressed once more in his imperial robes, had been brought from the dungeon in which he had been confined for eight years and propped up on the golden throne of Byzantium. There, in his stiff brocade, perfumed, encrusted with gems, he sat motionless like some gorgeous idol. It is doubtful whether, after his long confinement, he could understand what was going on. Con-temptible though Isaac may have been, he had suffered for his sins. Surely even the hard hearts of the crusaders must have been touched.

A fortnight later, the Young Alexius (as Alexius IV) was crowned joint Emperor with his father. Isaac Angelus ratified his son's agree-ment with the crusaders, though, with his mind weakened by suffer-ing, it is unlikely that he was aware what he was doing.

Because of the mutual animosity between Latin and Greek, it had been thought prudent to quarter the crusaders in the suburbs of Galata and Pera; but even though they were supposed to be sepa-rated by the waters of the Golden Horn, there was constant brawling between the two factions, often provoked, no doubt, for his own pur-poses by Dandolo. Before long, this skirmishing was the cause of another fire. Churches, palaces, and whole streets of houses were burned. When it was over, bales of valuable merchandise still lay in the open, smouldering and ruined. It need hardly be said that each side blamed the other.

For months, too, there was wrangling among the crusaders themselves. Many felt that they had been defrauded of the rich plunder which they had been promised and they bitterly resented not being allowed to sack the city. To make matters worse, Alexius was unable to pay the large sum of money which he owed to the crusaders; and when, in his efforts to do so, he imposed new taxes and melted down church plate, he increased the anger of his own people who could not forgive him for trying to unite the Greek and Roman Churches.

Insecure on his throne and sure that he would have short shrift if the crusaders withdrew their support, he pleaded with their leaders to remain in Constantinople for a year, offering to pay all their expenses. A sojourn in that city of luxury was not without its attractions and was infinitely preferable to the perils of a winter voyage with a levanter blowing a gale. But that this puppet should offer more money when he could not pay what he already owed must have struck the crusaders as grimly humorous. Urged on by Dandolo, they continually renewed their demands for payment until even the pliable Alexius became tired of being browbeaten.

The climax came when the crusaders sent six emissaries, including de Villehardouin, to confront the two Emperors in their own Blaquernal Palace. Again the audience took place in the splendour of the presence chamber. The Emperors sat side by side on two thrones, surrounded by perfumed, soft-spoken courtiers in jewel-encrusted robes of heavy silk, brocade and cloth of gold, and by their tall Viking guards who must have looked like men among women.

That audience was disastrous. It had always been the custom for envoys, however noble, to prostrate themselves before that almost sacred personage, the Emperor, crawling humbly to the foot of the throne, like the slaves of some eastern satrap. But those three Frenchmen and three Venetians, with their swords by their sides, made their reverence standing boldly upright like free men and soldiers. According to de Villehardouin, they spoke frankly, almost defiantly, warning the Emperors that they would obtain their due by any means in their power. "You have heard what we have said," they concluded bluntly. "It is for you to take counsel thereon, acording to your pleasure."

To say that this bold speech created a sensation would be an understatement, for even Alexius was not prepared to swallow this public humiliation. The audience ended in tumult; and if the envoys had not had the good fortune to escape in the confusion, they would have died where they stood under the axes of the Varangians. As it was, they mounted, spurred for their lives, and found a boat to carry them across the Golden Horn to safety.

The die had now been cast, and Latin and Greek prepared for a renewal of the war. The soldiers and the people closed the gates of Constantinople and then set about finding those few unfortunate Frenchmen who were still inside the walls. From hole to hole they were hunted like rats and done to death when they had been brought to bay. While the hunt was on, Alexius must have wondered when his own turn would come, for he knew that he had as much to fear from his own subjects as from the crusaders. The inevitable happened. Certain Byzantine noblemen who regarded him as a traitor and a collaborator risked torture and death by searching out a new leader. They found one in Alexius Ducas, First Lord of the Wardrobe and nicknamed Mourzoufle because his shaggy eyebrows nearly met. An opportunist and quite unscrupulous, he was ripe for any intrigue.

Predictably, Mourzoufle's first move was to eliminate Alexius. Gibbon tells us that the young Emperor was roused from his sleep by a false alarm and urged to escape from his bedchamber by a secret stair which, as he was to discover too late, terminated in a dungeon. There he was stripped and chained to the wall; and there, a few days later, in the presence of Mourzoufle, they killed him, whether by poison, the club, or the strangler's cord is not known. The official explanation, of course, was that he died of natural causes, which may account for the otherwise inexplicable delay before he was murdered. A very short time afterwards, his father Isaac was dead too—some say of fear, some say of a broken heart, some say of poison.

Mourzoufle's path to the throne was now clear. As Alexius V, he donned the imperial robes and scarlet buskins and tried to revive his dying city empire. This new usurper was a murderer and a villain, and before long he was to pay for his crimes by being hurled from the Column of Theodosius, a pillar of white marble 147 feet high. But before the end came, before he was seized and tried, his behaviour was not unworthy of an Emperor of Byzantium. Even while one abhors Mourzoufle's evil deeds, one can also pity him and almost admire him for his vain efforts to rouse his people to action. He had both energy and courage, qualities which were in short supply in the Constantinople of those days. And he was a leader—or would have been if he had had enough men worth leading. He erected wooden defences and installed powerful trebuchets and mangonels on the seaward walls over which the Venetians had stormed the city; regularly, mace in hand, he inspected the guard posts on the ramparts; and at the head of such cavalry as he could muster, he patrolled the outskirts of the crusaders' camp, cutting off foraging parties and generally keeping the enemy on the alert. Mourzoufle even did his best to raise a militia in the city, but the Byzantines loved their ease too much to take kindly to discipline. The canker of nonresistance had eaten too deeply into a people who, generation after generation, had been taught to despise soldiering. One cannot raise warriors from a supine stock which has had all the mettle bred out of it. When it comes to the test, craft and diplomacy are no match for virile manhood. One can always try to stiffen the sagging ranks. But often it is too late.

Two months passed. In the camp of the crusaders, long before the attack came, the remains of the great Byzantine Empire, calmly and in cold blood, were divided among its enemies. It was all set down in a treaty: three parts of the plunder were to go to the Venetians; the remainder to the French. The robbers' share-out of the loot (for the transaction deserves no more dignified description) was to take place in one of three churches which had been earmarked for the purpose. One-quarter of the Empire was to be ruled by a new Emperor, chosen from among themselves; the other three-fourths were to be divided between the Venetians and the French. All the trading rights and privileges of the Republic were to be restored and she was to be paid the 50,000 silver marks owing to her.

Dandolo had almost achieved his ambition. By cunning and a will of iron he had turned the whole crusade to the enrichment of Venice and the fulfilment of his own desire for revenge. Now, after these months of preparation, came the hour for which he had planned and intrigued and, quite possibly, prayed. At last he had ample excuse for the fight to a finish which had been his real object from the beginning: revenge for the barring of the city gates and the massacre of the Latins, the death of the Young Alexius and the seizure of the throne by his murderer. No longer was there any need to hold back his impatient followers.

On the eighth of April, 1204, an attack was launched by the Venetians on a two-mile front against the seaward walls, which were considered more vulnerable than the land-walls of Theodosius. But Mourzoufle's siege engines played havoc with the extended line of ships and the Venetians were forced to retire, licking their wounds. Four days later, however, they made another assault, concentrating on a smaller area so that not so many trebuchets and mangonels could be used against them. From ships lashed together to increase their stability and driven on to the shore by a strong wind, flying bridges were swung across to the ramparts from masts and high wooden structures on deck, while the Venetians' own engines on the ships kept up a continuous bombardment. One of the Byzantine towers was knocked out, and the attackers swarmed across the swaying bridge and over the ramparts. The Byzantines met them hand-to-hand but they could not stop the maddened crusaders, inflamed by greed and the lust of battle. Shields advanced and heavy swords swinging, they had soon cleared the wall walks, fought their way down the steps and opened one of the small postern gates. Then other gates were opened and the French knights and men-at-arms came riding in, driving the enemy before them in hopeless confusion. To cover any further advance, the French and Venetians set fire to the houses, but their destruction was unnecessary. The fighting petered out and by nightfall the entire northwest angle of Constantinople was in their hands. Mourzoufle had tried to rally his men but nothing could strike fire from the Byzantines now. They had fallen back from the walls to the streets. Whole regiments melted away and disappeared among the people. Even the famous Varangian Guard, renowned for its courage and fidelity, chose this moment of all moments to strike for arrears of pay!

All that night the crusaders were on their guard against a counterattack. But nothing hapened except one hopeless onslaught led by Theodore Lascaris, one of the few remaining Greek officers who deserved the name of soldier. Mourzoufle was no coward but he was a realist and he saw that all was over. In bitterness of heart he fled from the Bucoleon Palace under cover of darkness for a short spell of liberty before his capture, trial and execution.

At dawn Constantinople lay wide open. The conquerers had only to take possession. And it is this lull which makes the enormity that followed so cold-blooded. If that great crime had been committed in the heat of action it would be deplorable but at least it would be understandable. Much of the horror lies in the fact that it was deliberate, coolly considered, and all part of a plan—that plan for which a Doge of Venice must bear a large share of the guilt. There were chivalrous knights in the host—men like Montferrat and the Count of Flanders—who did their best to enforce discipline. But what could a few do against an army which was getting out of hand?

For three days that glorious city was given over to the sack, and every atrocity that the mind can conceive was inflicted on men, women and children. There was no organized massacre, but at least three thousand helpless civilians were butchered in a holocaust of rape, looting and murder. And there was no resistance. Houses were broken into and wrecked; churches and monasteries were profaned; in Sancta Sophia itself a harlot was enthroned in the Patriarchal chair to delight those Soldiers of the Cross with her obscene songs and dances. A number of priests were with the army but they did nothing to restrain the mob: it has been said that they were too busy looking for sacred bones and relics with which to enrich their own churches.

"Oh, for one hour of blind old Dandolo!" That was what Byron wrote of a man who knew neither remorse for his own treachery nor compassion for his victims. Different times, different values. The reaction of our chronicler, Geoffroi de Villehardouin, speaks for itself. He said: "The booty gained was so great that none could tell you the end of it: gold and silver and vessels and precious stones, and samite, and cloth of silk, and robes vair and grey, and every choicest thing found upon the earth. . . . And greatly did they rejoice and give thanks because of the victory God had vouchsafed to them—for those who had been poor were now in wealth and luxury. Thus they celebrated Palm Sunday and the Easter Day following."

The loss in literary and art treasures was incalculable. Constantinople had been the repository for much of the learning and beauty of the ancient world; but now many priceless manuscripts, mosaics and frescoes disappeared forever. Churches, palaces, obelisks, and statues were wantonly destroyed. When the pillaging was over, more than £800,000 or $2,250,000 in gold bezants and silver had been collected, but even that was not enough to satisfy the rapacious horde. Into the melting pot went the lovely Heracles of Lysippus, the Hera of Samos, Paris with the Golden Apple, Helen of Troy, Romulus and Remus—wonderful bronzes collected by Constantine and his successors—to emerge as copper coins, for money was the only treasure those vandals could appreciate. The Venetians were an exception, for they had an eye for beauty so keen that it even enabled them to overlook the Eighth Commandment. Among other things their Doge sent home were the four bronze Horses of Lysippus. For centuries they had looked down on the chariot races in the Hippodrome, but ever since his men stole them—except for a short trip to Paris in Bonaparte's time and their removal to a place of safety during the two World Wars—they have adorned the facade of the Basilica of St Mark.

The Pope said sadly that of such a conquest no good could come. And he was right. The crusaders set up their Latin Empire with Baldwin of Flanders on the throne, but it did not endure; and although, fifty-seven years later, Michael Palaeologus threw off the Western yoke and founded a new Imperial line, Byzantium—the real Byzantium—never fully recovered.

And Venice? Now at least the Serenissima ranked as a great power. Her merchants were masters of the Levant. Her capital city was made even more beautiful by the newly acquired collection of gold and gems and precious marbles. And her ruler could now call himself by the resounding title of Doge of Venice, Dalmatia and Croatia, Lord of one-quarter and a half-quarter of the Roman Empire—her share being the Aegean and Ionian Islands, Crete, the ports of Albania and of the west coast of Greece. She also gained territory near the Dardanelles but nowhere did she penetrate far. Land did not interest her. Her sole aim was to acquire seaports and centres for her commerce. Most important of all to the merchants on Rialto was the almost incredible news that Constantinople, their greatest rival, need trouble them no longer. By courage, adroitness and a little treachery, the Venetians had ruined her.

But although retribution was slow in coming, they had also ruined themselves.

7. Marco Polo

The Mongols
The Silk Road
Far Cathay
The Homecoming

It used to be said that the history of a nation was the history of its famous men. Nowadays we take a larger view and insist that, whenever possible, history should primarily concern itself with the affairs of ordinary people. By either standard, a figure looming large in the story of Venice is Marco Polo, who gave Western Europe its first glimpse of the Far East and whose travels are to the Republic what the voyages of Drake and Raleigh are to the history of England.

Marco Polo, a citizen of Venice, ranked as noble (*nobilis vir*), but he was an ordinary merchant whose family lived in the parish of San Giovanni Grisostomo and maintained a counting house in Constantinople for the conduct of their business in gems. He was also a great man in the best and truest sense of the word. With his father, Nicolo Polo, and his uncle Maffeo, he journeyed to the ends of the earth and lived not merely to tell the tale but to bequeath to the world the finest travel book that has ever been written.

In the middle of the thirteenth century, Venice was approaching the zenith of her power. Like a cloud the size of a man's hand, the Red Cross of Genoa was looming over the horizon. But the Byzantines had been humbled; the Republic had made her peace with the Church; and she reigned undisputed mistress over the Eastern Mediterranean. Her trading colonies flourished in every port of the Levant, skimming the cream of the merchandise, and bartering wood, iron, raw wool and the manufactured products of Europe for rare exotic luxuries out of the mysterious East: from Cathay and Manji, which are now China, from the islands of Zipangu which we call Japan, and even, it is said, from the unknown realm of Prester John, that Christian monarch of the Orient who had seven kings for his vassals.

For generations the Far East had seemed as remote and unreal as the fabulous Gardens of the Hesperides or the Mountains Beyond the North Wind, until, at the beginning of the thirteenth century, the Asian steppes which, nine hundred years before, had spewed forth the Huns, let loose another horde of barbarians under the Mongol, Jenghiz Khan. Taking what are now Mongolia and Manchuria in their stride, wave after wave of mounted archers had penetrated the Great Wall of China, conquered nearly the whole of that country, and then swept westwards with fire and sword through Bokhara and Samarkand, till first Khorassan and then the whole of Persia and Asia Minor lay under their heel. They were irresistible. There had been nothing like them since the days of Attila. Fresh Mongol hordes swept across the Indus to take Peshawar, Lahore and Herat, and then drove on to levy tribute from Afghanistan and Tibet. Another few years and those ruthless yellow men with eyes like black pebbles had overrun most of Russia, then Poland and Hungary, till in a very short space of time they had won the vastest empire that the world has ever known: it stretched from the Hoang-ho to the Danube and from the shores of the Arctic Ocean to the Straits of Malacca.

Then, in 1227, Jenghiz died and gradually the tide turned. Withdrawing from their outlying provinces (from many of which, however, they still levied tribute) the Mongols fell back on the four central khanates of China, Russia, Central Asia and Persia. There they settled into cities and cultivated the arts of peace, adopting all that was best in the ancient civilizations which they had overrun, encouraging trade with the nations of the West, allowing complete religious freedom, and welcoming any learned foreigners who came to live among them. Certain friars who visited Jenghiz's grandson in his new capital of Cambaluc (Peking) found Kublai Khan, overlord of all the Tartars—or the Grand Khan, as he was called—to be no savage barbarian but a kindly and cultured Chinese Emperor, first

of the noble line of Yuan and a model to all mankind of an enlightened and civilized ruler.

Mongols and Moslems were at daggers drawn; and influenced
by reports which filtered through, the crusaders began to visualize
these Tartars as potential allies. Together, striking from east and west,
they might crush the Saracens between them, while there was even
hope that the Mongols might become true believers. Here and there
among them were little bodies of Nestorian Christians; and it may
well have been from one of these that there arose the legend of
Prester John, just as it may have been reports of their teaching which
first interested Kublai Khan in that strange gospel of love. For interested he certainly was. He even sent envoys to the Pope with a request
that a hundred learned priests be sent out to expound the Faith to the
Grand Khan's people, and that they bring a bottle of holy oil from
the lamp in the Sepulchre of Christ. The Grand Khan's envoys to
His Holiness were two wealthy Venetian merchants. Their names?
Nicolo and Maffeo Polo.

Authorities differ about the date but it was probably in 1255 that
the brothers vanished into the unknown. Nicolo's wife was pregnant
when he set sail for Constantinople. Shortly afterwards she gave birth
to a son, but her husband never saw her alive again, and when he
came back to the Casa Polo, young Marco was fifteen. That was what
it meant to be a merchant adventurer in the Middle Ages.

In 1255 the Levant was reaching boiling point again. Michael
Palaeologus was preparing to wrest Constantinople from the Latin
Emperor, Baldwin II, an enterprise which was to culminate five years
later in the Battle of Pelagonia, the last great victory of Byzantine
arms. Therefore the political climate in the Eastern Mediterranean
was not overhealthy for Venetians, and the Polo brothers found it
expedient to change their plans and make for Soldaia in the Crimea,
where they had another counting house.

From there, inspired by the adventurous spirit of the Venetian
trader, they pushed on through the land of the Golden Horde to
Sarai on the Volga, where a Khan of the Kipchak Tartars held his
court. In those days travellers took their time. The brothers spent a
year in Sarai, intending, no doubt, to return as they had come—by
way of the Black Sea. But war had broken out in the area to their rear

between the western Kipchaks and Hulagu, Khan of the Persian Horde. So, having no wish to walk into trouble, they again changed their plans and went on to the great mart of Bokhara in what is now Russian Turkestan. There they remained for another three years until, in that mud-walled city set in gardens and famous for its silks and sabres, a chance encounter changed the whole course of their lives. For they met emissaries of Kublai Khan, returning to their master's court, and these emissaries persuaded the Venetians to travel with them to China.

At Shang-tu they received a gracious welcome from the Grand Khan who, after entertaining them in a princely manner, decided to make them his ambassadors, and despatched them on their mission to the Pope. He furnished them with a cavalry escort, with letters to His Holiness, written in the Tartar language, and with the almost sacred *tchikouei*—a tablet inscribed with golden ideographs, which was at once a passport and the Grand Khan's order that these privileged travellers should be given every help on their way.

The Polo brothers reached Acre in 1269, only to hear from the Papal Legate that Clement IV had died the year before and that a new pope had not yet been elected. The papal interregnum was exceptionally long. After two years at home in Venice, the brothers decided that they must return to the East, for they were men of honour and considered themselves bound by their promise to the Grand Khan; and they took Marco with them. In the days of her greatness Venice was a school for heroes.

They were furnished with a letter to Kublai Khan explaining the long delay, for even the most enlightened of eastern potentates can be touchy and they had no wish to lose their heads or to be shaken to death between two carpets. After making a short detour to Jerusalem for the holy oil, they set off again and had reached the Armenian port of Layas on the Gulf of Scandaroon when they heard that the legate, Tebaldo di Piacenza, whom they had met at Acre, had been elected Pope Gregory X. So back they went to Acre to accomplish their mission, only to meet with disappointment. Obsessed with the petty strife that was still going on between rival Italian factions, the Roman Catholic Church lost this unique opportunity of converting Asia to Christianity. Instead of the hundred learned priests that Kublai

Khan had requested, the Pope sent two Dominican friars, both of whom lost their nerve and turned back. This short-sighted policy was surely one of the great mistakes of history.

About November 1271, Nicolo, Maffeo, and Marco Polo left Acre on one of the greatest journeys of all time. In the famous record of his travels, Marco tells us that their route lay through Turcomania, in Asia Minor, where they saw Ararat, "an exceedingly large and high mountain, upon which, it is said, the ark of Noah rested." They skirted the Caspian sea, where Marco noted the oil wells at Baku; and then for many days they travelled southeast, past Mosul and the ruins of Nineveh on the Tigris, and down through Bagdad to the port of Ormuz on the Persian Gulf. Apparently their plan was to continue the journey by sea; but they found the heat excessive, and this may well have been one of the reasons why they chose to endure intense cold rather than face the long, broiling voyage across the Indian Ocean and China Sea. At any rate, they turned northwards through Persia and traversed lands which (save by Benedict Goes, the Portuguese missionary and explorer) were not to be described again by a European for six hundred years. They crossed the arid wilderness of Kerman where, says Marco, "little water is met with and that little so impregnated with salt, green as grass, and so nauseous that none can use it as drink." And so to Balkh, in Khorassan, a city once famous but then lying in ruins after the passing of Jenghiz Khan.

At this stage of their journey they travelled on the ancient Silk Road, that transcontinental highway along which the bales of lustrous fabric had been borne when China still held the monopoly and, in the western markets, silk was worth more than its weight in gold. They slept in the huge caravanserais, and all day long they heard the clonk of the bells on the long strings of pack animals—asses, mules, yaks, little Tartar ponies, and the woolly Bactrian camels—whose precious bales were worth many fortunes: copper, tin, raw wool, wine, honey and amber from the West, carpets from Turkestan, silk, porcelain, jade and ivory from China, spices from India, and the rubies and lapis lazuli of Balashan.

In Balashan, not surprisingly, Marco Polo fell ill, and they waited a whole year while he recuperated in that pure mountain air. A quiet interlude. But now came the worst part of that incredible journey, for they had to ascend the upper Oxus to the High Pamirs, that icy plateau which travellers call the Roof of the World, where the altitude makes breathing a burden, where the driving snow blinds, and where all the winds of the universe seem to come howling across Asia. Then came the long descent to the cities of Kashgar, Yarkand and Khotan, where the streams from the Pamirs again make it possible to cultivate the land. They rode through those markets of Tartary (no other European following them until 1860) and reached the town of Lop, where no doubt they rested before they faced the thirty days' hell of the Gobi Desert.

Marco has much to say about the Gobi—"the abode of evil spirits," he called it. For him and his companions it was a miserable and dangerous trek from water hole to water hole, for it was those stinking, brackish pools which alone made the journey possible. On the way, a man might be the victim of mirages and even think that he saw his own fellow travellers luring him away from the track. And there were strange sounds. He might hear voices—voices that he knew—calling his name; he might swear that another caravan was passing at night, when there was none; or stand to his arms at the sound of Chinese warfare—shouting, drums, bells and gongs—which made him believe that they were being attacked by robbers.

It was a test of endurance to try any man's courage; but at last they arrived at Tangut on the extreme northwest frontier of China. Their journey had taken them nearly four years, for it was in 1275 that the Grand Khan gave them a cordial welcome in his new summer palace of Shang-tu. Seeing a young gallant with the Polo brothers, Kublai Khan asked who he was. Nicolo bowed. "That is your servant and my son." A Venetian merchant was not only soldier and sailor. He had to be a courtier as well.

For seventeen years Marco Polo, his father and uncle, remained in the service of Kublai Khan, living the life of wealthy mandarins. And for three years Marco was Governor of Yang-chow. As he had learned to speak the Tartar (though not the Chinese) language fluently, he was sent on confidential missions which took him, among other places, to Shansi, Shensi and Szechuan, to the old Tartar capital of Karakorum far beyond the Great Wall, to Cochin-China, Burma, and the fringe of Tibet—even, it would seem, to Southern India.

The young Venetian possessed qualities which appealed to the Grand Khan, including his acute observation and graphic power of description. For while the reports of other envoys were strictly confined to the business in hand, Marco allowed himself a free rein to describe strange scenery, customs and people, in all of which his master was keenly interested. He remembered everything and, years later, he caused it to be written down: a tale of marvels for which his contemporaries were quite unprepared. His audience was sceptical; but, looking back across the centuries with the wider knowledge which time has given us, we can see that he opened a door to disclose all the wonders of the East—a door which was soon to be slammed again for six hundred years.

In his book he takes us to the land of Cathay (North China) and to Kublai Khan's new capital, Cambaluc—now the so-called Tartar City which forms part of modern Peking. Its commercial prosperity and its high standard of law and order astonished those travellers from the more backward and turbulent West. Every day a thousand packhorses and carriages brought traders and their wares through the gates of the city. There was a police force, and at night the curfew rang from the great Bell Tower.

Not far from Cambaluc was the Grand Khan's winter palace, built on a scale which would have astonished the citizens of Venice. It must have been rather like one of those Chinese nests of boxes set one inside the other. The whole area was an exact square, surrounded by a wall each side of which was eight miles long, pierced by a gate and crowned by buildings. Then came an open space a mile in width, where Kublai Khan's bodyguard of over 10,000 cavalry could exercise. Inside was another square of similar walls, but these were only six miles long and had six gates, three in the north side and three in the south. Within the space thus formed were gardens and a park for horses, deer and other animals; and lastly there was a third square of walls, white and crenellated, which enclosed the palace proper. There was a solid platform of marble, ten feet high, on which rose a complex of fantastic, curly-gabled buildings roofed with glazed tiles of red, green, azure and violet, and surrounded by a

marble terrace with a parapet and steps. Inside was a maze of apartments which included a treasury, a harem for the imperial wives and
concubines, and vast halls decorated with carved and gilded dragons,
birds and warriors.

Farther south, too, in Kinsai, the city which we call Hang-chow,
there were commerce and luxury on a scale undreamed of in Western
Europe. This Celestial City was built by the side of a lake and, like
Venice, was intersected by numerous canals. Marco Polo is eloquent
about the size of the ten principal squares, the splendour of the
buildings, and the multitude of shops and warehouses. The Rialto
Bridge which he remembered was Ziani's wooden erection; but the
main canals in Kinsai were spanned by bridges which must have
looked rather like modern highway overpasses, with long gentle slopes
for carts and pedestrians, and yet with arches so high that junks in
full sail could pass beneath them. When one reads of the lost beauty of
Kinsai, one can almost hear the tinkling of the little bells on the pago-
das. One can see the lovely ladies of China, motionless as painted dolls
as they are carried by in their palanquins; and imagine oneself strolling
in the lantern-lit pleasure-gardens, where gentlemen in silken robes
listen to the clear minor notes of the bamboo flute, or discuss the
philosophy of Chu Hsi as they sip their wine under the willows.

Yet Marco Polo, for all his sterling qualities, was of the earth
earthy. He dwells at great length on the paper money with which
the troops were paid and commerce conducted—money which, on
request, could be exchanged for gold at the mint; and on the fine caravanserais and post houses which were situated at twenty- or thirty-
mile intervals on all the main roads. At each of these houses a number
of fast horses were kept for the use of despatch riders on official
business; while supplementing the post houses were relays of run-
ners with bells on their girdles to warn the man at the next stage
that they were coming and that he had better stand by. It was a most
efficient system. "Fruit gathered in the morning at Cambaluc, could
reach the Grand Khan at Shang-tu by the evening of the following
day, though the distance is usually considered ten days' journey."

A man of the early Middle Ages and bred in the traditions of a
warlike republic, Marco Polo had nothing but contempt for the quiet
merchants of Su-chow: "a pusillanimous race, and solely occupied
with their trade and manufacture." He tells us that if they had been

as enterprising, manly and warlike as they were ingenious, they might have subdued the whole province of Manji. He makes no mention of the great artists who were flourishing at the time: men like Chao Mêng-fu, noted for his paintings of landscapes, horses and flowers; and Wu-chèn, known as the Priest of the Plum-blossom, who also loved to depict the beauty of the bamboo. Indeed, all through his book, reading between the lines, we can see that Messer Marco Polo, a typical westerner of his time, preferred the virile Mongols to the industrious and peaceful Chinese.

So the time went by till at last Marco Polo, his father and his uncle became homesick. It took them seventeen years to do so; but in the end they began to long for the green glint of the Grand Canal, for the dark little shops of the Merceria, and the rippling gold of the lagoon in the glory of a Venetian sunset. So they sought an audience with the Grand Khan, and with all the tact of the skilled diplomats which they had become, they asked leave to go home.

Kublai Khan refused.

That he was as suave and smiling as they were goes without saying. But he was very firm. They were unable to leave China until 1292, and then it was only by an unexpected stroke of good fortune.

It happened that the Khan of the Persian Horde lost his favourite wife, whose dying wish was that her successor might be, like her, a Mongol. So Persian envoys arrived in Cambaluc and a beautiful Tartar princess whose name was Kukachin was chosen. The Venetians made friends with these emissaries, who begged the Grand Khan to allow the three foreigners to go back with them to Persia. In the end, very reluctantly, he gave his consent, loading the men who had served him so well with gifts, which they had the wisdom to exchange for easily portable gems.

Seventeen years after first setting foot in China, they set sail from the port of Zaitan, crossed the Gulf of Tonkin and made for Sumatra, where they were delayed for five months by the blowing of the contrary monsoon. They had a fair wind to Nicobar, the Andaman Islands and Ceylon, but off the southern coast of India there was another long delay. At last they reached Ormuz in the Persian Gulf, where they had first set out for the wilds of Tartary all those years before; and, having safely delivered the Princess Kukachin into the hands of the authorities, the three adventurers set off overland through Persia and Armenia to Trebizond on the Black Sea. Then on to Constantinople and Negropont, arriving in Venice in 1295, at the end of an odyssey which lasted for twenty-four years.

Their homecoming savours of *The Arabian Nights*. It is said that when three bearded strangers in outlandish clothes knocked at the door of the Ca' Polo, in what is now the Corte della Saboniera, they were not recognized, for even their Italian was a little uncertain. The next we hear of them is that they gave a great feast for all those friends and relatives who had listened to the story of their great adventure and great wealth with ill-concealed scepticism. One is forced to the conclusion that Messer Marco Polo was not unduly troubled by modesty. When he talked of Cathay, its cities and its people, he talked in millions; when he spoke of his own wealth, it was in millions; in short, the word figured so often in his conversation that the Venetians, who have a sense of humor and a short way with braggarts, soon coined a name for him: *Il Millione*. Marco, his father and his uncle, however, had the last word, for they made a flamboyant gesture which was not only an effective reply but the stuff of which immortal legends are woven.

At the banquet the returned travellers greeted their guests in long gowns of crimson satin, which they then took off and presented to their friends. But after the first course they retired, to reappear in even richer robes of crimson velvet. Then, after the next course, they delighted their guests with even more sumptuous costumes of crimson brocade which, like the other gowns, were taken off and presented as gifts to the company. And last of all, when this fashion display must have been becoming a little wearisome and smiles a trifle strained, they came down in the shabby old Tartar clothes in which they had arrived home, but—and this was the grand finale— they slit the seams with a knife and out rolled a priceless hoard of gems: rubies, diamonds, emeralds, rolling, clinking, glittering, shimmering, cascading all over the table, convincing proof of Kublai Khan's munificence. The fact that the story has been told so often does not mean that it is true. The Ca' Polo was burned down long ago: only the doorway remains. But it is significant that the courtyard of the house—and indeed its surroundings—are still called the Corte del Milion.

Just two more scenes: a battlepiece and a prison. From 1253 the Republic had been at war with Genoa; and three years after that famous homecoming, Marco Polo, sailing his own galley as *supra-comito* or gentleman commander, went out under old Dandolo's great-grandson to meet the enemy in the Adriatic. In a battle off the island of Curzola the Venetians were routed and Marco spent a not uncomfortable year as a prisoner of war in Genoa. While in that mild captivity he found a ready audience for the tale of his travels; indeed, it has been suggested that the popularity thus gained shortened the term of his imprisonment. And he had as fellow-prisoner a poor writer from Pisa named Rusticiano, to whom he dictated his book.

We know very little more about him. He married a lady whose name was Donata and by whom he had three daughters. In 1324 he made his will and shortly afterwards he died. Marco Polo deserved the fame and riches which were the reward of his labours, though centuries were to pass before the truth he told was wholly believed.

8. The Struggle for Power

The Closing of the Great Council
Rebellion
The Council of Ten
Marino Falier

During the thirteenth and fourteenth centuries the Bride of the Sea was growing in beauty, a beauty enhanced by the gifts that her bridegroom lavished upon her. They were troubled times. There were long years of war and civil strife—even one period when the Republic was nearly overthrown by Genoa. Yet somehow timber was being replaced by brick, and brick by stone and marble. All over Venice and especially along the banks of the Grand Canal, the fortified houses of the nobility, with their crenellations, courtyards and angle towers, were giving place to stately mansions adorned with frescoes or inlaid with decorations in serpentine and porphyry, while here and there arose something new; the semi-oriental glory of Venetian Gothic.

Most of the Doge's Palace, as we know it today, belongs to the fifteenth century; but the rebuilding begun in Ziani's time was proceeding steadily and soon the city would be enriched by that wonderful colonnade surmounted by its carved loggia and pale apricot upper storey of delicately diapered, creamy Istrian stone and red Verona marble. The noble church of the Dominicans, San Giovanni e Paolo—or San Zanipolo, as the Venetians call it—was rearing its walls of rose-coloured brick above the Canal of the Beggars, while far away across the Grand Canal the building of its rival, the great Franciscan church called the Frari, had begun. Then, as now, one could hear the slap of the water against the bows of a gondola and the gondolier's warning cry, *Stalì!* as he turned the corner of some rio, the deep booming of the bell from the high Campanile, and the eerie, whirring sound of wings as the pigeons of St Mark rose in alarm from the Piazza—a continual reminder of the glory of the Republic for, according to one account, they commemorated the day when Blind Dandolo's carrier pigeon brought news of the fall of Constantinople.

But there were other changes in the air, more important than the rebuilding of palaces or even the eclipse of Byzantium, for they were to affect the life of every man and woman in the city. And as one considers the internal affairs of the Republic it should be remembered that until almost the end of the fourteenth century the war with Genoa dragged on, now smouldering in an uneasy truce, now flaring into flame. It drained Venice of blood and gold, and almost brought her to her knees. Many brave men fell but the most notable victim was freedom. She died at home by the hands of her own sons, and the story of her death is simple. Venetian democracy had had its day: from now on, as long as the Republic endured, the many were to be ruled by the few. Already the Doge had been bridled and curbed; now it was the turn of the people, though the patricians never realized that in disenfranchising the majority, they were unwittingly forging fetters for their own limbs.

Now that the Doge was becoming more and more of a figurehead, there is no longer any need to follow the succession closely. There were, however, some holders of the office who should be mentioned. Marino Morosini, who was elected in 1249, reigned only for three years, but it was in his time that the Inquisition first found a foothold in Venice. The Venetians were, on the whole, devout Christians; but, as we have seen, they did not take kindly to interference by the Church, and the introduction of fanatics, still redhanded after suppression of the Albigenses in Southern France, was met by hostility from the common people and firmness by their rulers. Not for the first time, the Pope resented the independent attitude of these stubborn islanders, who reserved for themselves the right to hunt heretics and to sentence them after they had been examined by the priests; but once again he was forced to admit that the Venetians were hard to drive, and it was not until 1288 that the Papal Inquisitors were allowed a little more authority.

Morosini's short reign also saw the institution of the *Signori di Notte*. At first this was simply a force formed to maintain law and order after dark, and especially to check the nocturnal assassinations which had become so frequent in the streets of Venice. Later, however, these Lords of the Night were to make themselves dreaded as secret police—the executive arm of that tribunal which was soon to be the real ruler of the Republic.

Another Doge, Giovanni Dandolo (1280-1289), one of the four Dandolo Doges and a man of liberal views, is chiefly remembered because, in a time of war and turmoil, he ordered the first golden ducats, or sequins, to be minted. They were noble coins, justly renowned for the purity of their gold, and they have afforded posterity an accurate record of the Doge's bonnet and vestments. The series of ducats remained in circulation for three hundred years—no mean memorial for a man whom his contemporaries called the Uncouth and who made no deep imprint on the pages of history.

Change was in the air indeed, for the time was at hand when the patricians were to make their great bid for power. For many years Venetian foreign policy had been based on the cool assumption that the Serene Republic enjoyed a monopoly of the Levantine trade which, since the Fourth Crusade, had become an ever increasing source of wealth. To conduct this trade, the Venetians declared, was the prerogative of their own citizens. But with a growing population and the acquisition of new territories, how was such citizenship to be defined? An answer was found, simple, audacious and quite shameless. The great commercial families—the merchant princes—decided to take the trade of the Eastern Mediterranean into their own hands. In order to do this, their plan was to close the Great Council to all but members of their own caste.

To ensure success it was necessary that the reigning Doge should be a die-hard patrician. The chance to set such a man on the throne came when Giovanni Dandolo died in 1289. Ruthlessly the nobles set aside the ancient right of the people to share in the choice of their own ruler and forced the election of one of their own kind: Pietro

Gradenigo. It was a bold and successful coup. The secret of their intentions was admirably kept; and on St Catherine's Day the crowd which had gathered outside the Basilica expected to hear that the popular candidate, Jacopo Tiepolo, was their new ruler. But although the election was not supposed to be valid until the people had approved the councillors' choice, on this occasion they were not even given a chance to express their opinion. Never in the history of the Republic had the election of a Doge been announced so bluntly and with so little ceremony. As the crowd which filled the square and overflowed into the Piazzetta and side streets subsided into silence, a deputy of the recently constituted *Quarantia* or Forty (the Supreme Court) appeared. He declared curtly: "Pietro Gradenigo is your Doge, if it please you." And then, without waiting for the customary *arengo* by which the people gave voice for or against the candidate, he turned on his heel and withdrew. The deed was done. Jacopo Tiepolo had been persuaded to withdraw from the contest and retire to his villa on the Brenta. The right man was in the saddle. No doubt fists were clenched and grumbling was heard in the taverns, but there seems to have been no real opposition at first to these cavalier tactics. Even now the people did not realize that their freedom was being stolen from them.

The nobles were in no hurry. They bided their time, and it was not until February of 1297 that they took the tremendous step of turning the Great Council, formed in 1172, into what we would now call a "closed shop." It was Pietro Gradenigo who brought forward and carried the measure whereby the *Quarantia* balloted for the names of all those councillors who had held seats during the last four years. Only those who received twelve favourable votes retained their membership. Further, commissioners were appointed whose duty it was to submit further names for membership, and they at once decreed that only those who could prove that a paternal ancestor had held a seat on the Council were eligible. As the great families of which it was largely composed reserved for themselves the right of reelection, this famous assembly which, in theory at least, had always been democratic was turned into the private preserve of a patrician oligarchy. Membership of the Great Council had, to all intents and purposes, become hereditary.

The position was now as follows. All who were councillors when the act was passed or during the previous four years were eligible for membership—and so were their sons. So, too, were those gentlemen—and their sons—whose ancestors had held seats on the Council. But all those men who had never been, or whose ancestors had never been, councillors were excluded forever. From now on, with very rare exceptions, no man of the people, whatever his ability, could hope to hold high office, for all such posts were now held by councillors whose names—with particulars of marriages, births, etc.—were inscribed in a register which eventually, in 1569, became *Il Libro d'Oro*—the Golden Book of Venice. The power of the Doge was still further limited and no longer were the people to have any voice in his election. It was barefaced dictatorship, not by one man but by a few great families of merchants who had elected themselves into an exclusive guild.

Reaction to these high-handed measures was violent and took the form of two revolts. The first was a rising of the people, led by a wealthy citizen named Marino Bocconio, whose hopes of a political career may well have been blasted by the new act. In the spring of 1300 he and his confederates conceived the idea of forcing their way into the Great Council and there murdering the Doge and all the nobles present. But even in those days Venetian security was seldom lax. Gradenigo's spies brought him news of this clumsy conspiracy and he ordered every councillor to come to the next meeting armed.

Details of what followed remain obscure; but, according to one old chronicler, the rebel leaders were lured from the shelter of the mob by a bland messenger who spoke of the possibility of seats for them on the Council, provided they presented themselves for election in parties of five. Surprisingly, they accepted this invitation to "walk into my parlour." The gates of the Doge's Palace closed behind them and they were never seen alive again. Once inside locked and guarded doors, and overwhelmed by numbers, Bocconio and the other ringleaders were stripped and thrown into a deep pit called the *Trabucco della Torresella*. When they did not return, the deluded people imagined that they had been elected, till the Doge and his councillors, still fully armed, came out and faced them. Whatever we think of their methods, the leaders of the Venetians certainly did not lack courage. Sternly the Doge ordered the people to disperse to their homes; and when they had done so, the naked bodies of the conspirators were exposed in the square, for what in that hot Italian sunshine was an unpleasantly long time, with the threat that anyone who dared to move them would forfeit his head. Rough justice even for the Middle Ages. Treachery by any standard. But it served its purpose. Those shopkeepers and gondoliers had learned who was master. Gradenigo was now free to deal with his other troubles. And he had plenty.

His next misfortune was a serious breach with the Church. In 1308 Azzo d'Este, Lord of Ferrara, died, leaving behind him a disputed succession. On his deathbed he commended to the protection of Venice both the city-state of Ferrara and his natural son Fresco. But Ferrara was nominally a fief of the Holy See, and Pope Clement V supported the claim of Azzo's brother, Francesco. The bastard Fresco, driven from the city, appealed to Venice; and Doge Gradenigo, with an eye to a foothold on the mainland, despatched a fleet of war-galleys to enforce his claim. The Venetians landed and clashed with Papal troops in the streets of Ferrara.

His Holiness had not forgotten the intransigence of the Venetians when he imposed the Inquisition upon them. Now would be the time to show them the strength of his spiritual weapons, so the dread sentence of interdict and excommunication was again pronounced. Some members of the Great Council were in favor of surrender, but the Doge was made of sterner stuff. After all, excommunication had not daunted Blind Dandolo, and Gradenigo would not willingly forgo this chance of dominating Ferrara. He pleaded eloquently that they should not desert young Fresco in his need.

Once again the Venetians had to face the thunder of the Church. A bell was rung, a book was closed, and a candle extinguished; and the citizens of the Serenissima were beyond the pale. All privileges granted by the Holy See were cancelled; all property owned by Venetians was declared to be confiscated; and, hardest blow of all, they were deprived of the sacraments. No marriage could be solemnized; no baby could be baptised; no man or woman, however devout, could be given Christian burial. In that Age of Faith it was a dread sentence, and Venetians soon had reason to believe that they had incurred the wrath of God. A crusade was preached against their city, Papal warships inflicted a severe defeat on one of their fleets, and all

over Europe the property of their merchants was pillaged. Pietro Gradenigo, who might well have been nicknamed the Unlucky, did not
live to see the end of the ban which was not lifted until 1312, when
Venice submitted to the Pope's demands and paid a fine of 100,000
gold ducats. But he saw only too clearly the repercussion of the
sentence, for in 1310 it was partly the cause of the second of the two
rebellions which marred his reign. This time it was more serious
than Marino Bocconio's futile revolt, for it was a conspiracy of powerful nobles, and the rulers of Venice were frightened as they had never
been before.

In those days, one of the most popular of the younger patricians
was Bajamonte Tiepolo, known to his admirers as *Il Gran Cavaliere*.
He was the son of the Jacopo Tiepolo who had been set aside when
Gradenigo became Doge; and in that land of the vendetta, men do
not easily forgive or forget. Pietro Gradenigo had never been popular
and there were many who railed against his pride and folly. The
Closing of the Great Council was still an open wound. Justly or un-
justly, he was blamed for the fact that many innocent people were
under the ban of the Church; and for the first time since the days of
Barbarossa, cries of Guelph and Ghibelline were heard in the streets
of Venice as citizens ranged themselves for or against Pope or Doge.

There were many who regarded Gradenigo as a usurper forced
upon them against their will and thought that Bajamonte Tiepolo,
as his father's son, had a moral right to the Dogeship. Power is a
heady wine; Bajamonte was intoxicated and only too ready to drain
the cup to the dregs. So a plot was hatched by the noble family of
Tiepolo, together with their friends the Querini and other patricians.
They planned to launch their revolt at dawn on the Feast of St Vitus.
With their retainers they planned to seize the Piazza di San Marco
and capture or kill the Doge, trusting that a popular rising would
follow, for Bajamonte, although an aristocrat, was the hero of the
people. One of the confederates, Badoero Badoer, was sent to Padua
to raise more men, while the others mustered at the Querini palace
on the right bank of the Grand Canal. From there they were to advance on the Piazza in two converging columns. One, led by Marco
Querini, was to march along the left bank of the Canal by the small
bridges and *fondamente*, debouching into the square through the
Calle dei Fabri: the other, under Bajamonte Tiepolo himself, was to

make its way through the Merceria, the narrow shopping street of Venice.

Everything went wrong. Although it was June, the weather was appalling. Thunder and lightning and rain were so loud that the noise of the storm drowned the rebels' war cries. Worse, they had been betrayed and the Doge was forewarned. A secret shared is seldom a secret much longer. There were too many in the plot and the inevitable traitor had emerged.

The Doge's reaction was swift and energetic. He sent an urgent call for help to the other islands of the lagoon; and Badoer, marching from Padua, was intercepted and captured by a force from Chioggia. When Marco Querini and his followers burst into the Piazza they saw, through driving sheets of rain, a long steel line of men-at-arms drawn up in front of St Mark's. They fought desperately but they were outnumbered. Marco Querini and one of his sons were killed, and the rest of the little force took to their heels.

In the meantime, Bajamonte Tiepolo, who knew nothing of Badoer's defeat or the fight in the Piazza, discovered that he had badly misjudged the mood of the people. Popular he had certainly been, while the Doge was unpopular; but, with Bocconio's rebellion in mind, it is not surprising that the Venetians preferred law and order to what, as they surely must have guessed, would merely be a change of masters. Instead of the cheers that he had expected, Bajamonte and his men met fierce opposition and had to fight their way along the Merceria in that grey, teeming dawn. To this day can be seen a plaque showing an old woman leaning out of a window and hurling down a heavy stone mortar. Venice was lucky in her old ladies. Five hundred years before, as we have seen, one of them had misled the invading Franks; and now another, a certain Guistina Rossi, broke the most dangerous rebellion that the Republic was ever to know. It was a lucky shot. Her mortar killed Bajamonte's standard-bearer; and when his disheartened men saw their banner with the word *Liberta* trampled in the mud, panic seized them and they ran for their lives, followed by their leaders. They recrossed the Grand Canal at Rialto, breaking down the wooden bridge behind them, and took refuge in the strongly fortified Palazzo Querini.

There followed parley after parley; and although Badoer was

beheaded, Bajamonte—thanks, no doubt, to the fact that he was, or had been, a popular idol—escaped with exile. His palace at Sant' Agostino was razed to the ground and a Column of Infamy erected on its site, while the Querini palace, the rebels' stronghold, was turned into a public slaughter house. The Venetian authorities had a grim sense of humour and a pretty taste in punishments.

As for Bajamonte himself, he became that all too familiar figure, the rebel in exile, the hopeless plotter, the fugitive with a grievance. For years, all over Northern Italy, he was kept under observation by the agents of Venice, hounded from little court to little court—a pathetic has-been forever trying in vain to stir up trouble.

And the old lady of the Merceria? What was Guistina Rossi's reward? She was promised that her rent would never be raised and she was granted the privilege on high days and holidays of flying the flag of St Mark. For one who had just saved the Republic, it could hardly be described as generous!

Bajamonte's rebellion was a fiasco, badly planned and badly timed. What makes it so important is that it was the direct cause of the formation of the Council of Ten: that sinister tribunal beloved by the historical novelist. A committee of magistrates whose task was to inquire into the recent conspiracy, it was made permanent in 1335. Its functions were to watch over the security of the State and public morals; and its great strength lay in the fact that it was above the law—or, rather, that it was a law unto itself. Its members, chosen from the noblest families, served for one year, after which they were no longer exempt from the justice of the tribunal. They received no pay, and acceptance of gifts was a capital offence. They could not be threatened; they could not be bribed; they ruled by terror; and they turned Venice into a police state. But if their courts were ruthless, there is no reason to suppose that they were not also just: in cases of extreme importance or difficulty, a small body of additional members called the *Zonta* was co-opted to make sure that the defendant received a fair hearing.

The two chief weapons of the Ten, as they were always called, were secrecy and a melodramatic atmosphere of mystery and horror. It was all handled very cleverly, and on an imaginative people like the Venetians its effect was terrific. Denunciations could be posted in the *Bocca di Leone*—a stone lion's head with an open mouth, just outside the Hall of the Ten, on the second floor of the Doge's Palace. In spite of the novelists, it is almost certain that anonymous accusations were never read, and the extent of its use may well have been exaggerated. The fact remains, however, that the Lion's Mouth (and other post-boxes) were dreaded instruments of intimidation.

Arrests were made secretly and usually at night by the *Signori di Notte;* trials were held in secret; and records of the proceedings were secret—so much so, that the reports of the transactions of the Council of Ten in the State Archives were not made public until the middle of the nineteenth century. If a suspect was found guilty, he simply disappeared. The spies of the Ten were everywhere and alarming rumours were spread, probably by the Tribunal itself, of torture and stranglings in the dungeons of the Doge's Palace. In case skeptics might be tempted to scoff at such stories, occasionally some unfortunate who had disappeared, suddenly reappeared, floating peacefully along a canal in a sack. Or Venetians might be greeted one morning by a row of dead men, each strung up by one leg, between the two columns on the Piazzetta.

So the Serenissima became subject to a secret tribunal which ruled noble and commoner alike with a rod of iron. It was truly Venetian in that it served the State and no one man. It was as terrible and as fantastic as anything in fiction; yet it continued in office for centuries when it could have been abolished at any time simply by not electing its members. The Venetians dreaded the Council of Ten but clearly it had its uses.

At this point, let us briefly consider the Venetian constitution. The solid foundation on which it rested was the Great Council, above which was the Senate, which dealt with all matters of war and peace, trade, finance and foreign affairs. On the same level with the Senate but outside the main stream of the constitution was the Council of Ten, who could, however, override the Senate. Still higher was the administrative and initiatory body, the *Collegio* or Cabinet, which passed down matters worthy of consideration to either the Senate or the Ten. Right at the top (in theory, at least) were the Doge and his advisers. He, with six councillors and three leaders of the *Quarantia*, together formed what later came to be known as the *Serenissima*

Signoria. But all the power—all the real power—was now in the hands of the Ten.

The first trial of importance involving the Ten, any rumour of which has come down to us, took place in 1355. In the Hall of the Great Council there are portraits of a number of Doges, but one frame is empty except for the representation of a black curtain on which is written: *Hic est locus Marini Falethri decapitati pro crimini-bus.*

Who was this Marino Falier or Faliero who was beheaded as a criminal? He was seventy years of age; he had, in his absence and against his will, been elected Doge; and he was married to a beautiful lady much younger than himself. Furthermore, he had the misfortune to come to the throne in troubled times, when the war with Genoa was at its height and the people in an ugly mood. All the ingredients of tragedy were there; and they were stirred, heated and brought to the boil by a young spark named Michele Steno.

In the fourteenth century the city was infested by gangs of dissolute patrician youths called *giovinastri,* who swaggered about the streets insulting women, singing bawdy songs, and decorating public buildings with *pollizini* or small placards on which were written obscene verses or pasquinades. In their setting of mediaeval Venice one can see those supple, leggy boys with their clubbed hair and tight, parti-coloured clothes, who made themselves a public nuisance, yet thought themselves safe because they had relatives on the Great Council or in the Ten. There is nothing new in callow youth cocking a snook at the establishment.

Such then were the *giovinastri,* and one of the worst of them was young Michele Steno—rich, gay, probably handsome, and as wild as an unbroken colt. It is said that he owned four hundred horses, all dyed a bright yellow, though where he exercised them we are not told. Perhaps on the sands of the Lido. (One thinks of Venice as a horseless city, but it was not so in the Middle Ages. There was jousting in the Piazza, and Venetian bridges had gentle slopes, not steps, to allow for the passage of horses.)

The trouble began on Holy Thursday when, during festivities at the Doge's Palace, Michele Steno made an improper suggestion to one of the Dogaressa's maids-of-honour and was thrown out for his pains. No doubt his boisterous companions laughed; but Steno swore revenge. The method he chose was to fix a lampoon on—of all places! —the Doge's throne. It was a short but scurrilous verse which insinuated none too delicately that although old Falier kept his wife, others enjoyed her favours.

The Doge was furious at this public ridicule; and he bitterly resented the insult to his wife. There is no doubt that if he had had his way, Michele Steno would have paid for his insolence with his life; and when, after arrest and trial, he escaped with one month's imprisonment and a small fine, Falier's rage burst its bounds. It was almost as if something had snapped in his brain; he became a changed man, filled with bitterness and resentment, not only against Steno but against the Republic he had sworn to serve.

The wrong festered until Falier began to show more of his real feelings than was prudent. When Stefano Gisello, Admiral of the Arsenal, came to him with a complaint, Falier countered by asking what hope Gisello had of justice when it was denied to the Doge. Gisello brought matters to a head by remarking significantly that if one cannot bind wild beasts one should kill them; and with a dreadful clarity the old man saw what he must do. He would show them that he could not be insulted with impunity. He would kill all the nobles, overthrow the Republic, and proclaim himself a prince. From now on Venice, like other Italian states, would be ruled by a single lord or tyrant.

So another conspiracy was born: a crazy scheme without a hope of success. But at that time and in that place, a plot—any plot—held an irresistible appeal for a race of men who seemed born to intrigue. Deep in the conspiracy were Gisello and old Falier's nephew Bertuccio; Filippo Calendario, said to have been one of the architects of the Doge's Palace; and other lesser men, including sailors and workmen from the Arsenal. But the amazing, the unheard of thing was that at the head of this conspiracy against the Republic was the Doge himself.

With so many in the plot, it is surprising that it was so long before any rumour of it reached the ears of the Ten. There was nothing subtle or clever about it: Doge Falier's plan was quite simple. The great alarm bell, the *Campana*, would be sounded from the Campanile and as people flocked into the Piazza, a rumour would be spread that a Genoese fleet was in the Gulf of Venice and attempting to enter the harbour. The whole city would soon be in an uproar; and in the confusion all the nobles in the Piazza would be cut down and Falier would be proclaimed prince amid shouts of "*Viva il principe Faliero!*" And that would be the end of the Republic—that accursed republic which turned its reigning Doge into a puppet and then let that puppet become a laughingstock. It all sounded so simple. But given a chain of conspirators, there is bound to be a weak link. In this case, it was a man who dropped a hint to a friend—a patrician—that it might be wiser to stay at home and not go out on to the Piazza. This gentleman smelt treason and, after a few private inquiries, communicated his suspicions to the Council of Ten.

Once on the scent, the Ten acted with commendable speed and efficiency. They received their warning on the evening of the fourteenth of April. Calendario was quietly arrested, spirited into the Palace, and questioned. Others followed. The truth was disclosed. And on the morning of the eighteenth Doge Falier was beheaded at the top of the stone steps leading down into the courtyard (not the Giants' Staircase, however, which was not built until 130 years later).

He had been given a fair trial: to ensure this, for the first time, the *Zonta* of twenty additional councillors had been summoned. At the place of execution the condemned man made a short speech in which he asked for pardon and acknowledged the justice of his sentence. The ducal *birettum* was removed from his head and he was stripped of his insignia. Then, dressed simply in black, he knelt down and with one sweep of a sword his head was struck from his body. The lesser conspirators were hanged in a row along the loggia of the Palace; but it is the tragic figure of the disgraced Doge that history has chosen to remember: Marino Falier, who was false to his trust and executed in his own palace.

And what of the other chief character in the drama—Michele Steno? Did he continue his progress along the downward path? Was he in due course punished for all the trouble that he had caused? No. On the contrary, the one-time *giovinastro* reformed, married a lady of exemplary virtue and strong religious principles, and in his seventieth year, after a long career of service to the Republic, became Doge himself—a "character" noted for his extreme garrulity, for once

9. War with Genoa

The Ottoman Turks
The Black Death
Carlo Zeno
Battle and Blockade

We must now retrace our steps and follow the course of the war with Genoa. It would really be more accurate to describe it as a series of wars which dragged on and on, from 1253, when the rival merchants first drew steel on each other at Acre, to the signing of the peace treaty at Turin in 1381. In the final stages of the conflict the two republics were battling for their very existence; but this war, like so many others, was caused by greed, and Venice and Genoa were equally guilty.

The establishment of the Latin Empire by the crusaders in Constantinople had given Venice a great advantage over her competitors. The most formidable was Genoa, cut off from the rest of Italy by the Ligurian mountains as Venice was isolated by the sea. For some time it had been clear that there was not room for two maritime powers in the Mediterranean, but the proximate cause of hostilities was a dispute over a church in Acre. The Venetian and Genoese merchants came to blows, and brawls escalated into bitter fighting. Lorenzo Tiepolo, a future Doge, rushed a squadron of galleys to Syria and was raiding enemy shipping in harbour before the Genoese even realized that he was in the Levant. The Venetians were victorious in several hard-fought engagements, and trophies of their prowess were brought home to grace the growing city: the four porphyry figures at the angle of St Mark's, near where the Porta della Carta now stands; the two square columns, adorned with flowers and lettering, on the south side of the Basilica; and the low porphyry pillar called the *Pietra del Bando* (Stone of Exil), from which all future laws of the Republic were proclaimed.

In need of allies, Venice now made a league with Pisa and with Manfred of Sicily, while Genoa cast bread upon the waters by helping Michael Palaeologus, who aspired to the throne of Byzantium. In 1261, taking advantage of the temporary absence of a Venetian fleet, the Genoese seized Constantinople and their ally was proclaimed Emperor, while the Venetians only returned in time to carry the fugitive Baldwin II to safety. The Latin Empire had run its course.

Once on his rickety throne, Michael Palaeologus decided that in his position the wisest course was to be friendly with everybody. Accordingly he graciously renewed the rights and privileges of both Venice and Genoa. Understandably, however, he inclined more towards his former allies than his enemies, and went so far as to grant Genoa the palace of the Pandocrater, formerly the residence of the Venetian Podesta or chief magistrate which was not even in the Genoese quarter of Constantinople. This and the fact that the new occupants promptly demolished the building and sent the stones to Genoa were regarded by Venice as a mortal insult; and soon the rivals were at war again. In 1264, off the coast of Sicily, the Genoese were defeated in the naval action of Trapani. As a result, the Byzantine Emperor found it expedient to desert them and Venice became the favoured nation again.

And now, to the thud of kettledrums and with the horse-tail banner at their head, the future scourge of Europe, the Ottoman Turks, came riding into history. It was perhaps the most important historical event of the thirteenth century. By this time their predecessors, the Seljuk Turks, had divided and subdivided Asia Minor into a number of principalities—easy prey for these fresh hordes of warriors who came pouring westwards from Khorassan. Once again the East erupted in a flood of slaughter and devastation. The Latin Empire had collapsed and the whole pattern of power was changed. In 1289 Tripoli fell to the invaders, to be followed in 1291 by Acre. This meant, of course, an abrupt end to the special trading privileges which

Venice had enjoyed in those cities. The Republic, however, had never had any scruples about doing business with the infidels and soon she again scandalized Christendom by courting the new conquerors of Syria and negotiating the restitution of all the rights which she had lost.

This, Genoa could not allow to go unchallenged, and as guardian of the conscience of Europe and her own moneybags, she immediately retaliated by closing the Dardanelles. She was in a strong position to do so, for not only was she in possession of the island of Scio (in fief to the Venetians!), but also she had several bases on the Black Sea and held the strong town of Caffa, which is the key to the Sea of Azov.

Closure of the Dardanelles meant a renewal of the war, and this time fortune favoured Genoa. In 1294 she won a victory in a sea battle near Curzola, an island off the Dalmatian coast of the Adriatic. Here at the hands of the Genoese admiral, Lamba Doria, Venice suffered a crushing defeat. Authorities differ as to the number of her galleys which were destroyed: sixty-five is one estimate, while the number has been put as high as eighty. In any case, the loss was crippling and many more of her ships were captured. Many of her fighting men, including Marco Polo, became prisoners of war; and among them, chained to his own mainmast, was their admiral, Andria Dandolo. But he preferred to die rather than grace Doria's triumph in the streets of Genoa, and with almost superhuman courage he dashed out his brains against the mast.

After this battle there was a lull in the fighting and in the same year an honourable peace was negotiated through the good offices of Matteo Visconti, Lord of Milan. But in 1348 both antagonists had to face a danger even more deadly than enemy galleys or even those terrifying new inventions, gunpowder and cannon. It was the Black Death. The scourge first struck Italy at Genoa; but there was havoc in Venice even before the plague came, for the islands of the lagoon were shaken again and again by an earthquake which lasted for several days. Towers and houses crumbled; canals were dried up; and then, while everything was still in confusion, the city was stricken by this bubonic plague from Asia, which gained its sinister name of the Black Death from the disfiguring hemorrhages which occurred beneath the skin. Boils, violent retching, death in two days: that was the usual sequence. It was a pestilence more horrible than any which

Venice had known. Fifty patrician families were wiped out; the quorum of the Great Council had to be reduced from thirty to twenty; and so many ordinary citizens died that the casualties have been estimated at three-fifths of the population. Burial became a problem. On religious grounds cremation was not even considered. But, on pain of a heavy fine, bodies were ordered to be cast into boats which patrolled the canals, and then buried in shallow graves on some of the smaller islands. Then the Black Death passed, as swiftly as it had come, leaving a wake of broken homes and desolation behind it.

It would have been thought that in those devout mediaeval days, such a visitation would have been regarded as a clear sign of the wrath of God—condign punishment on all those principalities and powers which, while calling themselves Christian, harried their neighbours with fire and sword. One would have thought that St Mark's Basilica and the Cathedral at Genoa would have resounded with Te Deums, while weeping congregations beat their breasts and cried *Mea culpa*. Perhaps they did—in the Middle Ages they were sticklers for propriety. But man was a fighting animal then as now, and within five years the two republics were at war again.

This time the pretext was a dispute about the fur trade of the Black Sea. In vain the Lord of Milan again intervened, even sending the poet Petrarch to plead with the Doge for peace. The Venetians' hands itched for their hilts, and Visconti's overtures to Genoa were equally unsuccessful.

At first the new outbreak of hostilities went well for Venice. Off the coast of Sardinia she won a naval action, capturing thirty-two galleys. In the brutal fashion of those so-called Days of Chivalry, four thousand Genoese prisoners were thrown into the sea. But retribution followed. The year 1354 saw the accession of the traitor Doge, Maria Falier, and it will be remembered that he mounted the throne unwillingly, in time of trouble. Not only were the earthquake and Black Death still fresh in men's minds, but the beginning of his short reign was marred by a crushing defeat. At Sapienza, in the Morea, the entire Venetian fleet was destroyed, leaving the islands of the Lido and the city itself open to attack. A chain was stretched across the port of the Lido, and once again, as in the days of the

Franks, the wooden *bricole* which marked the deep-water channels were removed. The *Campana* which was to have given the signal for Falier's abortive rising would have been rung in grim earnest, but the Genoese failed to follow up their success. One bold assault and they might have been masters of the Mediterranean, but for some reason the attack never came. Perhaps, like Venice, Genoa had been bled white. Certainly the effects of a war which must have seemed interminable to those who fought in it can be traced throughout the remaining years of the rival republics' history. They were like two game but savage dogs, battered and bitten, who, even though almost exhausted, still struggle to reach each other's throats. There was another lull; then in 1379 the conflict entered its final phase.

The story of Venice now becomes, in some degree, the story of two very great men, Carlo Zeno and Vittore Pisani: both Venetians, both admirals, and both endowed with all those qualities which we associate with the splendid and once honored name of gentleman.

Carlo Zeno the Unconquerable. He was only of middle height, this born leader of men, but broad-shouldered and burly. Quick-witted, versatile, he had a weakness for walking into danger and for delivering long, rousing speeches on every possible occasion. In his old age he bore the scars of forty wounds, but he died serenely in his bed. Carlo Zeno's whole life had been a romance. He was the typical knight-errant of the Middle Ages.

The feudal system never took root in Venice and there were no orders of chivalry, so he did not receive the accolade until late in life, and then from—of all people—a Scottish prince with whom he became friendly while on a pilgrimage to Jerusalem. Born into one of the oldest and noblest Venetian families (his mother was a Dandolo), he was destined for the Church and endowed by the Pope with a canonicate at Patras. He was sent to study at Padua; but, like so many of the men who turn out best in the end, his youth was wild. He lost all his money at play and even, it is said, deserted the University for several years to serve with a troop of freelances. At Patras he was a square peg in a round hole and the inevitable happened. Having spent most of his time fighting the Turks, he fell foul of the Greek Governor and was deprived of his canonicate. The Church's loss was the Republic's gain.

It was then that Carlo Zeno's adventures, both military and matrimonial, really began. In Constantinople he risked his life in a most hazardous enterprise on behalf of the dethroned Emperor; he travelled all over Italy, to France, Germany, and even to England on a political mission; and during these years of wanderlust he was learning the ancient art of war. As soon as he was free from the bonds of the Church, he had married a wealthy lady of Chiarenze. When she died, he returned to Venice and, sobered by sorrow, settled down to the comparatively quiet life of a merchant on Rialto. It was several years before he married again—this time, a lady of the noble family of Guistiniani. Then war broke out again and Carlo Zeno's ability was recognized. He was given high command.

As security for a debt, the Byzantine Emperor John Palaeologus had ceded the island of Tenedos (now Bozcaada) to Venice—a concession disputed by Genoa. The Venetians were determined to forestall another attempt to close the Dardanelles; and with Tenedos, the key to the Straits, in their possession, it seemed unlikely that anyone would challenge them. Tenedos, however, belonged to Venice in name only; and when the old Emperor's son, Andronicus, rose in rebellion against his father, he offered the island to Genoa in return for her help. The help was forthcoming. But the islanders remained loyal to John Palaeologus and the Venetians went into action: Admiral Tron sailed to Tenedos with a strong fleet while Carlo Zeno, based on Negropont, began to harry enemy shipping in much the same way as, centuries later, Sir Francis Drake harried the Dons.

At this time the Republic had the powerful Duchy of Milan as her ally; but the Genoese were able to bring a formidable league against her, including Padua, Verona, Naples, Hungary and the Duchy of Austria. The once mighty Byzantine Empire was now in its dotage, feeble, impotent, and quite useless as an ally, so Venice was reaping the first fruits of that dastardly betrayal and sack. A strong Byzantium, as in the past, might have proved a good friend in the hour of need. A strong Byzantium might have acted as a barrier against the Ottoman, a task which now devolved on Hungary, Poland and the mountaineers of the Balkans. Foolishly the aged Emperor tried to make a pact with the Turks and suffered the fate of all weaklings who truckle to a race of warriors. Sunk in debauchery, he deserved the contemptuous answer of the Sultan Murad: "Close the gates of your town and reign within the circuit of its walls, for all without that circuit is mine."

When fighting was resumed the Genoese were quick to seize the initiative. In May 1379, another admiral of the Doria clan, Luciano Doria, sailed into the Adriatic and routed the main Venetian fleet off Pola in Istria. For the first time, in the land fighting against Padua, Venice had made use of the great clumsy bombards, but in a naval engagement gunpowder was still unheard of. Galleys rammed each other with their beaks or steered alongside an enemy ship, snapping off the banks of oars like matchsticks and turning the rowing benches below decks into a shambles. From the high wooden castles at bow and stern, and from the crows'-nests on the masts, archers, crossbow-men and slingers launched a storm of missiles, while down below in the waists of the ships the combatants grappled and boarded: swar-thy, half-naked sailors, and men-at-arms led by warriors in full plate with closed visors like pointed snouts, and emblazoned jupons over their armour. The scene was like an inferno: a confusion of swords, spears and maces; the sky criss-crossed by a sleet of shafts; the water that churned round the heaving vessels darkened by the red tide from the scuppers; and the cries of the gulls drowned by shouting, scream-ing, the blare of trumpets, and a clatter and clanging like the sound of some diabolical smithy.

The Venetians were outmatched by their enemies. Again their fleet was completely destroyed; their admiral, the gallant Pisani, was one of the few who escaped; and when at last the victors sailed away, bedraggled banners bearing the Lion of St Mark were trailing in the water behind them.

Once more Venice lay open to attack. Her rulers were in despair and in this time of trouble they looked round for a scapegoat. They found one in Vittore Pisani. He was deservedly one of the most revered and beloved men in Venice. But he had been defeated and that was a crime which the Council of Ten never overlooked, even when the culprit was an idol of the people. For high command in the Venetian Republic could be compared to walking a tightrope: if you refused to accept it you lacked loyalty—and that was, to put it mildly, unwise; if you accepted and were defeated you paid the penalty of failure; while if you were victorious—too victorious—you might well be suspected of becoming overambitious in a community that dreaded supreme power in the hands of any one man. Pisani was fortunate. He was ordered to stand trial before the Ten, but his sentence was a light one: loss of all his appointments and six months in a dungeon.

The dethroned Queen of the Adriatic now had to endure all the terror and shame of defeat. From the Campanile watchers had the humiliation of seeing a Venetian merchantman taken and burned within sight of the city. A barrier of old ships chained together barred the port of the Lido; but with the honourable exception of Castello delle Saline, which held out obstinately until the end of the war, all the forts along the coast surrendered, Palestrina was captured, and on August 16, 1379, after a three months' siege, the island town of Chioggia that commands the southern entrance to the lagoon was taken by yet another Doria—Pietro—with a loss of 6,000 Venetians killed and 3,500 taken prisoner.

News of the fall of Chioggia brought Venice to the edge of panic. The Venetians were not in the habit of suing for peace, but now the situation was so grave that envoys were sent to the Lord of Padua in the hope that he might be willing and able to arrange reasonable terms. Francesco da Carrara passed on the message to his ally, Doria, who rebuffed the envoys in that insolent answer which has become famous—there would be no peace until Genoa had bridled the bronze horses of St Mark.

It was to be a fight to the finish and Venice had little hope of victory. Doria's plan was to blockade the city and starve its inhabitants into surrender; but in this emergency the Doge, Andrea Contarini, another of Venice's brave old men, delivered a fighting speech to the excited crowd in the Piazza. He was in his seventies, with a voice too feeble to be heard at the other end of the square, so his mouthpiece was Pietro Mocenigo (not to be confused with a future Doge of the same name). But if the Doge's voice was weak, his courage was strong and he knew his people. He promised nobility to those families that served their country best, and he ordered Mocenigo to ask for donations of money and jewels. He called for volunteers to defend the city and—this was a clever touch—for counsel. What did the citizens wish to do? Back came the answer in a roar—from senators, sailors, traders, gondoliers, from the very beggars of the alleys: "To arms!"

His harangue shamed the citizens out of their panic. They were ready now to dare anything. But who was to lead them in action? Carlo Zeno with their remaining squadron was far away in the Levant; and although a small, fast ship was sent to recall him, he moved so quickly in his guerilla campaign, seeking out and sinking every vessel he could find which flew the red cross of Genoa, that there was a long delay before he heard the news of the disaster at Pola and his city's peril. Even when the messenger who had followed him from port to port at last overtook him, Carlo Zeno did not race back at once to the Adriatic. Perhaps he underestimated the gravity of the situation, but perhaps he may have succumbed to temptation. For rumours had reached him of an immense enemy galley, the *Bichinogna*, carrying a valuable cargo and, in addition to her crew, two hundred noble Genoese, all senators or the sons of senators. It was too good a chance to be missed. Zeno was a patriot and a hero but there was also a strain of the buccaneer in his character. After a long chase he overhauled the huge ship, delivered one of his fiery harangues, and then led his boarders over the side. The *Bichinogna* was seized and towed into the harbour of Rhodes, where Carlo Zeno burnt her and distributed the booty among his men. Then only did he hoist his lateen sails and lead his squadron at full speed back to the beleaguered Venice.

In the meantime, inspired by their Doge, the Venetians were straining every nerve to meet the emergency. One of their best commanders, Taddeo Guistiniani, had been made Captain-General; but the question of the supreme command was still a cause of dissension, for there was only one man in whom the majority of the people had absolute confidence, and he was in a dungeon. This was no time for half measures, and a crowd besieged the Doge's Palace, demanding that Vittore Pisani be set free. The Council of Ten in their wisdom knew when to give way; and disregarding the objections of certain envious patricians, they ordered Pisani to be released and restored to his command, though a second demonstration was needed before he was allowed to supersede Guistiniani. It is interesting to note that the man who unlocked Pisani's dungeon door and congratulated him on his liberty was the aged Michele Steno, whose misbehaviour in his youth had brought about the execution of Doge Marino Falier. Now, nearing the end of a long and honourable career, he was in trouble again. Apparently he had committed some misdemeanour while accompanying the Army as *Proveditore* (a kind of political commissar) and had been deprived of all his appointments for one year. There can be no doubt that his ascent to the throne was up a long and slippery slope. But his spirit was indomitable and when the time came he went with the fighting men to Chioggia.

Nothing ever became Pisani better than his bearing after he had been released. He had insisted on spending the previous night in his dungeon, where he was visited by a priest and made his confession. As soon as it was light he went to church and received the Sacrament; then calmly he presented himself before the *Signoria* without betraying the slightest trace of bitterness or malice. His only thought was for Venice.

The first necessity was a fleet. Somehow one would have to be improvised. But by great good fortune, Doria played into Pisani's hands. The Genoese blockade of Venice was complete and an all-out assault might well have meant the end of the Republic. With already such a stranglehold, however, the Genoese commander was not inclined to push his advantage and risk heavy losses of men and ships in those treacherous channels through the mud. He preferred to starve out his enemy, and this gave Pisani what he most needed: time.

The Venetians poured out their gold and gave their labour, each according to his means. They worked as men have seldom worked; and on the twenty-second of December, 1379, six patched-up old galleys and a number of smaller craft sailed out into the mist and bitter cold of the lagoon, bound for Chioggia. They were crammed with eager volunteers, and on the poop of the foremost galley, clad in armor, their undaunted Doge, Andrea Contarini, went out to share the honour and the hardship with Vittore Pisani. It is said that his presence gave a tremendous boost to morale.

The admiral's plan was simple. But it had a touch of genius about it. He had decided to turn the besiegers into the besieged. In that wild winter weather the Genoese had not dared to risk having their fleet scattered by storms. They had therefore retired from the open sea to the shelter of the Porto di Chioggia, and there Pisani was determined that they should remain, blockaded as Venice had been, with all their supplies cut off.

He blocked the harbour like a fox's lair. Every way out into the lagoon was closed by chains of sunken hulks filled with stones. The channels at Malamocco and San Antonio were the first to be barred, and they were followed by the Lombardy Canal and the straits of Brandolo and Chioggia. Now the trap was sprung and the Genoese could only be relieved by a fleet coming in from the sea. That, of course, was the great hazard. If a squadron flying the red cross appeared, the war was as good as over and the might of the Serene Republic would soon be only a memory.

Conditions were so appalling that almost at once the volunteers' enthusiasm began to evaporate. In the teeth of the gales barricades were raised on the sand spits; but the men toiling at the chains and the blockships had to work up to their armpits in icy water and mud, for the canals round Chioggia are so shallow that they are only navigable by flat-bottomed boats. The arrows sang past their ears, and every now and then a ponderous stone ball from a bombard splashed into the water or crushed some little group of besiegers into a bloody mash. There were times, too, when storms lashed the grey Adriatic into a fury. Then all work became impossible and enforced idleness was made even more of an ordeal by the fear that their ramshackle little fleet would be dispersed by the tempest. Already the men's spirits were low and there was grumbling by those who were beginning to regard their position as hopeless. Where was Carlo Zeno? Had their cry for help never reached him? Would a squadron from Genoa arrive first? The cold and the mist and the lively Italian imagination were becoming more dangerous enemies than Doria's men-at-arms.

Pisani kept his head, for he had faith in his plan. He moved among his men, outwardly calm, though his heart must have been sick within him. But before long there were signs of insubordination almost amounting to mutiny. Reluctantly the admiral was forced to agree that if reinforcements did not reach them in the next few days, he would raise the siege.

Very occasionally history provides a climax as dramatic as anything in fiction. On New Year's Day 1380 the sky was clear; and those anxious watchers discerned a faint blur on the horizon which, after what seemed an eternity, resolved itself into ships. Eighteen galleys. But were they friend or foe? Had Carlo Zeno come at last or was it another of the Dorias with a squadron which would cut off their retreat and drive them onto their own barriers? Life or death?

New hope or an end to that city in the sea for which their fore-fathers had toiled? In that biting cold, desperate men confessed their sins and sharpened their swords. Then someone with keen eyes made out the device on the ships' banners. It was the Lion of St Mark.

Carlo Zeno brought with him men, food and money, and now the Venetians pressed the attack on Chioggia by land and sea. Before long the Republic was able to muster a small army of 6,000 merce-naries: Italian, French, English. They assembled on the sandbanks at Pelestrina and were then landed on the shores of Chioggia, not far from the town. According to Bishop Jacopo Zeno, Carlo's grandson and chronicler, this was the first time that the Republic employed these soldiers of fortune; and in view of the experience gained, it is astonishing that it was not the last. This polyglot force was supposed to be under the command of the famous English captain of freelances, Sir John Hawkwood, but for some unrecorded reason Sir John went "absent without leave." His courage was never in question, so one can only conclude that he had accepted another, more lucrative en-gagement. Certainly it must have been at about this time that he was awarded a generous pension by the *Signoria* of Florence.

Carlo Zeno, used to dealing with foreigners, was appointed to the vacant post of commander, and he was helped by the loyal coopera-tion of another Englishman, William the Cock, of whose fidelity and courage his chronicler speaks highly. It would be tedious (even if it were possible) to narrate in detail the story of the engagements that followed: forgotten skirmishes, attacks and sorties, varied by insub-ordination and treachery among the mercenaries—including a strike for double pay, in the face of the enemy! But Carlo Zeno never lost his nerve—he had his spies in the ranks and was kept well informed —even when a rascal named Recanati incited his comrades to open mutiny and threatened that if their demands were not met, they would go over to the Genoese. Suave, smiling, firm when need be, Carlo Zeno dealt with each new crisis as it arose, countering every hostile move, daring the dagger in the back, and leading assaults in which the English, some of them, no doubt, like Hawkwood himself, veterans of Crécy and Poitiers, proved themselves second to none in valour and did much to wipe out the bitter memory of Sir John's desertion.

The battle was by no means won. The Chioggia garrison was in a desperate plight, reduced to eating rats and mice; but it was still touch and go when an unexpected stroke of good luck brought victory to Venice. During an attack on the Chioggian fort of Fossone, a ball from a bombard demolished a tower, and the Genoese commander, Pietro Doria, was buried under the rubble. The command was taken over by Napoleone Grimaldi, who tried to fight his way out of the town but was repulsed with heavy losses. The heart had gone out of the garrison and on June 24, 1380, Chioggia surrendered at discretion. The Doge made a triumphal entry and the banner of St Mark was hoisted on the Campanile.

On his return to Venice, Doge Contarini received a hero's welcome and there were services of thanksgiving for this almost miraculous deliverance from the gravest danger that the Republic had yet had to face. In fulfilment of the promise made when things were at their worst, thirty of the most deserving families were ennobled. At a solemn Mass, in the presence of the Doge and Senate, those new patricians, the Nobles of the War, as they were called, took the oath of loyalty and—a typical Venetian touch—of secrecy. It is strange how this instinct for security, for not letting the left hand know what the right hand is doing, runs like a dark thread through the intricate pattern of the Republic's history. It manifests itself not only in the tortuous machinations of the Ten, but in the masks of latter-day Venetians and a love for such melodramatic devices as peep-holes, sliding panels, private stairs, and the warning mirrors fixed to the window sills of many modern flats. Intrigue has always been in the air of Venice, and the atmosphere still lingers.

For over a year after the recapture of Chioggia the war dragged on; but only seven weeks after the Te Deums for their victory in the lagoon had died away, the citizens were saddened by the news that Pisani, fighting the Genoese off the coast of Dalmatia, had been killed in action. Venice mourned him for the noble-hearted patriot that he was and buried him with sombre ceremony in the church of San Antonio.

After Vittore Pisani's death the gonfalon of Supreme Commander was handed to Carlo Zeno; but like Pisani, he soon discovered that the reward for distinguished service was too often distrust and ingratitude. He was summoned home to answer charges in connection with certain misdemeanors which, it was alleged, he had committed during operations in the Adriatic. But Zeno was not the man to be bullied, even by the Great Council. He flatly refused to obey the order until he had provided for the safety of his fleet. That done, he faced his accusers as boldly as he had faced the Genoese, but he was treated with little ceremony and it might well have gone hard with him if the crowd in the Piazza had not made it clear by their clamour that the man whom the Council saw fit to abuse was the hero of the people. With the cheers of his fellow-countrymen ringing in his ears, Carlo Zeno was set free to return to the camp and the fleet where he was at home. The city of Venice did not see him again for ten years.

The long war was nearly at an end. Through negotiations set in motion by the Duke of Savoy, a peace conference was held in Turin, and on the eighth of August, 1381, a treaty was signed by representatives of the two great maritime republics. But each was to pay a heavy price. Genoa never recovered from her defeat; while Venice, although for a time she remained mistress of the Mediterranean and Levantine trade, lost Treviso and Tenedos and was forced to surrender the whole of Dalmatia to the King of Hungary. It has been said that there are no victors in war and in this case it seems to have been true, for Venice was permanently weakened by the long drain on her resources.

10. Expansion on the Mainland

The Cities of the Plain
The Lord of Milan
Verona and Padua
"A dead man makes no war"

During the war with Genoa, Venice had faced the danger of starvation caused by an enemy blockade, and this was partly responsible for a momentous change of policy which draws a sharp dividing line across the history of the Republic. With an ever increasing population and no means of growing her own food, she was faced with the problem of how to feed her people in time of war. There was also the question of the cheap passage of merchandise on the overland route to Western Europe. Venice was now the great central market for the exchange of goods between East and West, but how could her position be made economically sound while neighbouring states levied heavy toll on her goods?

To the Venetians of those days the answer was simple. Territorial expansion. By fair means or foul they must gain control of the roads and rivers along which their merchandise travelled on its way to the Alpine passes. And to supply their larder they needed at least a large share of the fertile plain of Northern Italy, which was divided among a number of independent city-states. These were the matters which occupied their minds, slowly hardening into resolution and action. It is easy to be wise after the event, but one wonders how many Venetians foresaw that a heavy price would have to be paid when the Lion of St Mark spread his wings over the mainland. For, by becoming a land power, Venice lost a position unique and almost impregnable, except against blockade. She laid herself open to attack; and to maintain her hold on this hard-won territory she had to endure a constant drain on her resources, already seriously depleted by the long struggle against Genoa.

This was still in the future. But new times brought new problems and new Doges to serve as the mouthpiece of the Ten. In June 1382 Andrea Contarini died, full of years and honours. A Morosini succeeded him but was a victim of the plague after only four months in office. There were many who clamoured for Carlo Zeno, but his place was in the field, and one cannot imagine him—free, independent— as the Prisoner of the Doge's Palace. So Andrea Venier, a hard, honest man, quite incorruptible, and a Spartan parent, mounted the throne. To his great sorrow, he had a son Luigi, as wild and dissolute a young ruffian as Michele Steno had been in his youth. Luigi had an affair with a married woman, and when she jilted him for another lover, he took his revenge by decorating her husband's doorway with a pair of horns and an obscene lampoon.

The cuckolded husband was a respectable citizen; understandably, he was furious. As a result of his complaint inquiries were made, and Luigi was apprehended, fined a hundred ducats, and sentenced to two months in a dungeon. This was before the time of the terrible *Pozzi* or Wells of the Doge's Palace; but he was confined in one of the lower cells which doubtless was damp and unhealthy enough. The boy fell ill and wrote letter after letter to his father, imploring to be released. But the Doge refused—and let him die. He would not abuse his high office by showing favouritism and he was determined to curb the vicious habits of the delinquent youths of Venice. Beyond question, the Doge was a man of the highest rectitude. And yet— Luigi was his own son!

This was the time when many Italian city-states, no longer free republics, were ruled by despots whose families had in one way or another seized power. It was the heyday of the *signori*—tyrants not only in the sense of being absolute rulers but also in the sense of being cruel and oppressive. One must not judge mediaeval men by modern standards or forget the many upright people who lived in the land which had given the world Francis of Assisi. But having said that, it can justly be added that seldom in the history of Europe are we confronted by so many examples of calculated wickedness as we find among the rulers of fourteenth- and fifteenth-century Italy. The most charitable thing that can be said about them is that they were corrupted by power and by the knowledge that they could trust no one, least of all their own kinsmen, legitimate or illegitimate. To them, almost without exception, statecraft meant dissimulation and treachery. Their favourite instruments of policy were the poison cup and the dagger in the dark; or, if they wished to do things in style, perhaps a dose of diamond dust, which is not particularly good for the stomach or the bowels. Some merely followed the trend: as they understood things, this was the way to rule. Some were cowards, living in daily fear of assassination. Many were sadists who found delight in inflicting unspeakable tortures: monsters like young Gian Maria Visconti (a pathological case, if ever there was one) who hunted his prisoners with hounds made savage by being fed on human flesh. Of the Scaligeri of Verona, the historian Sismondi says that they hardly ever attained power without first having got rid of their brothers. And although many of these tyrants feared their fellow men, few of them seem to have feared God. When another member of the Visconti family named Barnaba was excommunicated for his sins by Pope Pius V, the ruffian forced the Papal Legate to eat the parchment bulls—lead seals, ribbons and all.

The most famous member of this family and a man of real ability was Gian Galeazzo Visconti, Duke of Milan and Pavia, and father of two sons: that evil boy Gian Maria, and Filippo Maria, each of whom, in his turn, was to become Duke of Milan. Rightly or wrongly, Gian Galeazzo's name had become a byword for timidity. He spent much of his time in seclusion, surrounded by guards; but this may well have been no more than a mask for his treachery and guile. After all, it suited him to be written off as a person of no account. He was a patient man and in no hurry to carry out the plans he had made for his uncle Barnaba who stood in the path of the power he craved.

After more than one plot against his life, real or imaginary, Gian Galeazzo declared that he would seek consolation in prayer and religious exercises. He filled his castle with priests and there was much talk of penance and pilgrimage. Then in May 1385, when he considered that he had created an image of himself as a man of piety, he announced that he was going as a humble suppliant to the shrine of Our Lady of Varese, near Lake Maggiore. Would not his uncle meet him there? Could they not offer up a prayer together? The message was couched in such honeyed words that even the wary Barnaba failed to read between the lines. Suspecting nothing, he walked blindly into the trap: he even allowed himself to become detached from his own escort. Uncle and nephew embraced lovingly till, unable to free himself from the smiling Gian Galeazzo, Barnaba suddenly saw that he was surrounded by men-at-arms and realized that he was a prisoner. He ended his days in a dungeon.

With his uncle safely behind bars, the way was clear for Gian Galeazzo Visconti to realize his own overweening ambition, which was nothing less than to unite all Northern Italy under his own rule. At first he was in league with Venice, but when those usually astute statesmen in the Doge's Palace came to realize that they were driving in double harness with a particularly dangerous beast, they freed themselves from an alliance more deadly than open enmity. Others were not so fortunate.

As early as 1339 Venice had gained some slight foothold on the mainland, but at the end of the Chioggian campaign she had reluctantly ceded Treviso to the Duke of Austria rather than see it fall into the hands of her enemy, Francesco da Carrara of Padua, sometimes called *Il Vecchio* to distinguish him from his son and grandson who were also named Francesco. But when Carrara promptly bought the town from the Austrians, the Venetians were furious and promised their help to the Lord of Verona if he would attack Padua.

During the war between Venice and Genoa, Gian Galeazzo Visconti had made considerable additions to his possessions in Lombardy; and now, from his castle in Milan, he watched the conflict between Verona and Padua, biding his time and secretly allying himself with both parties so that, whatever happened, he would emerge on the winning side. At first the tyrant of Verona, Guglielmo della Scala, had the worst of several engagements, but when Venetian aid was forthcoming the tide began to turn in his favour. Visconti watched and waited. Then in 1387 he saw his chance and intervened on the side of Padua. The Scaligeri were ousted and Verona came under his rule.

It was at this time that Carrara of Padua made a double protest against the Venetian-Milanese alliance: to the Visconti for being in league with the Republic which had backed Verona; and to the Venetians a protest which also contained a secret warning against that most treacherous of allies, Gian Galeazzo Visconti. He had pretended to support Verona only to stab her in the back. Who could doubt that, when it suited him, he would treat Padua in the same way and thus consolidate his position for an eventual attack on Venice? It was sound sense, and the Venetians must have been alive to their danger; but for the time being they did nothing, so deep was their hatred of the Carrara family which had fought on the side of Genoa.

In 1388 a peace treaty was concluded at Turin, by which Venice regained Treviso and secured several fortresses on the mainland, while, as Carrara had feared, the city of Padua was given to Milan. Hopelessly lost in the maze of Italian politics, Francesco de Carrara was forced to abdicate in favour of his son, Francesco Novello. He retired to Treviso, which had not yet been handed over to Venice; but eventually he was seized and spent the remaining years of his life as a prisoner of Milan.

It was never intended that Francesco Novello should rule Padua, but he was a brave man and he made one desperate attempt to remain in possession. Backed by the enthusiastic support of his people, he ignored the terms of the treaty, perhaps hoping that after his father's warning Venice would intervene and deliver his city from the Visconti. But the hostility of the Republic towards the House of Carrara remained unabated.

Nor was the Republic's attitude unreasonable. It was not so long since Novello had abused the sacred person of one of her heralds by sending him back to Venice with cropped ears and slit nostrils. For years, too, the Republic had been plagued by the efforts of the Carraresi agents to bribe or seduce influential Venetians from their allegiance. In some instances they may have succeeded, but usually the Ten were too clever for them and the traitors ended their careers strung up in a row between the two columns of the Piazzetta. One such plot had been the Gobba Conspiracy of 1372, so called because it was hatched in the house of a humpbacked procuress (*gobba,* it will be recalled, meaning hunchback). Unfortunately for the plotters, their plan became known to certain ladies of the town who, in pursuit of their profession, had indulged in careless talk. Horrifying rumours had spread among the imaginative Venetians, including lies about arson and the poisoning of wells.

The plot, as a plot, was a failure and it was only one of many. But it is worth mentioning lest, in view of what follows, the Carraresi should appear as innocent victims of the Ten. In this long and intricate chronicle, the characters, like all of us, are a mixture of good and evil. Only here there are no halftones: like Venice itself, they should be painted in either the brightest or the darkest colours. These men were capable of gallant deeds and of the most shameful treachery, of cruelty which can still make us shudder and of almost saintly compassion. But, above all, they were subtle: candour and frankness they despised. They smiled on their enemies and hid their hand until the dagger was slipped from the sleeve, and they considered it foolish to strike when there was risk of retaliation. So in judging these mediaeval Italians, one must remember that different games have different rules. Theirs were not ours. But they understood their own very clearly.

On the day after Novello's accession and flouting of the peace treaty, heralds in their emblazoned tabards again pricked their horses up to the gates of Padua, sounded a flourish on their trumpets, and delivered the cartel and defiance of Venice and Milan. And this time they returned unharmed, for the bluff had been called. The allied armies of mercenaries would soon be on the march. Resistance was useless. Francesco Novello da Carrara was obliged to surrender and, with his brave wife, Taddea d'Este, became that all too familiar figure in the Italy of those days, the noble fugitive. He had been granted a castle at Asti in which to spend the years of exile, but he preferred to escape to France and, after many adventures, eventually made his peace with the Venetian Republic. He cut a gallant figure in adversity, and at last the wheel of fortune turned again in his favour. The insatiable ambition of Gian Galeazzo Visconti could no longer be disregarded, and Venice had to face the fact that this megalomaniac was a menace, not only to the Republic but to the whole Italian peninsula.

Characteristically, the first to defy him was the exiled Novello. Greatly daring, with only a small force behind him, he returned to

Padua and received a rapturous welcome from his faithful subjects. Church bells clanged in the *campanili* as the people rose in arms against the Milanese garrison; the arcaded streets echoed with war cries and the clash of steel, and when the fighting was over, a Carrara ruled again in his native city. This time he did not lack strong allies. Venice, now fully awake to the common danger, formed a league with Padua, Florence and Bologna against the Visconti. In 1397, at the battle of Governolo, the army of Milan was routed, and the campaign was ended by another peace treaty which, it was hoped, would ensure security for at least another ten years.

Now, for a brief space, the scene shifts from Verona, Padua and Milan, for all Eastern Europe was threatened by a new tidal wave of conquest. The Emperor Manuel, who ruled the last remnant of the once glorious Byzantine Empire, was a feeble decadent and quite helpless against the armies of the Ottomans under their Sultan, Bajazet Ilderim. Fortunately the Turks bypassed Constantinople; but they threatened all the frontiers of Christendom; and Venice, Genoa and Hungary, temporarily reconciled by the common danger, had hurriedly concluded an alliance in an attempt to turn the tide. Carlo Zeno was sent to France and England to raise funds; and thoughtful statesmen among the Venetians must have condemned the folly of their ancestors who had so wantonly destroyed the Byzantine barrier.

In 1400 Michele Steno had reached the top rung of the ladder. It had been a long and arduous struggle for the erstwhile *giovinastro* but he had done everything possible to atone for the sins of his youth; and now, in his seventieth year, he was proclaimed Doge of Venice. Inevitably the thought of his succession carries with it a certain piquancy. Splendid in his cloth of gold, as he walked between the ranks of courtiers in their long houppelandes to take his place on the ivory throne, did he, one wonders, remember the young delinquent who had once had the impudence to defile that same throne with a bawdy rhyme? Insofar as a ruler with no real power can be held responsible for crimes committed in his name, there was, as we shall see, one ugly blot on his record. But on the whole, history has treated him kindly and the *enfant terrible* lived to be revered as one of the "good" Doges. He was no genius but he was a brave and honourable man who was perhaps the more likable for his human foibles.

Three years after Steno became Doge, Venice found herself at war with Genoa again. But it was soon over. Carlo Zeno, although he was growing old, had lost none of his skill as a commander and he gained another brilliant victory at sea. He had not been called the Unconquerable for nothing. And so, with the Genoese again defeated, but the Allies in Eastern Europe reeling under the hammer blows of Bajazet's Turks, the complicated story of Venetian expansion on the mainland continues.

On the third of September, 1402, Gian Galeazzo Visconti died of the plague. Masses were said for his soul, but all over Northern Italy people must have offered up prayers of thanksgiving for this great deliverance. Gian Maria, still in his teens, succeeded his father as Duke of Milan, and his brother Filippo Maria became Duke of Pavia, the dowager Duchess of Milan acting as her sons' regent.

The recent peace treaty had not prevented Gian Galeazzo from adding to his dominions. During the four and a half years before his death he had taken Siena by force of arms and acquired Pisa by more subtle methods entirely typical of the man. First he had instigated the assassination of the rightful ruler; then, with his own puppet in control, he had bought the city for 200,000 florins—with three islands thrown in. No doubt he regarded the transaction as a master stroke of diplomacy. Perugia, Bologna and Lucca had all come under his rule, and when he died he was besieging the capital of another of the Allies, Florence. But on his removal from the chessboard, the knights and pawns could move again, and many a Lombard and Tuscan town welcomed home its former tyrant.

In earlier days Francesco Novello had been regarded, with some justification, as a romantic and heroic figure; but now, with Gian Galeazzo dead and Padua his own again, his character deteriorated. Some flaw which must have been there from the beginning gradually revealed itself; and as a flaw in the rock face can widen into a fissure, so this beau ideal of chivalry began to lose all sense of honour. With surprising ingratitude he transferred his friendship from Venice to Milan. The Duchess rewarded him with the towns of Balluno and Feltre, but ambition is a heady wine and these were not enough. He sent one of his sons, Francesco Terzo, to besiege the neighbouring city of Vicenza, while he himself, acting in consort with the exiled Guglielmo della Scala, took possession of Verona by even more questionable means. The details are still somewhat obscure. The returning Lord of Verona, his two sons and Francesco Novello rode into the city together on April 7, 1404. But by the end of the month both Della Scala's sons were under arrest and he himself had died mysteriously—some say of poison. It was all very odd and most convenient for Novello who now, strangely enough, found himself tyrant of Verona.

Meanwhile, the Duchess of Milan's councillors had persuaded her to break with the Carraresi—a common procedure in those days of changing sides and shifting loyalties. Milan now became the ally of Venice, and a Venetian army of mercenaries quickly raised the siege of Vicenza. This meant war between Venice and Padua, and both Padua and Verona were invested by the troops of the Republic. Verona soon fell, and another of Novello's sons, Jacopo, was captured as he tried to escape over the city wall. But Padua was bravely defended and endured all the horrors of a long siege. Repeatedly the Carraresi were offered the most reasonable terms, but Novello always refused to accept them, hoping for help from Florence. That help never came.

The Venetian forces were commanded by a Malatesta from Rimini, while Carlo Zeno, now over seventy, accompanied the army as *Proveditore*. He must have done so with mixed feelings, for during his wanderings he had become friendly with Novello, and while the latter was poor and in exile Zeno had, with characteristic generosity, helped him with a loan of four hundred ducats, a transaction that he was to regret. But the veteran had no thought now of the trouble to come, and he had lost none of his old spirit. He was here, there and everywhere, far exceeding his duties. He quelled a mutiny among the mercenaries; and defying the rheumatics of old age as once he had defied Turks and Genoese, half-wading, half-swimming, he led reconnoitering parties through the swamps around Padua.

The siege was long and arduous, for Francesco Novello was desperate. To the Venetians he had been a false friend and a treacherous enemy, and if he fell into their hands he had no right to expect mercy. But it was not until November 1405, when food and water were short, disease was rife, and all hope of relief had faded, that the Carraresi surrendered, apparently on the understanding that their lives would be spared. Whether Malatesta deliberately deceived them with the promise of a safe-conduct is not known; but Novello and his two sons were taken to Venice and there, after being tried and condemned by the Council of Ten, they were all brutally strangled in the dungeons of the Doge's Palace.

Doge Steno has been held responsible. Yet can he be blamed for this judicial murder? He was wholly in the hands of the Ten, and the Ten considered that an execution was necessary. They had summoned the *Zonta* to see justice done and there is no reason to suppose that the trial was not conducted fairly. Even by the standards of those days, however, they had no conceivable right to strangle three prisoners of war. But much as one may deplore the action of the Ten, in fairness one must remember that except for the time when, to suit themselves, they had courted the friendship of Venice, the Carrara family had been implacable and deadly enemies of the Republic. In fact, there seems to have been evidence that they were conspiring with Venetian traitors right up to the time of the siege. Officially the three Carraresi died of catarrh and they were buried with sombre magnificence. But the dry, biting, unofficial comment was their true epitaph. "*Uomo morto non fa guerra*," said the Venetians. ("A dead man makes no war.")

Venice, already in possession of Vicenza, now held dominion over the famous cities of Padua and Verona. It is remarkable that whatever changes of fortune took place in that long-drawn game of war and intrigue, the Republic nearly always contrived to scoop the pool.

The submission of Padua and Verona was made the occasion of a gorgeous ceremony in the Piazza. After the fashion of those days, many of the buildings were glowing with frescoes or were picked out in gold, blue, crimson and violet. The Doge, his courtiers and the Senate were seated on a raised platform in front of the Basilica; the Piazzetta and the mouths of all the alleys were packed; and every window, balcony and roof swarmed with an excited, gesticulating crowd of multi-coloured spectators. Padua was the first to pay homage. Music played as the sixteen ambassadors advanced slowly towards the platform. They were all splendidly dressed in scarlet and their attendants wore green. In token of submission they bent the knee in a deep reverence and presented the great gonfalon banner of Padua to Doge Steno, who received it graciously and delivered one of his interminable speeches.

Then, while the trumpets shrilled and the long drums thudded, it was the turn of Verona. She had sent twenty-one envoys, all dressed in white and mounted on horses with white trappings. They rode across the square almost to the foot of the dais and dismounted. Drawn up in three ranks, they bent the knee to the Doge. They handed him the keys of Verona and two silken standards: that of the People—a golden cross on a blue field; and that of the Commune—a silver cross on red. (These flags were later hung up as trophies beside the High Altar of the Basilica.) More oratory followed from His Serenity, including some ill-timed scriptural tags; then, as a sign of reconciliation, the aged Steno presented the envoys with banners bearing the Lion of St Mark.

Not long after this great event, the Council of Ten met again to consider serious charges against no less a person than Carlo Zeno. When Padua fell, he had been made Governor of the conquered city. Then he was replaced by another man and soon found himself in trouble. It will be remembered that when the murdered Francesco Novello was in exile, Carlo Zeno had lent him a sum of money. In due course the loan was repaid, and that should have been the end of it; but the new Governor, Carlo's successor, going through the Carrara papers, found one that puzzled him and aroused his suspicions. It was a memorandum of four hundred ducats paid by Novello to Carlo Zeno.

The over-zealous governor informed the Ten, and the great commander was ordered to appear before them. One can imagine him standing there, facing them: a burly, thickset figure, white-haired now, a little bowed, but still with the old fire in his dark eyes and the rasp in that strong voice which had ordered the boarders over the bulwarks and quelled mutineers. Boldly he denied having taken bribes or trafficked with the enemy, and told them the truth about the trifling loan which they seemed to think so important.

Those smooth, supple councillors who had been squalling in their cradles when Carlo first strapped on his sword did not believe him; and they sentenced him to a year's imprisonment and the loss of all his appointments. When Carlo Zeno came out of prison he returned to the East and, incredible as it may seem, he resumed his life of adventure. In Jerusalem, as previously mentioned, he received the accolade of knighthood, and on his way home the indomitable old war dog managed to put in a little fighting—as a freelance in Cyprus. He gave the Genoese another beating; then at last, reluctantly we may be sure, he hung up his sword and settled down. When nearly eighty he married again, for the third and last time. His bride was a lady of his own age, a patrician of Istria; and he married her, his biographer Bishop Jacopo Zeno tells us, "to secure domestic government, and a consort and companion."

We have one last picture of him, propped up in his bed, as was his custom on a cold winter night, poring slowly over huge leather-bound volumes of Scripture and philosophy. Those forty old wounds must have ached in the chill and damp of a Venetian winter, when the rain came teeming down or the sea fog was lying low over the lagoon. After a long life of action, serene old age and honour untarnished: what more could he desire? For if ever a man had lived to the full it was Carlo Zeno the Unconquerable.

He died in the year 1418 at the age of eighty-four, and he was buried in the now vanished church of Santa Maria della Celestra. The priests, as usual, would have carried his coffin, but the seamen of Venice contested their right to do so and appealed to the Doge. So it was on the shoulders of the sailors who had loved him, working in relays in order to give every man his turn, that the great commander went to his rest. He had served Venice well, but now she was a different Venice, with rich possessions on the mainland. She could no longer rely on fleets of galleys to defend her from her enemies. From now on she must give hostages to Fortune by employing armies of mercenaries.

11. The Condottieri

Soldiers of Fortune
The Passage of the Ships
The War Game
Carmagnola

By the church of San Zanipolo and overlooking the Canal of the Beggars stands the bronze statue of a *condottiere* in full armour: Bartolommeo Colleoni, who twice commanded a Venetian army against the Milanese and twice led the armies of Milan against the Republic of Venice. The work of Andrea del Verrocchio, with the pedestal completed after his death by Leopardi, it is said to be the finest equestrian statue in the world. There is another armoured horseman in the Piazza del Santo at Padua, erected in honour of Gattamelata, *nom de guerre* of a man named Erasmo da Narni. Quite apart from any merits of the sculpture, Gattamelata is remembered for his deeds; if it had not been for Verrocchio, Colleoni might well have been forgotten.

In Italy, just as the fourteenth century was the age of the admirals, so, in the hundred years that followed, the wars between the city-states were fought out on land by the *condottieri*, those hired leaders of mercenaries whose very names resound like the rattle of drums: Colleoni, Carmagnola, Gattamelata, Piccinino, Facino Cane, Bande Nere, Sforza and others. They were captains who lorded it like princes and who held the fate of Italy in their mailed hands.

In Venice it was the rule that no citizen should serve the Republic in war as a soldier: her commanders had always been the admirals, and her galleys were manned by Venetian sailors and by mercenaries hired for the occasion. As the history of Imperial Rome proved, a standing army could be a menace, especially if it was led by a popular hero, and the abiding fear of the Serenissima had always been power in the hands of one man. It was for this reason, together with freedom from the feudal system and the reluctance of prosperous citizens to spare time for military training, that the rulers of Venice, in common with other Italian cities, had put their trust in the free companions who plied for hire throughout the Peninsula.

The best of the *condottieri* were men of imagination and enterprise. In the depth of winter, when the passes were closed, Gatta-melata made a famous forced march across the mountains to the north of Lake Garda; and when in 1439 it became necessary for the Venetians to send supplies to the beleaguered city of Brescia, he ordered one of his subordinates (some say that it was Colleoni; others that it was a Candian engineer named Sorbolo) to transport a small fleet overland from Verona to the shores of Garda, a roundabout journey of about sixty miles.

There were two full-sized galleys and three smaller ones, together with a number of other craft, some of which were carried on carts. But to move the whole flotilla over the mountains took hundreds of men three months and was a notable feat of engineering requiring the utmost resolution and powers of endurance. The ships were taken up the River Adige, past Rivoli and Mori, and then manhandled over rough mountain tracks to the little lake of Loppio. A great number of trees had to be cut down to provide logrollers and the rafts on which the keels of the vessels rested, while the motive power was supplied by teams of oxen and by gangs of men hauling on cables. Slowly, yard by yard, they dragged the galleys up the pass, while other men toiled and sweated, shifting the logs to provide a constant succession of rollers. Lake Loppio gave them a short respite; then that terrible, heart-breaking haul began all over again as the ships were heaved up the mountain side to the village of Nago, high above Garda.

And then the descent began, down a watercourse where a rough path now runs between olive orchards. The descent is steep and the men had to strain at the ropes to prevent the ships getting out of control and crashing down into the valley. It is probable that this was the hardest part of the whole operation, but it was accomplished at last and the flotilla was launched on Lake Garda at Torbole near Riva.

At Nago, in what is now the Strada Santa Lucia, a stone tablet commemorates this tremendous feat, while in the castle of Malcesine, on the shore of the lake, there are diagrams and models which show the passage of the ships from Verona to Torbole. There are pictures of the galleys on their rafts, moving over the logrollers, the teams of oxen, the drivers with their long whips, and the gangs toiling at the ropes as they manhandled the big ships up and down the mountain slopes.

A wonderful example of ingenuity and fortitude—but those men would have done as much for anyone else who had hired them. Gone were the days of Sir John Hawkwood and the small companies of freelances. War had become big business. The leading *condottieri* now controlled quite large armies, mostly heavy cavalry in full plate; and with or without their troops, they could be bought like so much merchandise. Under other, more renowned soldiers of fortune, Colleoni served Venice for many years; then, probably in the hope of higher pay, he sold his services to Milan. The suspicious Visconti questioned his loyalty and imprisoned him for four years at Monza. When he was released, Colleoni returned to Venice, hoping to be made Captain-General. His hopes were disappointed, but by now Visconti was dead, so Colleoni reentered the service of Milan. Then the Venetians offered him a higher price, so back he came to Venice, to be appointed Captain-General in the year 1455 and to attain immortality in the shape of Messer Verrocchio's masterpiece.

There was no sentiment in this soldiering, no loyalty, no hatred, and very little danger, for Italy in the days of the *condottieri* was the scene of some of the most extraordinary battles in military history. Armies fought all day, and at the end of it there were hardly any casualties. At Zagonara in 1423, for example, and at Molinella in 1467, there was a great deal of noise and confusion and shouting but as battles they were almost bloodless. Mercenaries fighting for money were not interested in cutting throats. Dead men paid no ransom;

and in any case, why injure old comrades with whom you had marched and diced and drunk wine and beside whom, next year, you might be fighting under the same banner?

Until nearly the end of the century, when savage Switzers, German *landsknechte,* and the Spanish sword-and-buckler men showed that war, even in Italy, could be a bloody, brutal business, a tournament might well have been more dangerous than a pitched battle. One need not question these men's courage, for they were not fighting for anything that was dear to them—except cash. They were free companions, soldiers of fortune, whose swords were for sale to the highest bidder and who thought nothing of changing sides as soon as their contract had ended. The justice of the cause did not concern them in the least: they were plying a trade and, to them, one lord or one city was as good as another.

It is not surprising, therefore, that they risked their lives as little as possible, preferring to rely on clever strategy and tactics. Their object was to outwit the enemy and take valuable prisoners. Often their generalship was brilliant. And when they were brought face to face with their adversaries, most of them were so completely encased in plate armour that it was sheer hard luck if lance or poleaxe found a joint in their harness. Casualties (if any) were usually the horses, a few half-armed footmen, and of course the helpless peasants who had their cottages burned and their women raped.

Such then was warfare in mediaeval Italy when there were no English longbows or Swiss pikes and halberds to turn knightly passages-of-arms into deadly earnest. And such were the *condottieri,* who taught men to play at war. One of them—perhaps the most famous—was Carmagnola.

He was christened Francesco Bussone but the soldiers called him Carmagnola after the village in the mountains of Piedmont where he was born. Reared as a cowherd, he preferred the more lucrative trade of fighting and almost before he had reached manhood he was serving under the Viper banner of the Visconti, Lords of Milan.

Fiery by nature, a flamboyant figure, from the very beginning he was arrogant and overbearing. He knew his own value. The great *condottiere* Facino Cane in whose *condotta* he rode for several years recognized his ability, and also, it would seem, his ambition, for when Carmagnola asked for promotion the mercenary leader re-

Venice from the air. In the foreground is part of the Lido. *Credit: Venice Tourist Board.*

Venice with the mainland in the background. *Credit: Venice Tourist Board.*

Top: General view of the Riva. *Credit: Radio Times Hulton Picture Library.*   *Bottom:*
The Molo, the Piazzetta, and the two columns. The column to the right is surmounted by the
Winged Lion of St Mark. *Credit: Radio Times Hulton Picture Library.*

Top: The Piazza, St Mark's Basilica, the Doge's Palace, and Campanile. *Credit: Venice Tourist Board.* *Bottom:* The Piazza under water. Abnormally high tides threaten the city today. *Credit: Venice Tourist Board.*

Top: St Mark's Basilica, the third on this site, begun after the disastrous fire of 976. *Credit: Radio Times Hulton Picture Library.*   *Bottom:* The interior of St Mark's. *Credit: Radio Times Hulton Picture Library.*

Top: The Hall of the Great Council. *Credit: Radio Times Hulton Picture Library.* *Bottom:* The Silk Route through the Gobi Desert. Along this road Marco Polo passed in about 1274 on his way east. *Credit: Radio Times Hulton Picture Library.*

Top: Sancta Sophia, Constantinople. The four minarets were added after the Turkish conquest in 1453. *Credit: Radio Times Hulton Picture Library.* *Bottom:* The Byzantine walls of Constantinople. These walls were breached by Venetians and Crusaders in 1204. *Credit: Radio Times Hulton Picture Library.*

Left: The Grand Canal. In the distance the Rialto Bridge. *Credit: Venice Tourist Board.*
Top: The Rialto Bridge. First built in the twelfth century—the current bridge was begun towards the end of the sixteenth century—this bridge was the only link between the two parts of Venice for 700 years. *Credit: Radio Times Hulton Picture Library.* *Bottom:* A campo, with Santa Maria Formosa in the center. *Credit: Italian State Tourist Office.*

Top: The statue of Colleoni by Verrocchio stands by the Church of San Zanipolo overlooking the Canal of the Beggars. Colleoni, one of the many condottieri, fought for Venice against Milan and for Milan against Venice. *Credit: Radio Times Hulton Picture Library.* *Bottom:* The Ca' d'Oro Palace, from across the Grand Canal. *Credit: Mr. & Mrs. Leonard Stevens.*

The Ca' d'Oro Palace. Built in the mid-fifteenth century, it is a "supreme masterpiece of Venetian Gothic." *Credit: Venice Tourist Board.*

Left: The Rio di Palazzo, with the Bridge of Sighs in background. *Credit: Venice Tourist Board.*   *Top:* The Bridge of Sighs. Built in 1600, this flying bridge links the Doge's Palace to the "new" sixteenth-century prisons. *Credit: Radio Times Hulton Picture Library.* *Bottom:* The Lagoon and island of San Giorgio. *Credit: Italian State Tourist Office.*

Top: A modern-day regatta on the Grand Canal. *Credit: Venice Tourist Board.* Bottom:
"Regatta on the Grand Canal" by Canaletto. *Credit: Radio Times Hulton Picture Library.*

Courtyard of the Doge's Palace, showing the well and the Giants' Staircase. *Credit: Radio Times Hulton Picture Library.*

A side canal. *Credit: Venice Tourist Board.*

plied drily that if this young man were advanced one step he would never be satisfied until he had reached the top. In mediaeval Italy one had to be wary of clever subordinates.

Then, on the sixteenth of May, 1412, Facino Cane died at Pavia on the very day when Gian Maria Visconti, Duke of Milan, was assassinated for his sins. He was that sadist with a lust for torture who hunted prisoners with hounds. The young Duke died unmourned, leaving his brother, Filippo Maria, as his heir; and with Facino no longer in the saddle, Carmagnola seized his chance. It is not recorded how he brought himself to Filippo's notice, but the Visconti saw that this big loud-mouthed peasant from Piedmont was wasted as an ordinary man-at-arms but might otherwise prove useful. Taking a hint perhaps from Facino's jest, he raised him from the ranks to command the army of Milan. It was shrewd. But then, for all his weakness and timidity, Filippo was a good judge of men. And in Carmagnola he had chosen wisely. The new commander secured Milan for him, killed a bastard claimant, and eliminated rival factions who would have disputed the succession.

Later Carmagnola was to prove his prowess in the field. He reconquered several cities which had risen against the Visconti; and in June 1422, at the Battle of Arbedo, he became one of the few *condottieri* who had forced a Swiss army to retire. The Swiss were not yet the power in warfare which later they were to become; but a force of four thousand men, mostly halberdiers, from Uri, Unterwalden, Zug and Lucerne, were not to be despised. Knowing that these unarmoured mountaineers had no fear of cavalry, Carmagnola dismounted his men-at-arms and charged the bristling Swiss phalanx with one solid column of steel. A false alarm of enemy reinforcements prevented him from following up his advantage; and the Swiss who for once were on the point of surrender retired in good order. But they suffered tremendous losses. As Sir Charles W. Oman has said: "The contingent of Lucerne had crossed the Lake of the Four Cantons in ten large barges when setting out on this expedition. It returned in two!"

At first, for a few years, Filippo Maria seems to have been grateful to the great *condottiere*: Carmagnola was on the crest of the wave. He was given the hand in marriage of a kinswoman of the Duke, together with the right to bear the arms and name of Visconti.

Honours and riches were showered upon him and he showed himself worthy of them. He gained more victories; above all, he humbled the Republic of Genoa. But one cannot mount on other men's shoulders without making enemies, and there can be little doubt about his swagger and his rough tongue—many a silken courtier must have winced when it lashed him. The court of Milan was a dangerous place, as Carmagnola was to discover.

It has been said that during the first year of his reign Filippo Maria showed courage in battle. But he was not a brave man. Power meant peril in those days; and fear of sharing his brother's fate made him almost a recluse, even in his own palace. Outside his own small circle he would see no one. Yet sneers and innuendoes about the *condottiere* reached him. Perhaps they frightened him a little. At all events, he decided that Carmagnola was becoming dangerous. The time had come to show him who was master.

The first sign of the commander's loss of favour was a sudden order to surrender the small troop of horse which was his own personal bodyguard and the apple of his eye. Other humiliations followed, but Carmagnola was not the man to take insults lying down. Failing to obtain an audience in the palace at Milan, he heard that the Duke had gone to the castle of Abbiate-grasso on the frontier of Piedmont. Bigli, the historian of Milan, tells us how the *condottiere* followed at full gallop, an escort jingling behind him. They rode on to the castle bridge, but their way was barred by the men-at-arms on duty. And Carmagnola was kept waiting. He was kept waiting for a long time. Fuming, he demanded to see the Duke and was told that Filippo was "busy." He kept his temper—*just*, explaining patiently that he had come to discuss certain matters which were for the Duke's ear alone. Again he received no satisfaction, and to make matters worse, he caught a glimpse of Filippo Maria at an upper window. Then Carmagnola flamed, and his great voice rang across the courtyard: "Since I cannot speak before my lord the Duke, I call God to witness my innocence and faithfulness to him." He said other things too, indiscreet things about how the people might one day feel the need of a man whom the Duke now refused to hear. Then, barking an order, he wheeled his horse and rode furiously for the border, never drawing rein until he reached the castle of the Duke of Savoy, to whom he offered his services.

Duke Amadeo was tempted. Here was one of the first swords in Italy for the asking. But he dared not offend the Visconti. So Carmagnola rode away, travelling secretly for fear of his enemies, into the hills and eastwards over a spur of the Alps, and so at last down to Venice.

The Serenissima welcomed him, though it has been said that agents of the Duke of Milan were arrested for trying to poison him. He was given command of the Venetian forces, a princely salary and, later, a palace near the church of San Stae (or Sant' Eustachio), for he was just the man who was needed to scotch this Viper of Milan. An alliance was formed between Venice and Florence, Mantua, Savoy and the Kingdom of Naples, and in January 1426 war was declared.

In March, the campaign opened with a night attack on Brescia. According to old Sabellicus, the librarian of St Mark's, Carmagnola's first move was an attempt to have the Governor assassinated. There is no proof of this, but certainly such an opening gambit was quite in accordance with the strategy of the time. In this, the century of Machiavelli, Italian generals, like the Byzantines, economized in human lives and did not believe in using force if cunning would serve instead. So Carmagnola saw to it that there was no unnecessary bloodshed. Two brothers who lived inside the walls were won over— perhaps bribed; and at about midnight on the Feast of St Benedict, the citizens of Brescia were awakened by the blare of trumpets, the shouting of orders, and the ring of hoofs on flagstones, to find their windows flooded with torchlight and, in the square, stiff blazoned banners and a dark forest of spears. But to take Brescia was one thing; to lay successful siege to the castle overlooking the town was quite another; and it was seven months before the Lion of St Mark flew from the ramparts.

In December 1426, Filippo made peace with the Allies; then, having signed the treaty and gained breathing space, he used the rest of the winter to strengthen his forces and prepare for a spring and summer campaign. There was an engagement between ships in the River Po; and in the heat of an Italian July, the army of Milan attacked Carmagnola at Casalsecco. This so-called battle was a farce. The heat was so intense that men were almost stifled in their armour and the dust rose in such clouds that visibility was almost nil. In the end, both sides had to withdraw without either claiming the victory.

So the war dragged on. The Venetians were not altogether satisfied with the conduct of their commander. In April 1427 Carmagnola had the misfortune to lose the town of Casamaggiore, and he incurred the displeasure of the *Signoria* by repeatedly absenting himself from the army—usually on the plea of ill health or the pain of old wounds—when his presence was urgently needed. The man was a law unto himself and Venice did not tolerate independence from those whom she employed.

Then, in October, Carmagnola won the famous Battle of Maclodio—famous because, even by the standards of those days, it was almost bloodless. There was in fact no slaughter at all. Carmagnola cleverly lured the enemy into marshes where they were at his mercy. The knights and men-at-arms floundered and splashed and surrendered in droves. "Five thousand horsemen and five thousand foot were taken prisoner," says Bigli, and adds cheerfully: "Those who were there affirm that they heard of no one being killed."

This extraordinary victory at Maclodio had the desired effect. Lords of small castles hastened to yield. Deputations of townsmen declared their undying allegiance to the Serenissima. And among the captives there were men of note: Carlo Malatesta, a young noble from Rimini, who had been given the command by Filippo over the heads of seasoned veterans; and the *condottieri* Nicolo Piccinino and Francesco Sforza—the last-named was one day to become Duke of Milan. Youth and experience shared the same fate, but with impetuous generosity Carmagnola set them free. From that ill-advised act of clemency can be traced his downfall.

It so happened that the Procurators of St Mark were in his camp, and on the morning after the battle they presented themselves in his tent to ask if it was true that he had released some important prisoners. Carmagnola was no respecter of persons and there must have been raised eyebrows and pursed lips when that big bronzed fellow in leather-and-steel reminded them, probably quite arrogantly, that he was in command and would do as he pleased. As they drew their robes of red damask round them and bowed themselves out of his tent, their faces must have been bland masks, their voices smooth as oil. Of course, of course. They quite understood—but possibly the *Signoria* might take a different view. The Carmagnola returned to Venice in triumph, but the damage had been done. From now on he was a marked man, though that by itself does not explain his misfortunes.

There followed three years of peace. Carmagnola's wife and children, arrested by Filippo, had been restored to him and he lived with them in his Venetian palace—in the eyes of the world a man to be envied, renowned and honoured by the Republic. Yet it was during this period of peace that his life became a riddle. For something happened, something which changed his whole attitude towards Venice and turned the doubts of the *Signoria* into distrust and suspicion.

In writing history one should confine oneself to facts and avoid speculation. But in this case the facts are missing: they have been missing for five hundred years. There is a human problem here, a tangled skein of actions, reactions and motives, which could best be unravelled by a psychologist—if the psychologist had any evidence on which to base his reasoning. Since it seems certain that we shall never know what happened in that house near San Stae, surely, for once, it is permissible to give rein to one's thoughts.

We know that Carmagnola's wife was a Visconti, though the Ducal family of Milan had given her no cause to love them. We have no right to doubt that she was devoted and faithful to her husband. But human nature is unpredictable. Who can tell what forces were at work? A clever woman could have ruined Carmagnola by persuading him to ruin himself. And, after all, why did Filippo release her? He may have had a good reason for doing so. No proof. No evidence. Nothing. But we must admit that the lady could just as easily have hated this illiterate peasant who had been forced upon her, and whose manners and conversation were still those of the camp. We do know that when he was in Venice, away from his familiar environment, Carmagnola was very conscious of his lowly birth; it may even account, in part, for his hot temper and readiness to take offence. There may have been other influences too, other characters in the drama. Of only two things can we be tolerably certain: that those three years in Venice hold the key to the mystery of his behavior and that day and night, at home and abroad, he was watched by the agents of the Ten.

He had his warnings. But this rough soldier was not subtle. The exact time is not known, but the tale is told of how, while on a visit to Venice, almost certainly during his next campaign, he met Doge Francesco Foscari coming out of the council chamber after an all-night sitting. The *condottiere* was hardly a wit, but he had been bred on barrack-room humour, and, according to the historian Sabellicus, he asked if he should say good morning or good evening "to those who watch over Venice while the rest of the world sleeps." His Serenity smiled and answered that among many serious matters which had been discussed, nothing had been mentioned more often than Carmagnola's name.

The double meaning should have been clear. Was the soldier blind to the danger that surrounded him, or had something—or someone—revived his old friendship with the Duke of Milan? The time was to come when men would be found to swear that he had been in treasonable correspondence with Filippo. That letters and messages had passed between them there can be little doubt, and we know that when war broke out again Carmagnola tried to resign his command. His resignation was not accepted. But the general who took the field against his old master was a different man from the fiery, self-confident victor of Maclodio.

The immediate cause of renewed hostilities was a Papal bull of Eugenius IV. The Holy Father solemnly admonished the lords and people of Italy, and, in order that fratricidal strife might cease throughout the Peninsula, he announced his intention of regulating affairs himself. But unfortunately His Holiness had been a Venetian cardinal, which was quite enough to alarm the Visconti. Milan flew to arms, and an unwilling Carmagnola was obliged to buckle on his armour and ride out again at the head of his lances.

The campaign opened badly for Venice with a defeat at Soncino. Carmagnola, forward with his advance guard, was surprised by his old enemy Sforza who took 1,600 prisoners. Carmagnola had to cut his way out of the melee and ride for his life. But he was able to rejoin the main body of his army and in the spring of 1431 he advanced on Cremona.

The ancient city of Cremona was used to war. It had been taken and sacked by Vespasian, by Agilulf the Lombard, and by the Emperor

Henry VII. Now, one May morning, the watchman on the Torrazzo Tower saw a glitter of arms among the poplars and dusty-green fields of the plain of Lombardy and, far away on the broad stream of the Po, the blazoned sails of a Venetian fleet. For this was to be a combined operation. Carmagnola, with horse, foot and bombards, was to invest Cremona by land while the Venetian admiral, Trevisano, sailed upstream almost to the walls. But the general's spies had failed to inform him that the enemy, too, had ships on the Po: ships lighter and swifter than his own, commanded by Grimaldi of Genoa and largely manned by Genoese seamen.

From the very beginning Sforza and Piccinino seized the initiative. When Carmagnola came within striking distance the Milanese *condottieri* made a feint at his main force; then, quickly retiring as darkness fell, they secretly embarked their men-at-arms in ships anchored under the walls of the city. At dawn they struck and, taking advantage of the current, bore down on the Venetian fleet.

The engagement was no longer a half-hearted clash of mercenaries. The sailors, Venetian and Genoese, were hereditary enemies and they fought like wildcats. Thus the battle on the Po was a long-drawn, sanguinary action. There were 2,500 casualties and the river was darkly streaked with blood. Locked together, crossbow bolts flying and boarders raging over the bulwarks, the vessels—many of them blazing—drifted slowly downstream while Carmagnola, in impotent fury, raged up and down the bank. His subsequent behaviour makes one wonder whether his anger was genuine.

Nicolo Trevisano fled and managed to reach the bank of the river in a small boat, carrying with him the war chest of 60,000 pieces of gold. Others who swam for it were less fortunate and either drowned or were bludgeoned by the peasantry, who had the upper hand this time and many wrongs to avenge. The truth is that the Venetians were outnumbered, outsailed and outmanoeuvered by the seamen of Genoa, and by mercenaries forced to fight for once or go overboard in their armour. The Venetians had no chance and their fleet was destroyed in the worst defeat since the Battle of Pola.

Carmagnola was blamed for the disaster, though it is difficult to see how he could have averted it once the battle was joined. He dictated a letter to the Senate, excusing himself, and the Senate graciously assured him that he was not to blame. But after the rout his conduct becomes inexplicable unless we are prepared to believe that he had gone over to the enemy. Either he had turned traitor or he had lost his grip. For days, for weeks, for eleven months, he and his men remained idle in their camp before Cremona. It is true that all over Italy a distemper had broken out among horses; but this would have affected the enemy too, and, in any case, he was not contemplating a cavalry engagement but an assault on a walled city. There was one insignificant skirmish. Apart from that, this great soldier, this famous commander, this man of action did nothing. He sulked in his tent and left what fighting there was to others.

One of his captains, Cavalcabo—supported, some say, by Colleoni himself—performed a daring feat of arms by making his way into the city with a small party of picked men. He captured a strong point and held it. All that he needed was reinforcement. One bold, decisive stroke and Cremona might have been taken. Cavalcabo sent back a message and then, when no answer came, of necessity retired with his men. For Carmagnola had made no attempt to help him. What was the reason for this strange inaction, for a lethargy not unlike that which overcame Napoleon at Waterloo? Was Carmagnola ill or had he, indeed, been seduced from his allegiance? The Council of Ten took the graver view and who shall say that they were wrong?

All through their history the Venetians feted and honoured successful commanders (until they showed signs of ambition) but they could be merciless towards failures. And here was a man suspected of treason. For over five years the agents of the Ten had kept Carmagnola under observation. They had given him plenty of rope; now at last, satisfied of his guilt, they tightened the noose—suddenly, quietly, without any fuss, as was their custom. With specious compliments and smooth phrases they requested him to return to Venice, to report on the progress of the war, to discuss new plans and possibly, it was hinted, to receive new honours for himself.

If Carmagnola had been wise he would have mounted his horse and made a dash for the border. The Florentines would have welcomed him. It is true that his wife and children were in Venice, but this was not the only reason why he walked into the trap. Although he could order a line of battle or contrive a cunning stratagem, he was at heart a simple soul. He obeyed the summons. At Padua he was met by a guard of honour and on the seventh of April, 1432, he reached Venice.

At the entrance to the Doge's Palace he was welcomed by a smiling party of eight patricians, who dismissed his few followers and ushered him courteously into the precincts. Accounts differ as to what happened next. It has been said that he addressed the Senate, who applauded his speech; another version, more likely to be true, says that he was refused an audience by the Doge, who pleaded indisposition. But all agree that the eight gentlemen, bland and soft-spoken, barred his way back to the courtyard and escorted him instead through narrow passages to the door which led to the dungeons. There *sbirri* (the contemptuous name given the dreaded secret police in the service of the Ten) disarmed him, loaded him with chains, and dragged him out of the friendly sunshine and into the darkness of a cell.

Was Carmagnola a traitor or merely a failure? We shall never know. But it is certain that he was put to the torture, so perhaps a turn or two of the rack revealed the truth—truth suppressed and not even recorded in the archives of the Ten. The Ten were ruthless, but there is no reason to doubt their justice or impartiality. The trial would seem to have been a fair one, for again they called on the *Zonta* in order to make absolutely certain that there would be no error. It need hardly be said that the proceedings were held under the seal of the strictest secrecy, though it is known that Doge Foscari pleaded for the soldier's life, recalling his past victories in the service of the Republic. But when all the evidence had been heard, the Ten remained implacable, and at the end of their deliberations, sentence of death was passed by a large majority.

Thirty days went by between the prisoner's arrest and his execution; then, on the fifth of May, 1432, Carmagnola's short life came to an end. On the Piazzetta, between the two columns, his head was struck from his shoulders. He was buried in Milan, but high on the wall of the Frari church in Venice can still be seen the rough coffin that was made for him. It contains the bones of a murdered patrician.

Always that touch of the theatrical. There was something about that soldier of fortune which was larger than life. He went to his death in his finest clothes: a crimson jerkin, scarlet hose, and a little Piedmontese cap set jauntily on his black curls. And in his mouth they had bound a gag. Why? What could he have told the crowd? Francesco Bussone—Carmagnola—was a mystery to the end.

12. The Zenith

Pomp and Pageantry
The Golden Boy
The Tragedy of the Foscari
The Fall of Constantinople

We must now go back to December 1413, when Michele Steno died. He was succeeded by Tomaso Mocenigo, another of the "good" Doges, though unfortunately for Venice he only reigned for nine years. In 1416 one of his fleets won a notable victory over the Turks at Gallipoli; but although he was ready to fight if the security of Venice required it, Mocenigo was essentially a man of peace. He would not agree to an alliance with Florence against the Visconti of Milan, for not only did he want to keep the Republic out of war, but he was wise enough to see that Venice would only be weakened by further military adventures on the mainland. In this and in other matters he was bitterly opposed by Francesco Foscari, leader of what might be called the War Party.

Apart from this, there is very little to say about Doge Mocenigo. It is almost a truism that a tyrant may commit wholesale murder and carry death and destruction into the territory of his neighbour, in the sure knowledge that his crimes will earn him not only infamy but a chapter in the history books; but the prince who goes quietly about his business, ruling wisely and winning the love of his people, may count himself lucky if the chronicle of his life fills one paragraph.

Such a man was Mocenigo. But one charming story is told about him. Owing to the drain on the exchequer caused by the long war with Genoa, all work on the uncompleted Doge's Palace had been abandoned. It was such a sore point with the Venetians that councillors were forbidden even to mention the subject, on pain of a fine of a thousand ducats. This project, however, was so dear to the Doge's heart that one day he appeared in the Hall of the Great Council with a heavy bag in his hand, from which he poured a stream of golden ducats. Then, having thus paid his fine, His Serenity proceeded to introduce the forbidden topic. His proposals for enlarging and embellishing the palace were approved and the thousand ducats went towards the cost of the building.

It was during the years following the death of Mocenigo that Venice reached the zenith of her glory. It is true that Cyprus was not yet hers, and she had still to bring more of the mainland towns under her rule; but she was the leading Mediterranean power and in the Adriatic her rule was absolute. Squadrons of well-equipped war galleys guarded her trading fleets, and from Cheapside to the markets of Trebizond her argosies brought the treasures of East and West to the teeming clearing house of Rialto. The descendants of those pitiful fugitives who had sought refuge from the barbarians on the sandbanks and mud flats now negotiated as equals with emperors and kings. In Italy, Venice disputed with Milan the leadership of the north. Her writ ran in Padua, Verona and Vicenza, in Feltre, Friuli, Belluno and Treviso. Her frontier stretched along the foothills of the Carnic, Julian and Raetian Alps; and by diplomacy or force of arms she had won a good half of the Lombard Plain—as far as the junction of the Po and the Adda, almost to the gates of Milan.

When Mocenigo died in 1423 he gave warning from his deathbed against the election of Francesco Foscari as his successor. Foscari had many qualifications. He had served the Republic as an ambassador and as President of the *Quarantia;* he had been a member of the Council of Ten and a Procurator of St Mark. Yet Mocenigo denounced him as grasping, deceitful, and a lover of war; and in this he was strongly supported by another great noble, Jacopo Loredan, who believed Foscari to have connived at the death of his father and uncle, and who, there is every reason to suppose, hoped to become Doge himself. Foscari won; and from that day, Loredan was his implacable enemy, tending and cherishing his vengeance and biding his time for thirty-four years.

Foscari's election was remarkable for the fact that for the first time a Doge of Venice was not elected by the will of the people. It had become a mere formality, but from time immemorial, when presenting their new ruler to the crowd that thronged St Mark's and the Piazza, the words had been used: "This is your Doge, if it please you." On the occasion of Foscari's election, however, at a meeting called to discuss the election oath or *Promissione,* some humorist asked what would happen if he did *not* please the people. There must have been a moment of stunned silence, but the question was taken quite seriously, and from then on the words of the proclamation were simply: "This is your Doge." The incident is important, for it marks the end of the pretence that the Serenissima was a democracy.

The early years of Foscari's long reign were prosperous and happy. As Mocenigo had predicted, the new Doge used his influence to conclude an alliance with the Florentines and embroil Venice with Milan. Soon war was raging all over Lombardy; but, on the whole, it was a victorious war, and captains like Gattamelata and Carmagnola won fresh laurels for Venetian arms. The Lion of St Mark was on the rampage and few had yet considered the cost of territorial expansion.

Venice herself was fast becoming the wonderful city that we know today, though in our mind's eye, to the familiar background of sparkling water, blue sky and marble we must add the costumes of the late Middle Ages. The gay primary colours of an earlier era had given way to a shifting kaleidoscope of the dim, rich hues we associate with the glowing canvases of the Old Masters. Velvet, satin and brocade, long houppelandes and the crimson damask of legislators stood out against the sombre middle-class fustian and the picturesque rags of the rabble—those common people who were to survive and preserve their integrity when the scions of their overlords had become as rotten as over-ripe apples.

Building flourished. It was in Foscari's time that the Doge's Palace gained its famous gateway, the Porta della Carta. More palaces, among them the incomparable Ca' d'Oro—that supreme masterpiece of Venetian Gothic—were rising along both banks of the Grand

Canal, while many older mansions were being refaced and embellished. The splendid waterway was often the setting for pageantry and spectacle, when from the crowded balconies hung carpets, tapestries and silks from the East, and musicians played on the old wooden Rialto Bridge, bright with emblazoned pennons and streamers.

Distinguished visitors were entertained. The illustrious Cosimo de' Medici, banker, diplomat and orator who had been banished from Florence for ten years, found a refuge in Venice and her cities on the mainland. And in 1438 the Byzantine Emperor, John Palaeologus, came as the guest of the Republic to beg the help of all Christians against the ever growing menace of Turkish aggression. He begged in vain. It was cheaper to give him banquets than war galleys and men. But his State visit to Venice was marked by an impressive display of pomp and splendour. The Doge in his vestments, attended by councillors and magnificos, was rowed across the lagoon to welcome him at the Porto di Lido. Then, on the next day, the *Bucintoro* moved slowly up the Grand Canal at the head of a stately procession. Beneath a canopy of rose-coloured silk embroidered with the Winged Lion in gold, Doge and Emperor conversed side by side, while in the wake of the great gilded barge there came the usual attendant train of smaller craft. Gondolas—still gaily coloured in those days—darted here and there across the surface of the water like dragon-flies. On the *Bucintoro* the Lord High Admiral was magnificent in cloth of gold; ranks of crossbowmen, splendidly attired, mounted a guard of honour; and the *Arsenalotti* or workmen from the Arsenal, claiming their privilege of toiling at the forty-eight oars, were arrayed in sumptuous gold-embroidered coats for this imperial occasion. The trumpets shrilled. The deep drums rolled. There was a continuous clamour of cheering. And as the banks of oars rose and fell, dripping and sparkling in the clear sunlight, the Doge delighted to show his guest the city which rode on the water and which men called Bride of the Sea. Francesco Foscari was a proud man that day. But the shadows were lengthening. The curtain rose on a pageant: it fell on a stage darkened for tragedy.

Foscari was fifty when he became Doge. He had married twice and had a number of children, of whom only one son survived: young Jacopo, who was destined to become the principal actor in the drama which involved both his father and himself in ruin. Much has been written about the Foscari. Many attempts have been made to inject romance into a rather sordid little story: it gave Byron his tragedy, *The Two Foscari;* Samuel Rogers a theme for his *Italy;* and Verdi the libretto of an opera, *I Due Foscari.* In five hundred years the pitiful tale has been embroidered with so many colourful details that it is difficult to distinguish between fact and fiction. But nearly all the different versions have one thing in common: they lay most of the blame for the tragedy on the Council of Ten. The truth is that in the case of Jacopo Foscari, the Ten behaved with exceptional forbearance and with a leniency that was quite remarkable, considering the age in which they lived. Jacopo—the Golden Boy of his time— was his own worst enemy. Flippant, frivolous, irresponsible, he could not be made to realize that those in authority meant what they said or that the laws of the Republic applied to the son of the reigning Doge.

The trouble began at his wedding. For years Venice had been at war with Milan; for years peace treaties had been signed which Filippo Maria Visconti broke whenever it suited his purpose. Then, during the siege of Brescia and the campaign in which Gattamelata hauled his galleys over the mountains to Lake Garda, Venice managed to entice Francesco Sforza from the service of Milan. A big bluff soldier whose father, like Carmagnola, had risen from the ranks, he was nevertheless enrolled among the nobles of Venice and given high command. He distinguished himself in the field, outwitting his late comrade-in-arms, Piccinino, and not only relieving Brescia, but saving Verona and Vicenza for the Venetian Republic.

Soon afterwards the war came to an end and yet another treaty was concluded. This was Filippo's chance to make peace with the famous *condottiere,* so he gratified Sforza's long cherished ambition by giving him the hand of his daughter Bianca in marriage, with the cities of Cremona and Pontremoli for dowry and a promise of succession to the dukedom. Francesco Sforza was triumphant, but like most of his kind he believed in having a foot in each camp. So, with his new wife beside him and the Duchy of Milan in his pocket, he judged it expedient to be an honored guest at another wedding— that of the Doge's son Jacopo to Lucrezia, a daughter of the ancient house of Contarini.

Even the Venetians had seldom seen such festivities. The bride, in silver brocade, went to St Mark's in a procession of boats; and after the ceremony there was feasting in the Doge's Palace and jousting in the Piazza. A temporary bridge had been thrown across the Grand Canal, opposite the Palazzo Foscari. Over it—and then clattering and slithering through the narrow alleys—rode a gay procession of a hundred horsemen on their way to the tourney: light-hearted young patricians dressed in velvet, satin and brocade; but all, we are told, in pied hose, one leg white and one red. They were Jacopo's cronies and courtiers; but, in spite of this splendid escort, he cut a poor figure beside the plain soldier. Sforza danced with the ladies of Venice and broke lances gallantly in the lists, while his wedding gift was magnificent: 2,040 gold ducats and some valuable pieces of plate.

Jacopo Foscari must have known quite well that it was absolutely against the law for any relative of the Doge to receive presents of this kind, especially from someone known to be hand-in-glove with the Republic's arch-enemy, Visconti. He may have been relying for protection on the fact that his father was Doge, but it is impossible to believe that he acted in ignorance, for the gold was carried surreptitiously to his house and carefully hidden, to be discovered, when the time came, by the agents of the Ten.

Very little escaped those gentlemen, but how that particular cache came to light we can only guess. Perhaps a disgruntled servant had information to sell, or perhaps one of Jacopo's rivals seized his chance to drop a letter into the Lion's Mouth. For some reason no immediate action was taken; and it was not until four years later, in 1445, that Jacopo was called to account. But he had already taken alarm and fled to Trieste. He was tried in his absence by the Ten and sentenced to banishment—some say to Naples, others to Nauplia in Greece. The precise location is of little importance, for when he pleaded illness the Ten relented, his place of exile was changed to Treviso, and shortly afterwards he was allowed to return home. That should have been the end of it. For three years Jacopo lived quietly in Venice. Then something happened which involved him in really serious trouble.

A certain Ermolao Donato, who had been a member of the tribunal at the time of Jacopo's trial, was leaving the Doge's Palace one winter evening when he was set upon and stabbed to death. It so happened that one of Jacopo's servants, a man named Oliviero, had been seen earlier lounging about the Piazza, as if waiting for someone. Then he had gone into the courtyard of the palace at just about the time when senators, having finished the business of the day, were going home.

In a suspiciously short time after the killing, this Oliviero was on the mainland near Mestre, and in reply to a friend's question, "What news?" gave him full details of the assassination. It is barely possible that he could have heard of Donato's murder before leaving Venice, while if he had had anything to do with it, one would have thought that commonsense would have made him keep his mouth shut. But this was not the view of the Council of Ten, who suspected that Jacopo might have instigated the crime. They may have had other sources of information; or when Oliviero was arrested and put to the question, the rack may have forced him to betray his master. According to Sanudo, the fifteenth-century diarist and historian, he confessed everything, though if so, one wonders why he did not suffer the death penalty. It would certainly seem that, in his agony, he said things, true or false, which implicated Jacopo. There were also rumours of a secret denunciation, though any accuser would have had to sign his statement and, if it was proved false, pay the penalty for perjury. For it will be remembered that any anonymous accusations posted in the Lion's Mouth were torn up unread. We do know that the tribunal waited some time before arresting their men. It would therefore seem that there was a thorough and careful investigation. Donato was murdered on the fifth of November, but it was not until January that Jacopo was seized by the *sbirri* of the Ten and brought to trial. The story that he was judged by his own father is pure fiction, for Venetian law explicitly stated that no matter concerning the Doge or his family could be discussed in his presence.

The servant Oliviero was sentenced to perpetual exile, a fate soon to be shared by his master. The trial of Jacopo was a long one, for though the tribunal was convinced that he was responsible for the murder, it could not be proved. He, too, suffered the torture of the rack, but he made no confessions; though when the winch creaked and his limbs stretched, certain unintelligible mutterings came from between his lips, which some of his accusers interpreted as prayers to the Devil. If Jacopo could have been proved guilty, the death penalty would certainly have been inflicted. As it was, he was banished for life—this time to Candia, the name then given to the whole island of Crete. His pension of two hundred ducats a year would have enabled him to live a life of leisure, while it was hoped that at such a distance from Venice his chances of becoming a public nuisance would have been considerably lessened.

The second trial of Jacopo Foscari had opened in January 1451, but it was not until March 29 that the *Signori di Notte* with a guard of their hated *sbirri* escorted him in their barge to a ship which weighed anchor that same night for Candia. Despite this severe punishment, Jacopo seems to have profited little from the experience, for a few years later he was engaged in a treasonable correspondence with the Duke of Milan, whom he implored to intercede with the tribunal on his behalf, and with the Turkish Sultan, from whom he begged a galley in which to escape from Candia.

Jacopo Foscari may have been a fool, but it is almost incredible that he should have thought the Council of Ten to be fools also. Although he had been brought up in the shadow of the Doge's Palace and bred in an atmosphere of intrigue, it never seems to have occurred to him that he was still under surveillance. He may even have been foolish enough to imagine that he, with his amateurish ciphers and codes, was a match for some of the cleverest secret agents in Europe. If so, he was soon disillusioned when, as the result of a report from the Governor of Candia, officials were sent with orders to search his house, papers and person, and then to escort the Doge's son back to Venice, there to stand his third trial.

There are two versions of what followed. One, favoured by sentimentalists, tries to turn the fool into a hero with a heart-rending story of Jacopo enduring torture for the second time but steadfastly refusing to incriminate himself. The other, for which there is more plausible evidence, insists that the trial only lasted for one day and that the accused, far from courting a second taste of the rack, confessed everything with almost unseemly haste and threw himself on the mercy of the tribunal. But both agree that the chief judge on this occasion was the pitiless Loredan, mortal enemy of the Foscari family.

Again, considering the heinousness of his offence, Jacopo escaped lightly. Again the dreaded Council of Ten showed that, on occasion, they could temper justice with mercy. This young man who had traded on his privileged position as the Doge's son, who had never been satisfactorily cleared of the murder of Donato, and who was responsible for the labour and expense of three trials, was condemned out of his own mouth and by his own correspondence. He had acted in the full knowledge that to appeal to a foreign power was an offence against the Republic, while his appeal to the Sultan to rescue him was inexcusable. And yet, possibly for his father's sake, the Ten were merciful. To be sure, the vengeful Loredan demanded that Jacopo should be beheaded between the two columns, but he was outvoted. The Council of Ten decreed that Jacopo Foscari should be returned to Candia, there to continue his exile; but that, on arrival, he should be committed to prison and remain there for one year. He should have considered himself fortunate. For lesser offences men had died.

Jacopo got what he deserved. But there were other innocent sufferers. Like many weak men, he had won his wife's devotion, and now she and her children were to be parted from him forever. And there was his father, eighty-four years of age and very ill. Francesco Foscari was heart-broken at the disgrace of his son, and there was a pathetic scene when Jacopo said goodbye to his family—not in a dungeon, as some would have us believe, but in a private apartment in the Doge's Palace. Francesco Foscari bore himself with calmness and dignity. He advised Jacopo to endure his punishment with fortitude and to cease trying to elude it. But when his son had been led away, he burst into tears, throwing himself into a chair and sobbing, "*O pieta grande!*" ("Oh, the pity of it!")

Six months later there came news from Candia that Jacopo Foscari was dead.

Broken by grave illness and the death of his only son, Francesco Foscari was unable to attend to the duties of his high office. It was not his fault that business was neglected, but obviously this state of affairs could not be allowed to continue. Several times in the years that had passed he had tried without success to resign the Dogeship. But now it was the Ten who proposed that he should be released from his vows and granted a pension of fifteen hundred gold ducats.

Then came the sting in an otherwise generous proposal: going beyond their powers, the Ten added bluntly that they must receive his answer within a few hours.

Foscari indignantly refused their offer, declaring that he could not violate the vows which he had taken. But the tribunal was adamant. While the old man was still in bed, worn out by trouble and illness, a deputation demanded an audience and repeated the offer in terms which admitted of no refusal. They went so far as to say that if he did not accept, his property would be confiscated. Francesco Foscari received this ultimatum with his usual courage, but in that hour he must have plumbed the very depths of misery, for this proud old man could not hide from himself that he was the first Doge of Venice to be dismissed by the all-powerful Council of Ten.

It was on October 21, 1457, that he was told that he must abdicate. In order to spare him humiliation, an announcement was to be made that, because of his great age and infirmity, he had felt compelled to resign his office. On the twenty-fourth the Great Council met and elected his successor, Pasquali Malipiero; and on Sunday, October 27, Francesco Foscari left the palace forever. In order to spare him, it was suggested that he should leave by a private stair which opened on the side canal now spanned by the Bridge of Sighs. But the indomitable old man refused, declaring that he would go down by the same stairs which he had ascended in triumph when he was made Doge. Leaning on the arm of his brother, he slowly walked down the great staircase and left the palace by the Porta della Carta. With a crowd watching in silent pity, he made his way to the Molo, where a gondola was waiting to carry him to the Palazzo Foscari.

On the thirty-first of October, Malipiero's election was announced and on All Saints' Day, November 1, Francesco Foscari died. Thus the story that the deathblow was struck by the bell in the Campanile ringing for his successor is clearly a fable. But there is another, more ugly story, in the true spirit of the vendetta, which may well be true, for it has become a tradition in the family histories of the houses of Foscari and Loredan. It is said that, many years before, Loredan, believing Foscari to have been an accessory to the death of the former's father and uncle, had entered his name on the debit side of an account book or ledger. Now, when he heard that his enemy had died, he made a terse entry on the credit side: *"L'ha pagato."* ("He has paid it.")

We now go back four years to May 29, 1433: one of the most momentous dates in the history not only of Venice but of western civilisation, for it was then, after a siege of fifty-three days, that the city of Constantinople was taken by the Ottoman Turks.

The founder and first Emperor of Byzantium had been a Constantine, and so was the last—the brother of John Palaeologus, who died in 1448. And the Turks had a new Sultan, Mohammed II, whose ambition it was to reign in Constantinople and hear the Koran recited in Sancta Sophia. It was not difficult for the aggressor to find a pretext for hostilities, and he declared war.

Mohammed had assembled fourteen batteries of cannon at Adrianople, including one enormous piece of ordnance cast by a Hungarian renegade which fired stone balls weighing 600 pounds (though only seven times a day, for fear it would burst) and which had to be hauled into position by a team of fifty oxen. He had a fleet of 320 vessels, including eighteen galleys; and an army of about 250,000 men followed the horse-tail banner. The *Capiculi* or regular troops of the Porte numbered only about 80,000 men—horse and foot—but the provincial bashaws levied a militia and there was a horde of volunteers and irregulars. The spearhead of the assault was a force of 15,000 of the famous Janissaries, recruited exclusively from Christian youths taken from their parents in childhood and brought up as Moslems. Their standard or emblem was a huge wooden spoon; they were armed with scimitar, shield and bow; and, subjected to an iron discipline and filled with fanatical zeal, they fought with the fury of men who sought through death to enter Paradise.

Against this formidable array the Emperor, with only about 9,000 men, could hardly hope to prevail. The citizens of Constantinople, softened by years of peace and luxury, and with all the fighting spirit bred out of them, received the call to arms with apathy. Concern for the altars of their God and the safety of their women and children was outweighed by their aversion to the use of arms—even in their own defence—and by their hatred of an apostate Emperor who had paid homage to the Pope of Rome. The historian Phranza, the Emperor's first chamberlain and principal secretary, was obliged to report to his master with shame that in a city of more than 100,000 inhabitants, only 4,970 men had the courage to man the walls.

There were a few—a very few—foreigners to form the core of the defence. The Pope sent a small body of mercenaries with a warlike cardinal to command them; from Genoa came that fine soldier, Giovanni Guistiani, with two galleys and 300 men-at-arms; and from Venice—an order to arm the workmen in her new factory at Galata! That was all the response which was forthcoming from the rulers of Christendom to the desperate call of the valiant Constantine. For a thousand years Constantinople had held Asia in check: now she was to be allowed to die like some decrepit beast in the slaughter house. It is just possible that Venice and Genoa would have been more generous in their help; but when Constantinople fell, their main fleets were still in harbour.

The siege began with a bombardment by the Turkish cannon, and very soon it became apparent that the battle was lost and won. These immense walls which had repulsed so many invaders in the past had not been built to withstand artillery. Soon they began to crumble, and breaches had to be repaired under fire. The wall walks of the ancient ramparts were too narrow for the Byzantine guns, the recoil of which shook the fabric, while there were not enough men to man the whole circuit of nearly thirteen miles. Old siege engines were used, side by side with the new mortars and cannon, and that once dreaded liquid, the Greek Fire, was discharged. But nothing could prevail against the powerful Turkish batteries.

The last of the Byzantine Emperors led his troops in person and made a gallant defence. All attempts by the enemy to force the harbour failed, but the hammering of the ramparts continued until at last Mohammed massed his Janissaries for the final assault. The besiegers' kettledrums were throbbing and all round the land walls the Turks had lighted a semicircle of fires. To the terrified inhabitants who thronged the churches, imploring God's help when many of them were too pusillanimous to help themselves, that flaming crescent must have seemed like an omen. To add to their misfortunes, Guistiani, who had been the mainspring of the defence, was mortally wounded by an arrow; and although a huge siege tower, rolling towards the walls, was overthrown and set on fire, the Emperor, fighting desperately, must have realized that the end was near.

The main force in the final assault was directed towards a breach in the Gate of St Romanus. But there were diversionary attacks on other parts of the land walls; and it was one of these which brought about the fall of the city, thanks to an accident which must be unique in the history of warfare. The *Kerkoporta*, or Gate of Fluted Wood, had been bricked up since the days of Isaac Comnenus; but a few days before, Constantine had ordered it to be reopened to be used for a sortie against the Turkish lines. By an almost incredible over-sight—or was it treachery?—it had been left unguarded, and now a reconnoitering body of Turks used it to enter the city. They were observed and slaughtered to a man, but the damage had been done. More and more of the enemy swarmed through the open gate; the defenders panicked and ran for their lives; and Mohammed, noticing that in this sector the walls were almost unmanned, set up his scaling ladders and poured in his men. Constantinople was in his hands. The Emperor, having done all that a brave man could do, prayed for a Christian to kill him; then, as no one would lift a hand against him, he plunged into the thick of the melee and went down, fighting, under the scimitars of the Janissaries.

For eight hours, the Imperial City was given over to rapine and pillage; then, attended by his viziers and bashaws, the Sultan Mohammed rode through the gate of St Romanus. In the Hippodrome, for one moment, he gave vent to his savage triumph and brought his iron mace crashing down on the twisted column of the Three Brazen Serpents from Delphi, breaking one of their heads. Then, once more master of himself, he entered the church—soon to be the mosque—of Sancta Sophia, packed with wailing refugees who had waited in vain for the miracle which had not been vouchsafed them.

Although about two thousand Christians were slaughtered when the Turks first broke into the city and half-crazed Janissaries and bashi-bazouks were running wild through the streets, it has been said to the credit of the conquerors that there was no wholesale massacre. Neither did they indulge in an orgy of rape and outrage as the crusaders had done. But there must have been many Byzantines who envied the fallen. Those who had refused to bear arms must have blamed their own folly or cowardice for a fate far worse than death in battle. For the restraint of the Turks was not inspired by compassion but by lust and avarice. In the slave market or the harem a captive was more valuable alive than dead.

The number of captives taken is said to have been at least 60,000. Age and sex were of no consideration. Old and young, men, women and children, all were herded together in a terrible equality: patricians, plebeians, soldiers, monks, great ladies, whores from the brothels, nuns driven screaming from their convents. In the eyes of the Osmanli, they all had their value. The men would be doomed to drag out the remainder of their days in hard labour, the women and children to life in the seraglio of some Oriental despot. Babies were wrenched from their mothers, families divided: in one hour the rich became poor, and the happy wretched forever.

One example will serve to illustrate the plight of these unfortunate people. The historian Phranza was himself a slave for four months; then somehow he managed to reach Adrianople and ransom his wife from her new owner, the *Mir Bashi* or Master of the Horse. But his two children, said to have been beautiful, were beyond his reach, for they were captives in the harem of Mohammed himself. His daughter died there, and so did his son, a boy of fifteen, who preferred a stroke of the Sultan's dagger to the infamy of his embrace.

Retribution had come at last and the Venetian Republic began to pay for that monstrous crime of the crusaders which she had instigated and in which her Doge had played the leading part. Before the sack of Constantinople in 1204, Byzantine fleets and armies had defended Europe against the hordes of Asia. In the early days of the Republic, the Greeks had been her friends and protectors; now when she was old and decadent and needed help, Venice, like other Mediterranean powers, had failed to answer the cry which had risen from the shores of the Bosphorus. The result was the ruin of Byzantium— and eventually the ruin of Venice. For centuries the bulk of her great wealth had come through the ports of the Levant; but now the doors of the East had been slammed in her face; every factory, warehouse and market was now in the hands of the Turks. Soon even heavier blows were to fall, one after another, in quick succession. From now on, the history of Venice is a sad story of decline.

13. The Italian Wars

The Acquisition of Cyprus
The Discoverers
The House of Borgia
The League of Cambrai

The capture of Constantinople by the Turks can be compared to the dropping of a pebble into a pool: the ripples spread outwards until at last it becomes impossible to set a limit to their expansion. The same may be said of the influence of this supremely important historical event. For centuries the Imperial City had been the repository of ancient learning, the centre of scholarship for all the western world. In her keeping had lain the legacies of Greece and Rome. But now the impact of an alien civilisation had put an end to all that. The scholars had fled, taking their treasures with them—their precious manuscripts and codices, their texts of the classics and works of art. In Italy they found a welcome, and with their arrival there came to full flower that revival of learning which we call the Italian Renaissance.

For generations there had been a growing interest in ancient art and literature. The dilettante had appeared, side by side with the genuine schoolman. Nobles were becoming amateurs of art and collectors of curios: one of the gifts for the acceptance of which young Foscari had been hailed before the Ten was a valuable codex; while in 1416 Cardinal Bessarion, a Greek from Trebizond who had been received into the Church of Rome, had presented Venice with those priceless manuscripts which formed the nucleus of the famous Library of St Mark. But now, with this fresh impetus, studies which formerly had given joy to only a few learned humanists became a great popular movement. The floodgates had been opened. Abstruse discussion was the fashion in every city and provincial town. Petty tyrants in their ancestral roccas perched up behind some mountain village might still hang prisoners by their thumbs and burn poor men's hovels about their ears; but bits and pieces of antique statuary had begun to appear in their "maschio towers" or "keeps," and some even professed an interest in Greek—the key to the New Learning.

The immediate consequences of the calamity were disastrous for Venice; but although the Levantine monopoly had been snatched from her hands, she made every effort to salvage what little she could from the wreck of her fortunes. Deciding again that it was more sensible to trade with the infidels than to fight them, she sent her envoy to negotiate with the Sultan, and in April 1454 a treaty was concluded in which it was agreed that a Venetian agent or *Bailo* should watch over the interests of the Republic in Constantinople. She must have foreseen that by doing this she would earn the execration of all Christendom, even if she did not realize that her days of power in the Levant were over. But such an agreement could not last, and within a few years she was at war again with the Sublime Porte. For a time she had an unexpected ally: King Corvinus of Hungary. Then he withdrew and for fifteen weary years Venice opposed the Turks single-handed. The nations of Europe, tired of her greed and jealous of her greatness, would not send a ship to help her; and Venice paid dearly for the selfish policy which for centuries had led to her monopoly of the eastern trade. She made a gallant fight for it, but it was an unequal contest, for the aging Queen of the Adriatic was no match for this young and vigorous opponent. Those exhausting wars on the mainland had forced her to dig deep into her treasury, and soon she had to face the unpleasant fact that the Turkish seamen were as good as her own.

She made overtures for peace, but this again aroused the anger of Europe. Shortly before his death Pope Pius II preached a crusade, but it came to nothing. Those who had promised support withdrew, and the Venetians, still alone, suffered a severe defeat at Patmos.

They fell back on the island of Negropont, and there, in the following year, the inhabitants had to endure all the horrors of a sea-borne assault by a cruel enemy. Women, too, played a valiant part in the defence—and, with their children, were brutally massacred when the islanders were overcome. To make matters worse, the Venetian admiral, De Canal, who had been sent to reinforce them, showed a reluctance to give battle and held back his ships until it was too late to intervene. He was recalled, tried, and sentenced to perpetual exile, but his punishment could not bring the dead back to life or lessen the disgrace to Venetian arms. The Republic also lost several towns on the mainland of Greece, and, as if her cup of bitterness were not already full, in 1479 Scutari in Albania capitulated to the Turks after a long siege. Another peace treaty followed; but the Venetians, who a few years before had dictated terms to the princes of the East, were forced to eat humble pie and pay an annual fee to the Sultan for trading rights.

There was one consolation in those bad times: the acquisition of Cyprus. The island came to Venice as a gift, thanks to a little adroit diplomacy and a well-timed display of strength. Long before, in the days of the crusades, Guy de Lusignan, titular King of Jerusalem, had bought the island from the Knights of the Temple. His dynasty had ruled Cyprus until the end of the fourteenth century when, during the wars between Venice and Genoa, the Genoese took Famagusta and held it for nearly a hundred years. Then they were driven out and the island was reunited under the rule of King Giacomo. Hoping for Venetian aid, he had married Caterina Cornaro, a wealthy patrician who, that she might more fittingly mate with royalty, had been created a Daughter of the Republic, and who took with her a dowry of 100,000 ducats.

A year after his marriage King Giacomo died, and the usual rumours began to circulate that he had been poisoned by the Venetians in order to hasten the transfer of his kingdom to the Republic. There were popular risings and riots in the streets, which gave Venice the excuse to send a fleet to help Queen Caterina. The admiral, Pietro Mocenigo, soon restored order and in doing so established his authority over the island. So it is not surprising that when soon afterwards the heir to the throne also died, there was a new crop of canards insinuating that Venice was responsible.

There does not seem to have been the slightest evidence of Venetian complicity in these murders—if indeed they were murders, which is extremely doubtful—and the truth may well be that this is yet another instance of the Ten being blamed for something of which they were completely innocent, this being part of the price which they had to pay for their policy and mode of action. That the rumours lied is surely proved by the fact that Caterina herself, the wife and mother of the supposed victims, quite voluntarily renounced the throne and placed herself under the protection of the Serene Republic. In February 1489, feeling unable to withstand the Turks by herself, she retired thankfully to Venice, where she was received with all honour and granted the castle of Asola in Lombardy for her residence. There she lived peacefully for many years, loved by all, as she had been loved in Cyprus, for her sweetness and charity. This daughter of Venice had borne the proud titles of Queen of Cyprus, of Jerusalem, and of Armenia; now she was content to live and die as the Lady of Asola. Her memory is still revered.

When the banner of St Mark was hoisted in Cyprus there must have been many Venetians who hoped that it meant the beginning of better things and that soon the Republic would again take her rightful place among the nations. But almost at once Fate struck another blow—and struck hard. In 1488, only a year before the acquisition of Cyprus, the Portuguese mariner Bartholomew Diaz with two caravels had reached the Cape of Good Hope; ten years later Vasco da Gama discovered the route round the Cape to India, while in 1492 Columbus sailed into the unknown and reached the Bahamas —the first white man since the days of the Vikings to set foot in the New World.

For Venice these voyages were catastrophic, for they shifted the hub of maritime traffic from the Eastern Mediterranean to the Western Mediterranean and Atlantic, and led to the emergence of powerful rivals at sea: England, the Netherlands, Portugal and Spain. The decline of the Republic was slow and shot with sudden gleams of glory. But when the Turks barred the way to the East and new sea roads led rovers westwards, the ominous writing had appeared on the wall for those with eyes to see.

Returning now to Italy, where misfortune still dogged the Venetians, we must go back a few years before the epoch of the great discoveries. On the Feast of St Stephen, December 26, 1476—that season of peace and goodwill—Galeazzo Maria Sforza, Duke of Milan, went to church. But three young noblemen were waiting on the porch of the Cathedral; and having the love of their country at heart, together with a misguided desire to emulate Brutus and Cassius, they stabbed him for his sins, which were many and lurid.

Then, inspired perhaps by their example, two years later there came the Pazzi Conspiracy against the Medici in Florence. There was not so much excuse for this crime; neither was it so successful. Gentle young Guiliano de' Medici was killed but his brother, Lorenzo the Magnificent, escaped the daggers. It is strange how the Renaissance mind worked. The assassins of Galeazzo Maria Sforza had heard Mass before they killed him; and now in this plot, which had originated in a sordid dispute over the ownership of a valuable property, the Pope's name was linked with the crime, the Archbishop of Pisa was among the conspirators, and again the murder was committed in church—the signal for the killing being the Elevation of the Host. In his *Florentine History*, Machiavelli declared that "The plot was revealed to the Pontiff before Giovanni left Rome and full assistance was promised." Giovanni Batista da Montesecco was one of the Papal *condottieri*, but Machiavelli could hardly be described as an impartial witness, and it is most unlikely that Sixtus IV was guilty of connivance. But the Sovereign Pontiff had been ill-advised enough to support the Pazzi clan so openly that inevitably his enemies associated him with the outrage.

And what, it may be asked, has all this to do with Venice? The answer is that it was the result of that mistaken policy of involvement in the affairs of the mainland. As the friend of Florence, it was inevitable that the Serenissima would be dragged into the quarrel. Her first move, after sending an envoy to convey her condolences on the death of Guiliano de' Medici, was an attempt to mediate between Lorenzo and the Holy See. But the Pope refused to listen: in fact, his actions were such that they gave new credence to those malicious rumours of his guilt. Furious that the attempt on the lives of the Medici had resulted in neither a revolution nor a change of government, he laid Florence under an interdict and then had recourse to arms. The Papal forces were commanded by the Duke of Urbino, and those of his allies the Neapolitans by the Duke of Calabria, eldest son of the King of Naples. Together they prepared to invade Florentine territory, while Venice rallied to the defence of her friend.

At first the war went badly for the Republic, while the Florentines were defeated at Poggio Imperiale. And now Lorenzo de' Medici took the bold but highly questionable step of visiting his enemy, King Ferdinand of Naples. He knew that he risked treachery and death, but his mission was successful and he achieved his object of making peace with both the Pope and the King. On the other hand—and this is what makes the whole manoeuvre so questionable—he did so without consulting his allies. The Venetians resented this and in revenge made no attempt to oppose the Turks when the latter landed at Otranto and laid waste the city. In the wars that followed—wars which convulsed Italy for many years—Venice and Florence fought on opposite sides.

Venetian troops were soon in action, laying siege to Ferrara which, in open defiance of the Republic's monopoly, was operating salt distilleries at the mouth of the Po. Failing to persuade Venice to make peace, the Pope again laid the city under the ban of the Church; but such was the cleverness of the Ten and the strength of their hold over the people that they were able to take effective measures to prevent the Bull being proclaimed and to ensure that the Venetians remained in ignorance of the interdict.

In the years that followed, the chessboard of Italian politics presented a spectacle so involved that only a master of the game could disentangle the moves: the constant shifting of bishops, knights and pawns, the subtle gambits, the unexpected checks and reversals of fortune. There was so much double-dealing and changing of sides, such tortuous and confused intrigues, that it will be enough for our purpose if we lift the curtain again on the year 1493. Columbus in the *Santa Maria* is sailing home from America; the Church's ban on the Venetians has been lifted by a new Pope; Lorenzo the Magnificent is dead of a fever and the gout; and the Republic of Venice is in alliance with the Pope and Lodovico Sforza, Regent of Milan—that same great man with a complexion so dark that people called him *Il Moro*, who was soon to be Duke and the friend and patron of Leonardo da Vinci. A strange trio to run in triple harness, and their purpose was even stranger. Fearing the growing strength and power of the Kingdom of Naples, they sought to redress the balance by letting loose a dangerous ally: King Charles VIII of France. With his Anjou blood he had some shadowy claim to the Neapolitan throne, so the trio persuaded him to invade Italy at the head of a French army.

The French came—and the rulers of Italy realized their error, as the Britons must have regretted calling in the war bands of Hengist and Horsa. When, at their request, the King of France invaded the Peninsula, his too successful intervention in Italian affairs caused his allies to turn against him. Venice contributed a force of the Albanian light cavalry called Stradiots in support of a new league formed by the Republic, Sforza of Milan, Gonzaga of Mantua, and "the foremost knight of the age," Maximilian, the German Emperor. And now it seemed as if all the devils in hell had been let loose on the land of Italy. For years the great wars raged as foreign armies made the Peninsula their stamping ground. The French king with a powerful force which included a contingent of Swiss mercenaries—those terrible Alpine warriors who had put an end to the bloodless manoeuvers of the *condottieri*—took Naples, occupied Florence, and marched on Rome itself. In 1495, he engaged the Allies in the Apennines and defeated them in a raging thunderstorm at the battle of Fornovo. But after retiring from Italy and then invading for the second time, King Charles died and his place was taken by the Duke of Orleans. The Duke laid claim to the Duchy of Milan, and surprisingly—or perhaps not so surprisingly for those days—found himself aided and abetted by a new ally. None other than Venice. In return for her action in changing sides, Louis of Orleans had promised the Venetians a large slice of Milanese territory; and, seeing that there were prizes to be won, the confederates were joined by Pope Alexander VI (Roderigo Borgia). The House of Borgia and the Venetians had long been enemies and rivals; but when there was a chance of rich pickings, His Holiness was not the man to allow scruples to stand in his way.

The alliance was too strong for Sforza. Forced to make friends where he could find them, he repaid the Venetians for their treachery by appealing for aid to the Turks. In September 1499 a Venetian fleet commanded by Antonio Grimani was routed by the Moslems near Sapienza, and Grimani (later to become Doge) was ordered by the Ten to be returned to Venice in irons. Somehow peace was again patched up between the Serenissima and the Sublime Porte; but the pretensions of the Venetians were contemptuously dismissed by the Turkish Vizier, who made it clear that times had changed. He said bluntly that although their city had once called herself the Bride of the Sea, that fickle element was now ruled by the Ottoman Empire— hard words and bitter humiliation for the successors of Carlo Zeno and Blind Old Dandolo.

Still following the story of Venice, we must now focus our attention on Rome—on the gilded halls of the Vatican, thronged with slippered priests, clanking captains in steel, and silken patricians who looked like court cards: kings, queens and knaves. There were plenty of knaves, for this was the abode of the Borgias, soon to be swept clean by better men who would restore its odour of sanctity.

For a combination of icy brain, beauty, brilliance and wickedness, it would be difficult to equal the record of this notorious family. Pope Alexander himself, the man who had turned the Vatican into a sty, was completely under the influence of Cesare, the fourth of his illegitimate children. It was Cesare who had frightened his father into condoning the murder of his brother the Duke of Gandia and of Alfonso of Aragon, the husband of his sister Lucrezia, about whose share in the family guilt there may perhaps be two opinions. There have been attempts to whitewash father and son, but the evidence is damning. Ruthlessly Cesare had eliminated the hostile families of Rome; by clever trickery he had drawn the teeth of the tyrants of the Romagna, for he was as ambitious as Napoleon and infinitely more unscrupulous. Italy, a united Italy—ruled, of course, by himself— was the dream that inspired him and nothing was to be allowed to stand in his way. The Papal historian, Onofrio Panvinio, mentions three, possibly four, cardinals who had been poisoned by the mysterious white powder of the Borgias (which was, in fact, nothing more mysterious than common arsenic); Cesare is said to have been

in the habit of roaming the streets at night with his guards and re-
ducing the number of his enemies; while the Venetian ambassador,
Paolo Capello, reported: "Every night four or five murdered men are
discovered—bishops, prelates and others—so that all Rome is trem-
bling for fear of being destroyed by the Duke (Cesare)."

The Borgias and their successors in power played an important
part in the eventual downfall of the Republic. When Pope Alexander
died and Cesare lay dangerously ill—owing, it was rumoured, to an
accidental dose of their own poison—Venice, although officially still
an ally of the Papacy, seized her chance to acquire land claimed by
the Holy See and to establish protectorates over the cities of the
Romagna. But not for long. Cesare Borgia, beset by enemies, fled
to the court of Naples; and soon the vacant throne of St Peter was
occupied by a strong man, Pope Julius II, who deeply resented the
Venetian desire for aggrandizement. In Bologna, Faenza, Rimini
and other places, the Borgia banner of the Bull had been replaced
by the Lion of St Mark, and the new Pope was resolved that this
policy of aggression must end.

Five years later, in 1508, Venice began to pay in full for her
treacherous and high-handed treatment of her neighbours. Again she
was under the ban of the Church, and she found herself alone and
friendless, facing the powerful League of Cambrai, an alliance of
enemies so strong that she could not hope to make headway against
them. According to the preamble to their treaty, the object of the
League was to combat "the insatiable cupidity of the Venetians and
their greed of dominion." The Pope, King Louis XII of France, the
Emperor Maximilian and Ferdinand the Catholic of Spain were
determined to humble the pride of Venice, to put an end to her
depredations, and to punish her for daring to make terms with the
Moslems. Also, it should in fairness be added, the Allies were
prompted by envy of the sheer greatness of the Republic, a greatness
which, in spite of the sins of her people, somehow enabled her to
survive in this time of adversity.

The Venetians responded to the challenge with a spirit which
proved that misfortune had not sapped their courage. Their Doge,
Leonardo Loredan, made a fighting speech to the Great Council and
was the first to send his plate to be melted down for the national war

chest. But more disasters followed, disasters so unexpected that they must have disheartened those who believed in omens. Both the Venetian Arsenal and the citadel at Brescia were badly damaged by explosions; precious archives were destroyed by fire; and a treasure ship carrying pay for the mercenaries sank on the way from Ravenna. Sabotage? They did not use the word then but they were familiar with the fact. Without evidence, it can only be called coincidence—but coincidence is always suspect.

Against almost overwhelming odds, Venice took the field alone. In April 1509 her troops encountered the French at Agnadello, on the banks of the Adda. The battle ended in a shattering defeat for Venice, and the Allies advanced to Mestre on the edge of the lagoon: from the Campanile, sentinels could see the watch fires of the enemy. Padua, which the Venetians had lost but recovered by a cunning stratagem, held against Maximilian; but other towns fell, one after another, before the invading armies. The fortifications of Venice itself were hastily repaired; stores of grain were brought into the city; and the people, patricians and commoners alike, prepared to defend their homes.

At the same time, Venice reinforced her arms by clever diplomacy. First she tried to persuade her enemies, one by one, to withdraw from the League. The Pope, the Emperor and the King of Spain were approached, but such was their hatred of the Republic that her envoys met with little encouragement. She next sounded out Henry VII of England and tried to tempt him with the suggestion that the time was ripe for another invasion of France. But Henry VII was not Henry V. He craved no Agincourt, no costly adventures on the Continent. Henry Tudor was not easily gulled and he had better things to do: England needed peace and a breathing space after the Wars of the Roses. It is true that in 1492 he had landed troops in France and laid siege to Boulogne for a few weeks. But an offer of 745,000 crowns had soon induced him to go home again.

So Venice fought on desperately, while in the diplomatic field she adopted a new policy which has been acclaimed as a masterpiece. With what was surely a touch of genius, she let it be known that she had relinquished all her possessions on the mainland, and at the same time she absolved all her subjects living there from their allegiance. This meant that cities which had not yet fallen could safely surrender and try to save themselves from the horrors of the sack without being guilty of treason to the Venetian Republic. It was a wise and generous action which showed great knowledge of human nature. And it reaped its own reward, for after the inhabitants of those towns had experienced occupation by foreign soldiery they proved only too willing to return voluntarily to the beneficent Venetian rule.

Although the Allied armies had advanced to within sight of Venice, all was not going well with the League of Cambrai. Its members began to quarrel among themselves, and Pope Julius was beginning to have second thoughts. His Holiness was heart and soul an Italian and it wounded him deeply to see his country overrun by foreign mercenaries whose methods of conducting a war were, even for those days, appalling. Arson, rape and murder were commonplace. Harmless civilians were tortured to make them produce nonexistent gold. The cold ferocity of the French men-at-arms, the gross brutality of the German *landsknechte,* and the savagery of Spanish veterans who had learned their soldiering in the rough school of the Moorish wars soon made the Pope realize that at all costs Italy must be freed from these barbarians, as he called them—especially the French, who if they were not checked would soon hold the whole country under their heel.

There was only one way to achieve this, and it must have cost Pope Julius hours of deep and anxious thought, for it meant nothing less than destroying the League which he, more than any other man, had helped to create. But, his decision once made, he set to work with a cold ruthlessness which his contemporaries understood and applauded, but which to us savours unpleasantly of double-dealing.

The simplest method of sowing discord among the members of the League was for the Pope to detach his own forces and form a new confederacy—a Holy League—aimed not against Venice but against the all-powerful French. So when he had recovered the Romagna towns, the occupation of which had been the chief cause of his quarrel with the Serenissima, the Pope began to put out peace feelers. By 1510 he had granted the Venetians absolution, and a year later their armies were fighting side by side with his own.

Maximilian the Penniless proved difficult as usual. As Holy Roman Emperor he considered himself lord and master of all Italy and he refused to relinquish one iota of what he was pleased to call his rights. But the King of Spain was a willing ally, and soon an army of Switzers in the pay of the Pope was marching down from the Alps into Lombardy. Pope Julius knew the quality of those sturdy Swiss pikemen and halberdiers; and already, in 1506, he had recruited his own bodyguard from among them. It is not for nothing that Swiss men-at-arms still mount guard at the Vatican. The new King of England, Henry VIII, regarded Venice as a bulwark against Islam. He had disapproved of the Treaty of Cambrai and refused to publish the Papal Bull. But he was ready to join any league against France, and two years later he crossed the Channel to win the Battle of the Spurs. He drew his sword, he said, "in the defence and support of Holy Mother Church." King Harry was to change his tune when he was beguiled by the bright eyes of Anne Boleyn!

In 1512 the people of Brescia rose against the French, while a Spanish army, advancing from Naples, laid siege to Bologna. The siege was raised by Gaston de Foix, Duc de Nemours and cousin of the King of France. Although he was only twenty-three years of age, the King had made him Governor of Lombardy, and already he had won such brilliant victories at Como and Milan that his soldiers called him the Thunderbolt of Italy. From Bologna he marched to Brescia, determined to punish the inhabitants for their rebellion. He stormed the city and sullied his honour by ordering—or, at least, permitting—an atrocious massacre of civilians, without regard for age or sex. It is curious to reflect that among the foremost of the attackers was that peerless knight, the Chevalier Bayard—he who was truly said to be "without fear and without reproach." With his customary valour, he was the first to scale the ramparts, and in doing so he was severely wounded. For speed in mounting the ladders, he and his companions had discarded their leg armour; now, with a pike thrust in the thigh, he was unable to take any further part in the fighting. But one wonders what that most chivalrous gentleman must have thought of the sack.

On Easter Monday of that same year was fought the bloody battle of Ravenna—the outcome of an attempt by Papal and Spanish armies to raise the siege of that city. A Venetian army covered the French flank, cutting off supplies from inland, while another Spanish force blocked all the coast of the Romagna. Gaston de Foix was again in command of the French, and in spite of his wound the indomitable Bayard had insisted on being present. The Papal and Spanish armies held defensive positions outside the city, and the engagement began with an artillery duel which caused heavy losses. The Frenchmen were too proud to lie down; and the captains of the foremost companies—perhaps as an example to their men, perhaps out of bravado—showed off their courage by parading like living targets in front of the ranks. Two of them, toasting each other in the face of the enemy, were killed by the same ball. As a result of these reckless gasconades, thirty-eight officers out of forty in one sector became casualties.

Then the French enfiladed the enemy. They drove their small guns, mounted on carts, to the extreme right of the Allied position, and from there they bombarded them all along the length of their line. The Papal infantry ran, but the fierce Spanish sword-and-buckler men, maddened by the fire of the culverins, climbed out of their trenches with shouts of *"Sant' Iago!"* and hurled themselves on the French men-at-arms and arquebusiers. Those crouching, leaping, savage swordsmen had grown used to victory; but there was no escape from the small brass cannon which continued to rake them from the rear, and, realizing that the battle was lost, the Spanish retired in good order to the shelter of the walls of Ravenna. This infuriated Gaston de Foix, who, rashly pursuing them with a few companions along a causeway between a ditch and the river, had his horse hamstrung and was then surrounded and killed.

The defeat of Ravenna was an almost overwhelming blow for the Holy League and may well have hastened the death of Pope Julius, which occurred suddenly in the following February. For a brief moment the brave Pontiff lost heart and was only persuaded to continue the struggle by the Venetians, who reminded him that more help had been promised by England and the Swiss. And, indeed, for the French it proved a barren victory. Their troops were demoralized by their losses—including the death of their commander—by the loot of Brescia, and by the defection of the Emperor Maximilian, who, on the eve of the battle, had recalled the German mercenaries who formed a third of the French army. The German commander, however, was an honest man. He might ply for hire but he was not prepared to bite the hand that fed him, and, after consultation with Bayard, he decided not to disclose the contents of the despatch to his men. They had been ordered to rejoin the Emperor "on pain of their heads," so he had good reason to fear that the *landsknechte* would obey the order and desert in a body.

On the day after the battle the city of Ravenna surrendered, and Ravenna was followed by Rimini, Cesena, Imola and Forli. The Gallic cock was still crowing, but Maximilian believed that, in spite of their victories, the fortunes of the French in Italy were on the wane. He had been sitting on the fence until he was quite sure which way things were going, but now he callously abandoned his ally and hastened to join the Holy League. He allowed passage through his territory to 20,000 Swiss who were on their way to fight the French, and he even made overtures to Venice—on a sound financial basis. Pope Julius urged the Republic to accept his peace terms and offered to lend enough money to satisfy the Imperial sponger.

But then the Pontiff died, and with the election of his successor the whole situation changed. Julius II had been a soldier pope, but Leo X (Giovanni de' Medici) was a man of quite different character, mild and conciliatory. He resolved to try different methods, for he had a sincere desire for peace; but although he was not lacking in guile, he met with more than his fair share of disappointment in that tricky game of changing sides and trumping one another's aces. In March 1513 Venice and France had signed the peace treaty of Blois, and to this he was asked to adhere. But the war dragged on. The French retired from Italy but were soon recalled by the Venetians as a check on the inordinate ambition of the Emperor Maximilian. There were more great battles, including Novaro (1513) where the Imperialists defeated the French, and Marignano (1515) where the French defeated the Imperialists. Marignano was another victory for the French mobile artillery, and the new French king, Francis I, followed it up by reoccupying Milan. In those fearful times, cities were like shuttlecocks, passing backwards and forwards from hand to hand: men went to bed as Milanese or Mantuans in the full knowledge that they might awake next morning as willing or unwilling subjects of France or the Empire. Only Venice was still impregnable behind her shield of shallow water. Her invitation to the French had brought her into open conflict with her former allies, and after the Battle of Novaro, Raimondo di Cardona, Viceroy of Naples, had advanced with his army as far as Mestre. The Venetians laughed at him as he halted on the edge of the lagoon; then, after firing a few futile shots, he was forced to retire whence he came.

The short reign of good Pope Leo was dedicated to his mission of peace and reconciliation. Soon after Milan was taken by the French he journeyed to Bologna for a personal interview and a conference at which a concordat with France was concluded. Then, in 1519, Maximilian died and Charles, King of Castile and Aragon, (who reigned conjointly with his mother, Joanna the Mad, until 1555) became Holy Roman Emperor. Francis I, who had hoped to be elected himself, immediately declared war; but at the Battle of Pavia in 1525, he was defeated and taken prisoner by the Emperor. The principal Italian republics gave Charles their support; under the impact of his armies, the French were driven out of Italy, and, as if this were not enough, the great Duke of Bourbon, Constable of France, deserted to the enemy.

These were bad days for the French. Her king, a captive in Spain, was not released until the following year, and once again Milan, the key city, was in the hands of the Emperor. But now there was a new Pope, Clement VII. He was justifiably alarmed by the ever increasing power of Charles V, so yet another league was formed, and once again the beautiful land of Italy was ravaged by war. Those conflicts of knights in full plate, and mercenaries in their gay plumage and strange, slashed, particoloured clothes may seem picturesque and romantic when viewed through the mist of four hundred years. Yet we, who are rightly shocked by modern methods of mass-destruction, may find it salutary to study those half-forgotten campaigns. We may even find that we have known very little about the horrors of war. To be sure, there were no bombs in those days; there were no rockets or napalm. But no prisoners were taken who could not afford to pay a ransom—and none at all by the Swiss. There was no Red Cross, no Geneva Convention, no restraint of any kind except the ancient code of Chivalry, which was wearing very thin.

Consider, for example, the sack of Rome in 1527. The Constable of Bourbon led Spanish and German troops to the storming. He himself fell in the first assault; but the city was ravaged by 30,000 of the most brutal soldiery in Europe, and the Pope himself was a prisoner in the castle of Sant' Angelo. Yet such was the changing pattern of events in those days when coalitions were formed only to be broken and when solemn treaties, signed and sealed, were not worth the parchment on which they were written, that before another year had passed we find England and France fighting as allies against the Emperor. And when at last all the pieces of the puzzle had fallen into place, the real ruler of Italy emerged as neither France nor Germany but Spain, that rising nation of warriors still flushed with the conquest of Granada and soon to be rich with the teeming gold of Mexico and Peru. With Spanish Viceroys lording it in Milan and Naples, supported by the Pope and the small subservient principalities, nearly the whole of Italy had become a dependency of Spain.

And Venice? She retained her liberty and her cities in the Veneto, although she never recovered from the loss of trade which followed the fall of Constantinople or her struggle against the League of Cambrai which had turned all Italy into a battlefield. Of their own accord the mainland towns had returned to her rule and in the midst of her lagoons the virgin city was still untouched. She was about to win undying glory in the realm of Art. But she was no longer a great power.

14. The Cinquecento (One)

The Arts of Peace
The Barbary Rovers
The Badoer Affair
The Inquisitors of State

The Cinquecento. The 1500s. Venice had passed the crest of the hill and all that remained was the long descent, yet this was perhaps the most glorious period in her history—not in war, although her fighting-men won new laurels at Lepanto, not in statecraft or diplomacy, but in the arts of peace. For when the sun set on her power she was vouchsafed an afterglow.

The Venetians were proud people; and when the inroads of the Turks and the emergence of Spain made it clear beyond dispute that they had lost their stake in Italy, they did not attempt to adapt themselves to their changed position: they ignored it. The outward show of empire was maintained. The banner of the Winged Lion still flew proudly before St Mark's; on Ascension Day the Doge still wed the Sea with ever increasing ceremonial, and from all the pomp and display one would have thought that the Serenissima was as mighty as ever. For all her brave show, she had lost the self-confidence—or arrogance—which had made her hated and feared, but which had enabled her to stand alone against the confederates of Cambrai. In a surprisingly short space of time her whole attitude towards other nations changed. The statesmen of Venice became more propitiatory in their dealings with their neighbours: weak and irresolute where they had once been strong; subtle and devious where plain resolution had often won the day. But the resolution had been backed by force and the will to use it if necessary. Now these were replaced by a welfare of words and a policy of pliability. Her battlefield became the council chamber, the boudoir and the back stairs.

In 1522 the island of Rhodes, which for over two hundred years had been held by the military order of the Knights Hospitallers, fell to the all-conquering Turk. After a noble defence in which wounded knights, sitting on chairs, still swung their swords with their brethren—a defence which is said to have cost the Moslems 90,000 out of 200,000 men—the Knights of St John were granted an honourable capitulation by the Sultan Suleiman the Magnificent, to whom the Serene Republic hastened to offer her congratulations. Another bastion in the East had fallen, another deadly blow had been dealt to her commerce; yet instead of a fleet of galleys, Venice must send her envoy, Pietro Zeno, to fawn and smile on the aggressor. That other Zeno, lying in his warrior's grave, would never have demeaned himself by running such an errand.

There seems to have been no outcry about this and other humiliations. A few of the more thoughtful citizens may have deplored their leaders' sycophancy, if only for the inevitable loss of security which must follow. But there were no public organs of communication to sound the alarm; and now that there was no enemy in sight, life in Venice could be very pleasant. Weary of war, the people were becoming complacent, and at the beginning of a new era which was to be glorious for its art, they took no notice of dark clouds looming over the horizon—clouds which for nearly three hundred years would be no bigger than a man's hand.

For a long time now the Venetians had been strangers to personal freedom, but their property was protected and they were ruled justly and well. It would be a mistake to imagine that at this time people lived in perpetual fear of the secret tribunal. That was to come later. But now anyone who had learned to mind his own business and curb that dangerous Venetian propensity for intrigue and conspiracy could live a long and happy life without ever knowing, except by evil report, the deep dungeons of the Ten.

With every year that passed the city was becoming more like the Venice we know. At the end of the fifteenth century its architecture had been at its loveliest, for the pointed arch introduced by Pisani two hundred years before had marked the beginning of the semi-Oriental Venetian Gothic which superseded the Byzantine style, and Palladio had not yet reintroduced the rounded Romanesque arch which is so typical of the Renaissance. It is those ogeed Saracenic windows and doorways, wrought in creamy marble and glowing above some green canal, which hold so much of the exotic beauty and the mystery of Venice. And this in spite of that later miracle, Santa Maria della Salute, shining like a white bubble above the Basin of St Mark.

The Doge's Palace was finished at last, with its noble gateway, the Porta della Carta, and the Giants' Stairs—though Sansovino's two statues were not added until 1554. Now, if one turned off the Piazza to look at the shops in the Merceria, one passed beneath the arch of the Clock Tower, with its white Lion of St Mark, its elaborate clock-face on a field of star-spangled blue, and its two bronze Moors who still strike the bell with their hammers. But in a quiet square, the Campo di Sant' Agostino, there was living in this pregnant cinque-cento a man whose work was as important as that of the architects and the builders, and whose victories meant more to the world than all the knightly exploits of the good Chevalier Bayard. For here was to be found the *stamperia* of Aldus Manutius, one of the greatest printers of fine books who ever lived. Printing from wood blocks had been carried on in Venice for a century; but when movable type was invented by Johannes Gutenberg of Mainz, it was not long before the new process crossed the Alps into Italy, to be brought to the highest pitch of perfection by this same Aldus Manutius, his son and his grandson. Their beautiful fonts of Greek and Latin type were used to print books which are now priceless, and their workshops became a rendezvous for all lovers of the New Learning. Here were to be seen famous historians like Sabellicus and Sanudo, and Pietro Bembo —one of the greatest scholars of his time.

To ordinary Venetians, knowing little and caring even less about politics, it may well have seemed that a new and brighter era was dawning and that they could afford to relax and drop their guard. It was a relief to turn from the brutality and waste of war to peace. But although it has been necessary to write of battles, sacks and sieges, we should remember that all this time—in Venice, at any rate

—the majority of men and women were leading quiet, uneventful lives: trading, laughing, quarrelling, falling in love, trying to read the message in bright eyes over peaches-in-wine in the moonlight, sitting down to a supper of savoury sea-food in some little *trattoria* on the Zattere, picking out a new air on the lute while drifting down some shadowy backwater, or visiting an artist's *bottega* to admire the new painting in oils.

This secret of painting in oils instead of tempera had been brought to Venice in the 1470s by Antonello de Messina, who had himself learned it from the Van Eyck brothers in Flanders. The story goes that a man disguised in the rich robe of a patrician visited Antonello's studio on several occasions, ostensibly to have his portrait painted, but really to find out all he could about the new process. This must be one of the earliest examples of industrial espionage.

That man, if rumour told the truth for once, was Giovanni Bellini, the younger of the two brothers who, with their father Jacopo, did so much to pave the way for the great masters of the Venetian School. It is beyond the scope of this book to attempt a detailed assessment of the work of the masters. It is enough to say that their composition and splendid colouring have never been equalled. Their work was like a breath of fresh air, blowing away the stiffness of earlier styles; they possessed a wonderful sense of movement; their architectural perspective was superb; and their sacred subjects, their Madonnas and saints, were inspired by deep religious feeling.

Those supreme artists of the Cinquecento were to surpass the pioneers; but the Bellini were remarkable men, all three of them. The brothers, Gentile and Giovanni, were taught by their father; and one of their first commissions was to paint the portrait of Caterina Cornaro, Queen of Cyprus, whom they visited after her retirement to the castle of Asola. In those days of huge canvases, painting was sometimes a combined operation. So later we hear of both brothers working together in the Hall of the Great Council on magnificent, flamboyant pictures glorifying the Republic and outstanding scenes in her history. The apotheosis of Venice—or her obsequies.

You will find pictures by the Bellini in the churches and galleries of Europe and America: Gentile, the elder, was famous for his professional groups and for his portraits; but Giovanni was the greater painter. His lovely *Madonna degli Alberetti* is one of the gems of the

Accademia, and his portrait of Doge Leonardo Loredan now graces London's National Gallery. But if he was a genius he was also modest, and when Albrecht Dürer visited Venice Giovanni was so impressed by the German's work that he had the humility to ask how it was done. They say that Dürer thereupon picked up a brush and painted a single lock of hair, so exquisite, so realistic, that it looked as if it could have been lifted from the bare canvas.

The Sultan Mohammed II saw one of Giovanni's paintings; and, although representations of the human form are contrary to the law of Islam, he requested that Giovanni come to Constantinople and paint him. For some reason the Senate sent the elder brother instead, but Gentile was well received by the Sultan and loaded with gifts. He stayed in Constantinople for several years, painting not only Mohammed and several of his wives, but his own self-portrait in a mirror, a feat which delighted his host.

And then in an evil hour, for his own pleasure, he began to paint a sacred subject: the head of John the Baptist on a charger. The Sultan expressed admiration but graciously pointed out that the artist had made a mistake. When a head is severed, he explained, the neck disappears. Gentile ventured to disagree, but Mohammed had his own way of settling arguments. He clapped his hands; a slave knelt; there was a quick rattle of Arabic. Next instant, a scimitar flashed and the slave's head rolled at the artist's feet. No more argument. No more fuss. Just an elementary lesson in anatomy. Signor Bellini could see for himself that the neck was no longer visible. Signor Bellini saw—and did not recover his peace of mind until he was on his way home to Venice.

Among the contemporaries of the two younger Bellini were Carpaccio and Giorgione. The former is justly famous for his delineation of character and for the vivid and varied incidents which enliven his paintings. Many of his works are still in Venice, and, apart from their beauty, they are a most interesting record of quattrocento Venetian costume. But of the artist's own life little is known.

Giorgione (Giorgio Barbarelli) was born at Castelfranco on the mainland, but he moved to Venice when he was a boy and lived there nearly all his life. He served his apprenticeship in the Bellini *bottega,* where Titian was one of his fellow pupils. When Giorgione died,

Titian completed some of his unfinished works, and so exactly did he imitate his friend's style and technique that experts find it impossible to determine where Giorgione ended and Titian began. But during Giorgione's lifetime this facility of Titian's led to a rift between them. Giorgione was a jealous man. In 1504 fire destroyed the Fondaco de' Tedeschi, the exchange of the German merchants near the old Rialto Bridge. It was rebuilt and it is still there—a big red building, now housing the Post Office. Giorgioni was commissioned to decorate its facade with frescoes, and Titian helped him; but when one of the younger man's paintings was mistaken for his own, Giorgione behaved very badly. He severed his friendship with Titian and no longer invited him to his house. A childish display of temperament which he may have regretted, for hardly any of those paintings were destined to survive: they were soon ruined by the salt winds blowing in from the lagoon. To paint in tempera out of doors was surely tempting fate, for as Vasari wrote after visiting Venice in 1541, "Personally I know of nothing which injures fresco so much as the sirocco, especially near the sea, where it always brings some saltiness with it." Many years later, all that remained of the frescoes was removed to the Accademia for safety.

Giorgione's life was a short one but from all accounts it was merry. A tall, handsome young man, immensely popular with a wide circle of friends, he seems to have been welcome wherever he went, but especially in patrician society which, in those days, was very gay. He was skilled in playing and singing to the lute; and perhaps we can catch some faint echo of festive evenings long ago in those semi-pastoral paintings of his in which young men and lightly clad girls "fleet the time carelessly as they did in the golden world." Sunlit meadows and music: that was Giorgione's background—that and the big untidy *bottega* where he worked like a slave. Or did he? He left few pictures.

Giorgione seems to have spent much time happily discussing art. On one occasion he got into an argument about the respective merits of painting and sculpture. His opponent maintained that sculpture was superior in that it showed all sides of a subject, whereupon Giorgione retaliated by painting the back view of a figure in the nude. The front of the man was reflected in a pool of water, while his discarded breastplate, lying on the grass, reflected the side view in its polished surface. A clever answer. But that is not the way in which great paintings are produced.

Giorgione was a genius but it seems doubtful if he was wholly committed. Except for that one jealous outburst, the big jovial fellow —painting, laughing, singing—is a singularly attractive figure. He was a young man in love with life, and that was his joy and his tragedy: he had to cram so much experience into such a few years. In 1510 the lady he loved caught the plague and Giorgione took it from her. He died, mourned by all who were young and gay. He was only thirty-two.

Critics have argued down through the centuries as to whether Raphael or Titian was the greatest painter who ever lived. It is outside our province to line up on one side or the other; for our purposes, it is sufficient to know that Titian produced his first masterpiece when he was twenty-three, that he went on producing masterpieces until he died at the age of ninety-nine, and that on his deathbed he remarked that he was almost ready to begin painting.

Titian (or Tiziano Vecellio) was born in 1477 of a noble family who lived at Cadore on the River Piave. As we have seen, he served his apprenticeship in the *bottega* of the Bellini and at first came under the influence of Giorgione. But he was much too original and inspired to remain a mere copyist of another man's style, however splendid. Soon he was painting in his own inimitable manner and the commissions came pouring in, both from private patrons and from the Republic. The man's whole life was a triumphal progress. He was rich and honoured. He talked with kings. The story of the Emperor Charles V stooping to pick up the brush which the master had dropped is well known. Not so well known, perhaps, is the fact that, at the age of seventy, Titian crossed the Alps in midwinter to visit the Emperor at Augsburg.

His life was as happy as it was long. He lived in the palace on the Grand Canal which had formerly belonged to the Barbarigo family, and when Henry III of France passed through Venice he honoured the artist by calling on him there—if a visit from King Henry III could be considered an honour! Titian also built himself a new house with a garden and orchard. It overlooked the island of Murano, and it was in this chosen retreat that he delighted to sup and entertain his friends, among them Sansovino the sculptor, and Aretino, the Tuscan poet whose scandalous and satirical verses were the terror of his enemies.

All through his life Titian loved to travel. In 1545 he went to Rome; it was there, in the Vatican, that he made a memorable faux pas. The artist Sebastiano del Piombo had been restoring some heads by Raphael, and it was he who was given the unenviable task of escorting the great man round the Papal picture galleries. Titian paused before the Raphael heads and then exclaimed in an enraged voice: "What ignorant and presumptuous hand has dared to injure heads like these?" History does not record poor Sebastiano's reply, but no doubt everybody talked very fast as the irate old gentleman was hurried along to the next picture.

Among those who created beauty in Venice there is no greater name than that of Titian. In his ninety-nine years he bridged the gap between the earlier and later generations of the Venetian School. He knew the Bellini, Carpaccio, Giorgione and many more of the pioneers; he was painting before Tintoretto and Paolo Veronese were born, and he was still turning out masterpieces when they were in their prime. Together these men introduced and established a new element of vigour and movement in painting. Their work was adult: it had lost all trace of mediaeval naïveté. Enriched by a love of pageantry and glowing, gorgeous colour, it was a true expression of the city which gave it birth.

Reluctantly, from art we return to war and intrigue. When, as the Republic had done in the past, Francis I made an alliance with the Turks and scandalized Christendom by inciting the infidels to harass his enemies, Venice rode on the wave of popular anger and fitted out a fleet. She went to war but—fatal error—she did so almost apologetically, protesting a little too much that she drew the sword in self-defence with no thought of her own aggrandizement. It sounded noble and it may well have been true. But it was foolish to say so. Suleiman must have realized that his enemy had no heart for the fight.

The Venetian admiral's first engagement was with one of the Sultan's most formidable subjects. A new menace to seafarers had appeared in the Mediterranean and elsewhere: those North African corsairs known as the Barbary Rovers, with whom Venice was to become increasingly involved. One of their number nearly turned the tide of battle at Lepanto; and two hundred years later, the last victory of the Venetian navy was scored against them. There had always been pirates in the Mediterranean, but none like these. Their *reisses* or captains—Ramadan, Dragut, "Drub-Devil" and others—made their names feared from Cyprus to Gibraltar and beyond. Many of the most redoubtable were Christian renegades. Owing nominal allegiance to the Sultan at Constantinople, their fast galliots and xebecs sailed from Algiers, Tunis, Sallee and the other ports of Barbary, attacking the ships of all Christian nations and enslaving their crews. In the following century they raided as far afield as Ireland and Lundy, and once they captured the whole of the Newfoundland fishing fleet. Incredible as it may seem, until well into the nineteenth century the nations of the western world, including Britain and the United States, paid an annual tribute—or, as we would call it now, protection money—to the Dey of Algiers. There was consternation when seamen on watch sighted those sinister pointed sails like sharks' fins above the deep blue of the Mediterranean and a fast xebec came darting out from under the lee of some island. But in the early days the corsairs usually operated in small fleets.

The most famous of their leaders at this time were two Greeks from Lesbos known as the Barbarossa brothers—or Khair-ed-Din and Baba-Aroudj, to give them their Turkish names. They were adventurers, playing for their own hands; and having murdered their predecessor, they reigned successively in the Kasbah of Algiers. It was Khair-ed-Din who in 1537 fought the Venetians and was defeated among the islands of the Greek Archipelago. Realizing that the battle was going against him, the corsair broke off the engagement and slipped away; then, with one of his lightning strokes, he took Corfu, and although the Venetians recaptured it, Khair-ed-Din again slid through their fingers, to ravage all the neighbouring islands with fire and sword. He carried away many captives to languish in the harems of Algiers or to labour in the quarries until they died under the lash, with only the saintly Fathers of the Redemption to minister to them in their sufferings. Members of the Redemptorist Orders, working under a special dispensation from the Pope, devoted their lives to succouring the prisoners of the Barbary corsairs, collecting their ransoms and even taking their places as slaves on the rowing benches of the galliots.

And Venice did nothing. Her men had fought well, but it seemed as if that one effort had exhausted them. Khair-ed-Din's victims went unavenged, though in 1538 the Republic signed a treaty with the Pope and the Emperor against the Turkish Sultan and his unruly vassals, the North African corsairs. She had sent as her envoy to Constantinople a diplomat named Alvise Badoer who was given the most precise though secret instructions. First, he was to attempt to carry matters with a high hand and to demand the return of all territory which had been seized by the Turks. If, however, this was refused, he was to modify his demand, even offering to pay tribute of 6,000 ducats for the towns of Nauplis and Malvasia, with, if necessary, a further 300,000 ducats as a war indemnity. A war indemnity from the Serenissima! And for defending her own possessions! Times had changed indeed. But that was not all. In the unlikely event of these terms proving unacceptable to the Sultan, Badoer was to yield the two towns and to make any further concessions that would bring the war to an end. The envoy never expected the Turks to drive a hard bargain, but, to his surprise and consternation, the Sultan demanded as the price of peace even greater concessions, including the handing over of several fortresses in Dalmatia. Negotiations dragged on; but in the end, to the shame of Venice, his terms were accepted, although the peace treaty was not concluded until October 1540.

The news of this abject surrender was received in Venice with incredulity, which rapidly gave place to anger. In the marble halls of their palaces, patricians expressed their opinion of the treaty in words which were bitter but guarded; on the Rialto, the merchant-adventurers spoke their minds more bluntly; and in the smoky little taverns of the sailors and gondoliers, men cursed the unfortunate envoy who had brought the Republic so low. All this was reported to the Ten, who did their best to allay public indignation by letting it be known that Badoer had only obeyed his orders.

Meanwhile, there had come even uglier news—at first no more than a rumour. It was said that the envoy's secret instructions had been "leaked" by some traitor. Before Badoer even reached Constantinople, the Turks had been aware that the first demands he would make were mere bluff and that they had only to stand firm to make him agree to almost any terms that would end the war.

This, too, was duly reported by the agents of the Ten, and the Council acted swiftly, for even in those days the quality of Venetian counter-espionage was of such high order as to make the lapse seem incredible. A thorough investigation was ordered and soon evidence came to light that one Maffeo Leone, secretary to the Senate, and Nicolo Cavazzo, secretary to the Council of Ten itself, had sold every detail of Badoer's secret instructions to the French, who had passed on the information to the Sublime Porte.

We are not told what happened to Leone, but Cavazzo was at once arrested by the *sbirri* of the Ten. There was another culprit, however, a certain Agostino Abondio, who somehow escaped the net and fled for sanctuary to the French Ambassador's palace in the Calle di San Moise. It was an awkward situation. But the Council of Ten was not prepared to stand on ceremony or allow justice to be baulked by a claim of diplomatic immunity. Bernardo Zonzi, one of the *Avogardori del Commun* (a body created in the twelfth century to deal with all civil and criminal cases), was sent at once to arrest the traitor; but he left his bodyguard in the courtyard, and the servant who admitted him rushed up the stairs ahead of him, shouting and raising the alarm. Another servant—armed—appeared, to whom Zorzi repeated his request for an audience with the Ambassador. The servant bowed and withdrew; but immediately, as if at a prearranged signal, armed men appeared on all sides, threatening and jostling the Venetian. Zorzi protested angrily but was forced down the stairs, and when he summoned his own men from the courtyard they were beaten back by the Frenchmen and driven out of the building.

Drawn steel in a foreign embassy: the fuse had been lit for a dangerous diplomatic crisis. But, having gone so far, the Venetian authorities were not prepared to give way. A stronger force was sent to the Embassy and Abondio was made a prisoner. Afterwards it transpired that before the traitor's arrest the French Ambassador had been inclined to have him strangled, lest, under examination, he make confessions which might compromise the King of France. In the end, however, he thought better of it and delivered him to the *sbirri*.

Abondio and Cavazzo were interrogated very thoroughly and made full confession: they were even persuaded to name other, hitherto unsuspected accomplices. Venice, as usual, was stern but just. The principal traitors were executed and the others sentenced to exile. But unfortunately it did not end there. The whole unsavoury affair had created a major scandal, the most serious aspect of which was that one of the culprits had been a secretary in the confidence of the Council of Ten. It was a bitter blow to officials who had always, and with good reason, prided themselves on the efficiency of their security service. But clearly something had to be done, and in 1539 action was taken, though none of those involved could have foreseen its far-reaching consequences.

The remedy of the Republic was to form an inner Council of Three, and in the end the remedy proved worse than the disease. The new tribunal consisted of three Inquisitors of State, each elected for a limited period: a red-robed inquisitor from the Privy Council of the Doge, and two in black robes. All three were members of the Council of Ten, from which they derived their authority, just as the Ten themselves were answerable to the Great Council. With the red inquisitor in the middle and a black inquisitor on either side, the Council of Three held their conclaves or sat in judgement in a small room on the second floor of the Doge's Palace, with private stairs leading to the prisons and to the torture chamber situated conveniently next door. The word inquisitor does not imply any connection with the Holy Office of the Roman Catholic Church, though the red inquisitor did deal with such offences as heresy, sorcery and witchcraft. At first the Three were concerned only with treason and the security of the State, and it could be argued that in the early days they did good work. Then gradually over the years, as Venice became more corrupt and decadent, they began to probe and pry into the affairs of ordinary people, and to supplant the Council of Ten itself, until at last their power was absolute.

The sad tale of the death of Democracy was moving inexorably to its climax. First there had been the closing of the Great Council to all but a chosen few, the curtailing of the Doge's power, and the exclusion of the common people from any voice in his election. Then had followed the curbing of the aristocratic oligarchy by the Council of Ten and the transformation of the Republic into a police state. And now, at last, the Venetians had saddled themselves with this sinister triumvirate who would one day rule them by terror and a network of spies far worse than anything that they had suffered under the Council of Ten. No peaceful citizen in his home would ever be certain that he was unwatched and unheard. No lady would dare to go to the theatre unless she was masked and wearing the style of dress ordained by the State Inquisitors. It all came gradually, slowly but surely, until the whole city and the Veneto were helpless in the grip of three ruthless men. The Three! It is possible, though not very likely, that the fear they inspired has been exaggerated, but it was not for nothing that the Venetians used to say: "The Ten send you to the torture chamber: the Three to your grave."*

---

* Quoted in James Morris. *The World of Venice* (London: Faber & Faber, 1960), p. 184.

15. The Cinquecento (Two)

Venice Adorned
Bianca Cappello
The Loss of Cyprus
Lepanto

We are still in those hundred wonderful years which we know as the sixteenth century but which the Italians, especially when they are discussing art, call the cinquecento. In the story of every nation there are certain periods, certain atmospheres and settings which, for no logical reason, so appeal to the imagination of every lover of the picturesque that they spring to the mind automatically whenever the history of that particular place or country is mentioned. They are not necessarily prosperous or happy periods, but invariably they have some literary or artistic association. In Venice such a period—together with the last years of her decadence—is the sixteenth century. It is a rich and varied tapestry woven of bright and sombre threads, and we can people it as we will: with Othello and the Merchant of Venice, sprung from the brain of Shakespeare; with that real-life ruffian of genius, Messer Benvenuto Cellini, or with the protagonists of uglier stories whom time has decked with a spurious glamour.

The late sixteenth century saw a second flowering of Venetian art. It was then that Andrea Palladio, the pioneer of modern architecture in Italy, reintroduced the Roman style and the round Roman arch into the churches which he built in Venice; while Jacopo Sansovina achieved immortality with his Library of St Mark and the adjoining *Zecca* or Mint which, with their perfect proportions and wealth of embellishment, are among the finest examples of Renaissance architecture in Europe. But they could belong to Rome or Florence: they are not uniquely Venetian as are the Ca' d'Oro or the Palazza Pisani-Moretta. There is one building, however, which is typical of the late Renaissance and yet, for all its classical arches, has become such an embodiment of the spirit of Venice that it is difficult to picture the curve of the Grand Canal without it. The Rialto Bridge.

When, towards the end of the sixteenth century, it was decided that the mediaeval wooden bridge had had its day, an open competition was held for the design of a new bridge in stone. There were many illustrious competitors, but the winner was Antonio da Ponte, with a bold conception of a single arch forty-five feet in height and with a span of ninety feet. Later this bridge was surmounted by two rows of small shops, and this is the Rialto that we know today. For three hundred years it was the only bridge across the Grand Canal.

Overlooking the Rialto market is the little church of San Giacomo, and just opposite it you can still see the ancient *Gobbo di Rialto*—a small statue of a hunchback man bent double beneath a heavy burden. From his pedestal, in the old days, the decrees of the Republic were proclaimed; and to petty criminals this queer old character brought blessed relief from pain; for when, for their sins, they were stripped naked and whipped all the way from St Mark's, this was journey's end. Once they had touched the statue of *Gobbo* they were safe from further chastisement. One cannot help wondering whether his name inspired Shakespeare's Venetian clown, Launcelot Gobbo, or even whether Shakespeare, of whom we know so little, once made a voyage to Venice.

But the architects and sculptors did not reign alone. In the last half of the sixteenth century there flourished the second generation of the Venetian School, which reached its apogee in the work of Titian and the two great artists who followed him: Tintoretto and Veronese.

Tintoretto was christened Jacopo Robusti and received his boyish nickname because he was the son of a dyer or *tintore*. It has been said that some of his later works show signs of having been finished in haste, but there is no denying that he had few equals in composition and colouring, while his historical battle pieces are almost deafening with the din of war. Ruskin called him one of the five supreme painters. One is not necessarily impressed by the mere size of a work of art, but for anyone who might hanker to see the largest oil painting by any great master, there it is in the Doge's Palace. This colossus is Tintoretto's *Paradiso* in the Hall of the Great Council. And it is not only in size that the *Paradiso* is colossal. There are over a hundred figures in it, and the whole vast canvas is vibrant with life and movement. It reaches out to all who look at it: saints and angels seem to come swooping down—circle upon circle of them—all centering on Christ and the Virgin, while on the lowest level is Tintoretto's daughter, who died while the painting was in progress.

Paolo Caliari (Veronese) was the son of a sculptor in Verona. In 1555 he came to live in Venice, where he made his fortune and earned the right to rank as the last of the Venetian great masters. He gloried in splendid architectural settings crowded with figures, sumptuously dressed; and after a visit to Rome, where the artists of the Roman School had considerable influence on his style, the movement in his pictures gained a new grace and dignity. The National Gallery in London owns his *Presentation of the Family of Darius to Alexander,* while his *Marriage Feast of Cana* is one of the treasures of the Louvre. In Venice there are, of course, many of his works. In the Accademia is another of his banquet pictures, *Feast in the House of Levi,* in which the artist himself figures prominently as the major-domo. It was for this painting that he was summoned to appear before the tribunal of the Holy Office, for he had given grave offence by introducing into a sacred picture dwarfs, drunks, German mercenaries, dogs, a cat and a parrot. He was ordered to correct the painting within a month, at his own expense. But they are still there: German halberdiers, buffoons, dogs, cat, parrot and all.

While all this superb work was being produced, the city which had given it birth and become a new centre and focal point for the arts of peace was steadily declining in esteem among the nations of Europe. Venice was no longer wooed as an ally or feared as a foe. Yet no stranger, ignorant of the place and dazzled by the opulence and luxury all around him, would have dreamed that the Queen of the Adriatic had been dethroned by younger rivals.

Venice in the late sixteenth century! Against the background of glittering water, festering slums, and pink, cream and amber palaces, a vigorous and colourful life surged along the lanes and canals, over humpbacked bridges, past the striped mooring posts, overflowing into the squares. Gallants in velvet doublets puffed and slashed in the latest fashion strutted like peacocks round the Piazza or lounged on the new Rialto Bridge. Gondoliers, half-naked and as brown as nuts, shouted their warning cry of "*Stali!*" as they slid round the corner of some rio. Beggars, mere bundles of noisome rags, mumbled for alms on the steps of the churches. Ladies in monstrous ruffs and farthingales watched the world go by from their balconies or, with waiting-women carrying their missals on velvet cushions behind them, went masked like conspirators to Mass at St Mark's. And those other ladies of leisure —the courtesans—the notorious courtesans of Venice—sat in the high loggias of their houses, bleaching their hair in the hot sunshine.

At night it became a city of mystery—black alleys opening out on little squares shining like mother of pearl in the moonlight, or grey with the sea-fog of winter and the steady, drenching rain. One had to walk warily at night, but the authorities did what they could to maintain law and order. The *Signori di Notte* provided a watch after dark and carrying weapons was discouraged.

Then when the sun in all its splendour rose again above the sea, barges laden with farm produce came sailing in from the mainland and islands. The fishing fleet put to sea, its multicoloured sails as gay as a drift of butterflies, the crews praying that nightfall would not find them slaves of the Barbary corsairs. The markets opened, their stalls piled high with flowers, vegetables and fruit; carnations and roses in season; oranges and grapes and melons; cuttlefish, scampi and steaks of tunny; golden slabs of freshly baked polenta and full-bellied flasks of Cyprus wine. And Venetian argosies still cast anchor in the Porto di Lido. The fleets were sadly depleted in numbers now but no one seemed to care. The men and women of this new generation were too young to remember the great days.

The noble families who had made Venice were losing their virtue but not their pride. In *Il Libro d'Oro*, as has been noted earlier, were recorded every legitimate birth and every marriage among the patricians. Moreover, every young nobleman whose name had been entered could, on reaching the age of twenty-five, apply for a seat on the Great Council.

And on one of the leaves of *Il Libro d'Oro* was inscribed the honoured name of Cappello.

And now, the overture ended, we find ourselves in what could almost pass for the world of grand opera. Indeed, it is surprising that Verdi or Rossini did not compose music for a libretto based on the life of Bianco Cappello. All the appurtenances of old-fashioned melodrama were there: frail lady, poor suitor, amorous nobleman, lurking bravos, an elopement by gondola, more than a hint of poison. Only this story happens to be true. Near the Ponte Storto you can still see the house where Madonna Bianca lived. She is important, for she was one of the very few women who left their mark on Venetian history. The record of her adventures is not romantic, but is rather the sordid story of a designing young woman with an eye to the main chance. Romance? No, only adultery and murder—themes as old as sin.

It was during the dogeship of Nicolo da Ponte that the affair began. Partly, no doubt, as a result of their long intercourse with the East, Venetian patricians segregated their women. They seldom left their palaces except for Mass, and never unescorted. Their activities were limited—or were supposed to be—to church, household duties and needlework: an infallible recipe for boredom. But in every city there are rebels, and Venice is no exception.

Madonna Bianca was young, rich and, we are told, beautiful, though judging from Bronzini's portrait, one can hardly imagine anyone less like a *femme fatale*. But no one could deny that Bianca had a marked talent for cajoling men: she used them as rungs on a ladder to power, for she was ambitious, promiscuous and completely amoral.

Even her first recorded love affair was apparently devoid of any real passion. From what we know, it is hard to believe that her elopement meant more to her than escape from a life that was little better than that of an Oriental odalisque.

Apart from her personal charms, she was no mean prize: she was of noble birth; she had inherited valuable jewels; and she was to receive 6,000 ducats from her late mother's estate.

Her lover was a young Florentine clerk, Pietro Bonaventura, and at first all that happened was an exchange of amorous letters. Pietro's uncle, who managed the bank in which his nephew worked, aided and abetted the lovers, so it is possible that he believed Pietro to have great expectations. The illicit correspondence continued; there were secret meetings; and then one night a gondola was waiting outside the house by the Ponte Storto. The lovers fled to the mainland and from there to Florence, where they were married. But now, for a time, Bianca's luck turned against her. This highborn lady found herself not only living in the comparatively humble home of Pietro Bona-ventura's father but even expected to do the housework. She had brought her mother's jewels with her but she could not touch the 6,000 ducats, for her father, enraged, had disowned her and de-nounced both her and her husband to the Council of Ten. And in his righteous anger he had offered the 6,000 ducats to whoever should deliver Pietro to the justice of the Republic.

In that house in the Campo San Marco in Florence, Bianca's thoughts must have been very bitter, for all her plans for advance-ment had gone awry. But she was not one to submit tamely to ill for-tune. Somehow—we do not know how—she made the acquaintance of a gentleman beside whom her poor clerk of a husband appeared very insignificant. He was Pandulfo Bardi, Count of Verino, and a lord in the household of Cosimo de' Medici, Grand Duke of Tuscany. It goes without saying that she allowed him to make love to her, and she used this love-making very cleverly to induce him to bring her to the notice of his master's heir.

Like Cesare Borgia, Louis XI of France and other rulers, Fran-cesco, son of Duke Cosimo, was in the habit of prowling the streets of the city incognito, after dark. He sought adventures, amorous or otherwise, though doubtless he persuaded himself that he had the more laudable object of learning something about the people over whom, one day, he would rule. It is not clear whether the Count of Verino had stooped to becoming his pander; but it was he who, on one of those night walks, first led the heir of Tuscany to the house in the Campo San Marco.

So Francesco de' Medici met Bianca and fell as others had fallen. Soon she became his mistress, and in the heartless fashion of those days the neighbours must have laughed to see young Bonaventura wearing the horns. At first it was only street gossip and bawdy jests. Who cared? But tongues began to wag in earnest in the Palazzo della

Signoria when the cuckolded husband rose in the world and was made Master of the Robes. The appointment gave rise to much scandal, but that did not trouble Bianca, for several eminent men were beginning to busy themselves on her behalf. Acting at the request of Francesco, no less a personage than the Apostolic Nuncio intrigued with the Florentine envoy in Venice to effect a reconciliation between the runaway and her family. They attempted, too, to restore her to favour with the Ten. But both the Council and the Cappelli were obdurate. Bianca had made her beds and she must lie on them. And if Pietro returned to Venice it would be to face criminal charges.

For seven years the wretched affair dragged on, with Bianca the acknowledged mistress of the Grand Duke's heir. The infatuated Francesco neglected his wife, Giovanna of Austria, and installed her rival in a splendid palace not far from his own. The lovers paraded their passion quite openly. They would have married if it had not been for Bianca's husband and Francesco's wife. But in 1572 the first of these obstacles was removed. Venturing out alone at night into the dangerous streets of Florence, Pietro Bonaventura was set upon by bravos lying in wait for him. He was stabbed to death, but no one knows for certain who hired the assassins: they may have been Venetian agents; they may have been Francesco's men; or Bianca herself may have decided that no one is more expendable than an inconvenient husband.

Six years later, Cosimo de' Medici died and Francesco became Grand Duke. Shortly afterwards that unhappy lady, his wife, died too. He remarried in almost indecent haste. Only two months later Bianca—or the Widow Bonaventura, as the people persisted in calling her—achieved the ambition for which she had schemed and sinned. At twenty-six, she became Grand Duchess of Tuscany.

The heir presumptive was her brother-in-law, Cardinal Ferdinando de' Medici; and he was her enemy, for he was a shrewd man and quite immune to her fascination. But now the Venetians had to change their tune. Bianca Cappello, who had run away with a poor clerk, was one thing: Bianca, Grand Duchess of Tuscany, was quite another. Florentine envoys, whose courteously veiled request was really a demand, begged that she might be created a Daughter of the Republic, which made her the equivalent of royal under a monarchy; and Bianca herself informed the Doge (surely with her tongue in her cheek) that she coveted the honour, not so much for herself, but as a means of strengthening the friendship between Florence and Venice. In those days, when allies were hard to find, the support of Florence was valuable, so Venice swallowed her pride, and the attitude of the *Signoria* changed almost overnight. All was forgotten and forgiven; the erring Bianca became a Daughter of the Republic—that same honour which Caterina Cornaro had borne with such grace and dignity; and, irony of ironies, it has even been said that she received the Golden Rose from the Pope.

For the next eight years her duty was to provide the Grand Duke with an heir; for she was determined, if possible, to thwart her enemy the Cardinal. And when no child was forthcoming, she did not flinch from certain desperate measures which involved passing off another woman's baby as her own. As a result of these clandestine transactions, there were rumours of another death—that of the woman who had produced the child and who shared Bianca's secret. Somehow an arquebus went off and the poor woman was in the way—in more senses than one. An unfortunate accident. No one worried. After all, she was only a servant.

But now Bianca's course was almost run. Power, riches, revenge on the Venetians who had condemned her: all were hers. Yet it is difficult to believe that in her triumph she was happy, for how could she enjoy being a grand duchess if she was not accepted? Hated by the patricians, despised by the commonality, she was still "the Widow Bonaventura." Her crimes had brought their own punishment.

Then quite suddenly, with a final touch of melodrama, the curtain fell. Francesco died, and on the following day Bianca died too. The Cardinal Grand Duke Ferdinando became the ruler of Tuscany, and one of his first acts was to order a post-mortem, for already it was being whispered that His Eminence was a poisoner. Bianca and her husband may have been poisoned—by the Cardinal or by another; but, on the other hand, many believe that the double death was due to colic. It is another of those unsolved mysteries with which history abounds. In the world of grand opera some corpulent tenor would have wept melodiously. But this was Florence on the Arno, whose citizens have long been expert in separating gold from dross. They knew the fascinating Bianca for the adventuress that she was and they denied her an honoured place among the tombs of the de' Medici.

She was buried in the common graveyard outside the church of San Lorenzo. There let her lie.

In front of St Mark's Basilica there are three vermillion flagstaffs on magnificent bronze bases by Alessandro Leopardi. On festive occasions they fly the flag of Italy and the Lion of St Mark, but they used to display the banners of the three lost provinces: Cyprus, Crete and the Morea.

Cyprus was the first to go. For thirty years there had been increasing discord between the Republic and the Turks. The trouble was caused by Istrian pirates who plundered the ships of both sides but for whose outrages the Turks found it convenient to make Venice the scapegoat. For they coveted the island of Cyprus and were glad of the excuse thus offered to make it their own. In 1566 their great Sultan, Suleiman the Magnificent, had died and had been succeeded by a lesser man: his son, who, in spite of the fact that he was a Moslem, has come down in history as Selim the Sot. Perhaps that is why he wished to acquire the famous vineyards of Cyprus. Venetian agents reported that he was assembling a large fleet, and the Republic prepared for action. Half-heartedly, it would seem, an armament was fitted out, and the galleys were feebly reinforced by the Pope and the King of Spain, from both of whom—such was her present weakness —Venice had implored aid. But the Allies, having no heart for a fight, were helpless against the Turks, who knew what they wanted and were determined to take it.

The Sublime Porte made no diplomatic approach to the Republic. There was no request for negotiations, not even a courteously veiled threat. Selim simply bided his time until things were going badly for Venice. Presently there was a poor harvest on the mainland and another disastrous fire at the Arsenal—a fire suspected of having been the work of incendiaries. The hour had struck. A Turkish fleet, under the command of Mustapha Pasha, set sail for Cyprus, and Venice was confronted with a peremptory demand for the surrender of the whole island.

So it had come: the war which the Venetians would have avoided at almost any cost. The enemy immediately laid siege to Nicosia, the capital of Cyprus, and the defence of Nicolo Dandolo proved quite inadequate. This descendant of the blind old crusader lacked his ancestor's fire and ability, and after a feeble defence he surrendered. But even this did not save him. The Turks were let loose in the city, which became a scene of horrible carnage. Dandolo himself was decapitated and his head flung over the walls of Famagusta as a warning to the garrison of what they might expect if they did not yield immediately.

But the Venetian commander at Famagusta was Marcantonio Bragadin, and he was made of sterner stuff than the spineless Dandolo. From April until August 1571 he put up a determined resistance, but at last, hopelessly outnumbered, he was forced to capitulate. Mustapha Pasha granted him honourable terms and a safe-conduct; so, carrying the keys of the city and sheltered by his red ceremonial umbrella, Bragadin, escorted by his captains, went out to meet his conqueror.

At first, all went well. The Pasha was affable and the conference seems to have proceeded amicably until a dispute arose over the alleged ill-treatment of some Turkish prisoners. Mustapha flew into a rage; he gave a signal; and there and then, the Venetian captains were cut to pieces by his guards. Compared with their leader they were fortunate: he was reserved for a worse fate. After being tortured for eleven days, with every refinement of cruelty that sadistic minds could devise, Bragadin was chained to a post and flayed alive in the main square of Famagusta. It is said that all the time they were tormenting him, he did not utter one cry.

His skin, stuffed with straw, was paraded through the streets on a cow, underneath the red umbrella which was the sign of his rank; then, lashed to the prow of the Pasha's galley, it was taken to Constantinople and displayed in the Turkish Arsenal as a trophy of war. Some years later, it was bought or stolen and returned to Venice where, having received the Church's blessing, it was given honourable interment in a stone casket high on the wall in San Zanipolo. It is still there—the pathetic relic of a very brave man.

The cruel death of Bragadin sent a thrill of horror through the civilized world. In Venice itself the news, like some tragic footnote to the loss of Cyprus, brought about a temporary resurgence of the old fighting spirit. If it had endured it might have saved the Republic, but the canker of ease and luxury had eaten too deeply for that. It was only a temporary revival, but while it lasted the great Orseolo and Carlo Zeno would have been proud of their countrymen.

The Turk must be stopped. Now, at last, others realized this as well as the Venetians; and what had been a half-hearted alliance of the Papacy, Spain and Venice, was metamorphosed into a strong and active Christian League of the Catholic powers, reinforced by the nominally independent princes of Italy and the Knights of St John. The tragedy of Famagusta was like a shot in the arm. The powers mobilised now in earnest. Their combined fleets mustered at Messina, and on September 16, 1571, they weighed anchor for Corfu.

It was a mighty armament. The supreme commander was that gallant knight, Don John of Austria, half-brother to Philip II of Spain; under him, as principal Spanish admiral in command of the reserve squadron, was a great hidalgo, Don Alvaro de Bazin y Guzmán, Marquis of Santa Cruz. The Papal fleet was commanded by a member of the ancient Roman family of Colonna; the Genoese by one of the fighting Dorias—those old enemies of Venice—and the Venetians themselves by that fiery veteran, Sebastiano Veniero, later to become Doge. In all, there were over two hundred galleys, some twenty transports, and about fifty lighter craft. There were also six great galleasses, propelled by both sails and oars: they had cannon mounted on decks raised high above the slave benches, and tall wooden structures fore and aft.

The fleet was manned by 50,000 sailors and carried about 30,000 soldiers, mostly arquebusiers. Don John's fire power was superior to that of the enemy, but he was slightly outnumbered in ships, and the morale of the Christians was bad. There were too many ancient enmities: jealousy and antagonism between the Spaniards and Italians led to drawn knives and bloodshed, and when Veniero ordered four Spaniards to be strung up to the yardarm for mutiny, Allied ships were on the point of opening fire on each other. But somehow, by tact and firmness, Don John preserved order; and early in October, as the result of information received, the Christian fleet set sail for Lepanto on the north side of the entrance to the Gulf of Corinth.

At sunrise on the seventh of October they came in sight of the enemy. At the mouth of the Gulf the Turkish fleet was waiting for them, drawn up in a crescent which almost stretched from shore to shore. Like the Christian order of battle, this crescent formation consisted of three squadrons, with a small reserve in the rear. In the centre the Turkish admiral, Ali Pasha, a brave and chivalrous enemy, flew his standard: red, embroidered with crossed scimitars and the Sultan's monogram in yellow. He had at his disposal about 300 ships, including 250 galleys. There were many galliots and smaller craft but no galleasses, and there were few musketeers among his men, who preferred the short but powerful Tartar bow. The main strength of his force lay in the ships of the Barbary corsairs; and the sixty galleys which formed the Ottoman left were commanded by one of the most formidable of them—Ochiali, nicknamed the Scurvied, a renegade Christian from Algiers and perhaps the finest seaman in the Turkish fleet. The squadron on the right was led by Mohammed Sirocco, Governor of Alexandria.

The sky was cloudless, the dark blue sea quite calm; and as the sun rose, it shone on those two fantastic fleets—on the pointed lateen sails, the crimson banks of oars rising and falling like slow-beating wing, on flags and pennants, on gleaming breastplates, morions and peaked burgonets, and on the towering headdresses of the Turkish Janissaries. From the Ottoman ships could be heard the clash of cymbals and the throbbing of drums; from the Christian vessels only the chanting of priests, for it was Sunday morning. Don John himself, with his officers, heard Mass on his flagship *El Real;* then he called for his pipers and, in full armour, danced a galliard before them all.

Half a mile ahead of the three Christian squadrons sailed the six galleasses, cumbersome but formidable, for they were too high to board, and in addition to their bow- and stern-chasers and a number of culverins and other light cannon, each of them mounted thirty guns on the raised platform above the rowers. Unlike the galleys, their broadside could be devastating.

Action was joined at about half past ten and the battle was in three phases. It began on the left of the Christian line when Barbarigo's Venetian galleys encountered the ships of Sirocco. The Venetians were preceded by two galleasses. The Turks carried out evasive action, but having sunk one enemy craft, the huge galleasses backwatered, swung round, and raked the enemy ships with their broadsides. The result was that when the Turks made contact with the main Venetian squadron, many of their galleys and galliots had already suffered severe damage. But once they were at grips with each other, the fighting was savage. Both commanders died: Barbarigo was killed by an arrow; while Mohammed Sirocco, badly wounded, fell overboard when the ships were locked together and the boarders were clambering over the bulwarks and was rescued by the Venetians, who promptly cut off his head. Remembering the death of Bragadin, they gave no quarter that day.

The centre squadrons came into contact at about eleven o'clock. The two flagships drove straight at each other and eventually rammed. Aboard *El Real* the pipes and clarions were sounding, though they must have been silenced when the galleys ground together and the banks of oars were splintered. Then the air was full of screaming as the fettered slaves were hurled into heaps. As we can see in old paintings of the battle, the sea was littered with broken oars; and when they snapped, one by one, with a sound like a giant's walking stick running along iron railings, the suffering on the wrecked slave benches must have been indescribable.

Three times before one of the ships rammed the other, the Christians boarded the *Sultana* and three times they were driven back. But at the fourth assault they held their ground, and for an hour they fought it out with sword, scimitar and yataghan. Both sides were continually being reinforced by soldiers scrambling up ladders from other ships' boats. Santa Cruz sent as many men as he could spare to *El Real,* and wave after wave of Janissaries swarmed aboard the *Sultana.* The last Christian boarding party was led by Don John in person and opposed by Ali Pasha, sabre in hand, at the head of his men. The Turks fought desperately but they were overcome, and the *Sultana* was captured and taken in tow. In the confusion of the melee Ali was cut down and his head was brought to the Christian commander elevated on a spear. It is said that Don John was outraged, which may well be true, for he was a man who could honour a gallant and humane opponent.

Meanwhile Doria, on the right of the Allied line, was in difficulties, completely outwitted by Ochiali. The Genoese had sixty-four ships and the corsair ninety-three, so, fearing that he would be out-flanked by the long-extended line of the enemy, Doria kept edging his squadron to the south, nearer and nearer to the shore. No doubt

Ochiali's original intention had been to use his superiority in numbers to turn Doria's flank, but the gap between the Christian centre and right was slowly widening and presently he saw the opportunity for an even more effective manoeuvre. He would alter course from south to northwest, drive through the gap that Doria had opened, and attack Don John's central squadron from the rear.

It was a typically bold plan and a good one, and it came very near to succeeding. On his way through the gap the corsair met and destroyed a small flotilla manned by the Knights of Malta; but this minor action delayed him and, just in time, Santa Cruz despatched six Sicilian galleys to the rescue, following them as soon as he could with the remainder of his reserve. Ochiali now saw that the battle was lost. Since to remain meant certain destruction, with consummate skill he extricated his Algerine galleys and sailed away to fight another day.

The casualties at Lepanto were appalling, for once the galleys were rammed and locked together there was no escape. There have been various estimates, but it is thought that the Christians lost about 8,000 killed and had about 16,000 wounded, among them Cervantes, whose left hand was shattered by a ball. It is believed that the Turks lost about 25,000 killed; but, significantly, the number of their wounded is not known. Those were cruel days and the Allies had much to avenge.

Lepanto was the last of the great galley battles, and thus is a milestone in naval history. To give his guns a better field of fire, Don John had had the steel beaks of his galleys removed; but in 31 B.C. when Mark Antony was defeated by Octavius at Actium, they used essentially the same tactics of ramming and boarding. In the Mediterranean, galleys were not discarded for another three hundred years; but from now on most battleships were propelled solely by sail, and ramming gave place to the broadside.

Lepanto was a great victory but it was a lost opportunity. The Turk had been checked and his growing reputation for invincibility destroyed, though it was not long before he reasserted himself in the Mediterranean and, like vicious mosquitoes, the corsairs again came swarming out of Barbary. For that, the Christian League must be blamed. The victory was never followed up. It was as if that one great effort had exhausted the Venetian Republic; and seventeen years later the Spanish hegemony came to an end when Sir Francis Drake and Lord Howard of Effingham, with God's "Protestant wind" to help them, drummed the Armada up the Channel. England was saved; and Catholic Spain, although the days of her greatness were not yet over, could no longer dictate terms to Europe or spare men and ships to chastise the infidels.

16. Years of Decline

The Prisons
The Great Interdict
Conspiracy and Espionage
The Loss of Crete

The plague, travelling in ships from the East, was no stranger to Venice, and in the late sixteenth and early seventeenth centuries the dreaded visitant struck hard. The outbreak which killed Titian in 1576 claimed at least 40,000 victims (one authority puts the number as high as 70,000) while in 1629 a quarter of the population died in a particularly virulent outbreak. Again barges plied the canals, collecting bodies for burial on the islands of the lagoon.

The survivors of pestilence sometimes expressed their thanks to God by building a new church. One such is Palladio's *Rendentore,* or Church of the Redeemer, begun in 1577, which is to be found in the Guidecca, the old Jewish quarter of Venice. And nearly eighty years later, another of these churches began to rise on over a million wooden piles. It took half a century to complete; but when the builders finished it, they had created an octagonal masterpiece of the Baroque, Baldassaro Longhena's *Santa Maria della Salute* (Our Lady of Salvation or Our Lady of Health). Together with the Campanile it dominates the Venetian skyline. Rising above the Customs House and the Basin of St Mark, or suddenly coming into view as one's gondola or water bus rounds the curve of the Grand Canal, the beautifully proportioned domes and cupolas are breathtaking in their beauty.

Also belonging to this period is the famous flying bridge which spans the Rio di Palazzo, linking the Doge's Palace with the sixteenth-century prisons. The Bridge of Sighs was built in 1600, and up and down its double slope prisoners could pass unseen from the lawyers' rooms into the Palace for examination by the Three and—unless they were very lucky—to a long or even indefinite term of imprisonment in the *Piombi* or Leads, those dreadful cells, icy in winter, furnace-hot in summer, which were situated immediately under the leaden roof of the Doge's Palace.

Much has been written about the prisons of Venice, some of it, no doubt, exaggerated. But connected by secret stairs with the *Piombi,* the torture chamber, and the Hall of the Three, were those even more terrible dungeons, the *Pozzi* or Wells, the floors of which some declare were below water level. There have been attempts to debunk the *Pozzi* and to make out that they were no worse than other dungeons of the time. But Casanova, who knew his Venice, had this to say about them:

"Those subterranean prisons are precisely like tombs, but they call them 'wells' because they always contain two feet of water, which penetrates from the sea by the same grating by which light is given, this grating being only a square foot in size. If the unfortunates condemned to live in these sewers do not wish to take a bath of filthy water, they have to remain all day seated on a trestle, which serves them both for bed and cupboard. In the morning they are given a pitcher of water, some thin soup, and a ration of army bread which they have to eat immediately or it becomes the prey of the enormous rats who swarm in these terrible abodes. Usually the wretches condemned to the Wells are imprisoned there for life, and there have been prisoners who have attained a great age. A villain who died while I was under the Leads had passed thirty-seven years in the Wells and he was forty-four when sentenced."

Casanova was certainly a rogue and probably a liar; but Charles Dickens was neither. He wrote of "two ranges, one below the other, of dismal, awful, horrible stone cells . . . quite dark," and in 1844, in a letter to Forster, he spoke of those "awful prisons deep below the water." Hans Andersen described the dungeons as "swampy cellars, deeper even than the water outside in the canals," while Shelley said: "I saw the dungeons . . . called the *Pozzi* or Wells . . . where the prisoners were confined sometimes half-way up to their middles in stinking water." From what these three famous writers, all of them eye-witnesses, have said, we can form our own judgement.

When, little by little, she shed her greatness, Venice became a city of pleasure—the Paris or the Las Vegas of the seventeenth and eighteenth centuries. But before the final cataclysm, when Bonaparte brought her to her knees, there were wars to be fought and rights to be upheld even though her strength was failing. At the dawn of the seventeenth century, the Republic was threatened by danger from two quarters: the Ottoman Empire and Spain. Turkish fleets and the Barbary corsairs were again scouring the Mediterranean; and although the defeat of the Armada and the invasion of the Prince of Orange had assured peace and religious freedom to England and the Nether-lands, the Spaniards, in close league with the Vatican, still maintained their hold on Italy. With Spanish grandees lording it in Naples and Milan, the Venetians still clung desperately to their freedom from foreign rule. Times had changed, but there were still occasions when the powder flashed in the pan; and those who provoked them found to their cost that even in their decline these islanders could still rally to the ancient cry of *"Viva San Marco!"* They proved this when in 1606 they again came under the ban of the Church.

The newly elected Pope, Paul V, was a saintly and dedicated man, but he misjudged the Venetians and failed to understand that the thunders of the Roman Catholic Church no longer terrified Christen-dom. All through history the Serene Republic had maintained a singularly independent attitude towards the Pontiff. In 1483 its rulers had prevented a Papal Bull from being proclaimed in the city; and now, in the winter of 1605, their defiance was even more flagrant. There were several points at issue. The Venetians had lately passed laws forbidding large donations or legacies to the Church or the erection, without special permission, of new churches and monasteries in their already crowded city. But above all, the new Pope bitterly resented an older law of the Republic which decreed that every Pa-triarch of Venice—and, for that matter, every priest—should be a Venetian by birth; and he was angered by Doge Donato's refusal to send a newly appointed Patriarch to Rome, there to be examined and have his appointment confirmed by the Pope. With this request (or demand) the *Signoria* had flatly refused to comply. It was a matter, they said, for Venice to decide, and Venice alone. If their man went to Rome at all, it would be merely to pay formal homage to His Holiness as Head of the Church.

There was also the question of discipline. Two priests had been charged with grave offences. Yet the Venetians refused to turn them over to the Holy Inquisition and insisted that they should be tried by the Council of Ten, the Holy Office having no right to inflict punishment within the bounds of the Republic. This was independence verging on insolence, which showed a shocking lack of humility.

Pope Paul also repeated Pope Clement's complaint that Venice was too lax in dealing with offences against the Church and that she was far too tolerant with heretics and members of other creeds. For example, not only was the English Ambassador, Sir Henry Wotton, known to receive cases of heretical books, but the Anglican rites were allowed to be performed in the English Embassy in Venice. To this the Doge replied bluntly that Sir Henry lived a quiet life, interfering with and offending nobody, and that it was not the Government's business to pry into an ambassador's baggage.

In all this the Pope was egged on by the influential and fanatical Spanish faction in Rome—the enemies of both the Venetian Republic and England. From their knowledge of the Ambassador's books, it will be seen that the Roman Catholic Church was well served by its agents. Yet one thing is certain. They were outmatched by that pleasant, friendly Englishman who appeared to be so harmless. How much information Sir Henry passed on to the Council of Ten is not known, but he had his own methods of inspecting the correspondence of the newly formed order of Jesuits and his activities were the perfect example of Intelligence disguised as diplomacy.

Finally, the quarrel came to a head, for Pope Paul, ever mindful of the dignity of the Church, was determined to stand firm and assert his authority. This Doge and his councillors lacked humility and must be brought to heel, so after a generous period of grace the whip was cracked and what has come to be known as the Great Interdict was launched. On the seventeenth of April, 1606, Venice was declared excommunicate, the Venetian Ambassador at the Vatican was handed his papers, and in every Catholic country it was made known that the dread sentence had been passed.

But again, times had changed. The Venetian *Signoria* responded with spirit. The Papal Nuncio was informed that he was no longer *persona grata*, and before dismissing him Leonardo Donato made it clear that he considered the sentence of excommunication to be invalid and that in all temporal matters the Doge of Venice acknowledged no superior but God. Priests were ordered to hold their services and administer the sacraments as usual—a gallows erected before a church with closed doors convinced one reluctant cleric that it would be wiser to comply. But most of the clergy (Venetians to a man) refused to obey the dictates of Rome. Only the members of the stricter orders—Jesuits, Capuchins and Theatines—remained loyal to the Pope and were expelled from the city.

The *Signoria's* wisest move, however, was to adopt as their theological expert and adviser Fra Paolo Sarpi, a Servite brother and one of the foremost scholars of the age. It is some measure of his quality that his friend Galileo, the famous astronomer and physicist, used to call the mendicant friar *maestro* and defer to his greater wisdom. This remarkable man—*Il terrible Frate*, as they called him in Rome—organized the defence in the long and ferocious war that followed. It was a war waged, not with swords, but with sermons, pamphlets, anathemas, fulminations, tracts and "apologies," over battlefields which ranged from the Pyrenees to the Baltic. Venice found that she did not lack friends, especially among the Protestant countries. Spain, of course, sided with the Pope, but the States-General of Holland gave strong support and Sir Henry Wotton went so far as to propose an alliance of Venice, England, the Netherlands, the Grisons and some of the German principalities, while France—the France of Henry of Navarre—offered to act as mediator. So, for that matter, did Spain; but though doubtless the gesture was appreciated, it needed more than Iberian courtesy to convince the wily Venetians that Spaniards could ever judge them impartially.

For over a year the state of excommunication continued—Pope against friar, for it was really Sarpi who bore the full brunt of the conflict. In Venice the services of the Church were held as usual. Babies were christened, people were married and buried, Mass was celebrated, as if priests had never heard of the ban. And soon the Pope began to see that he was in an impossible position. He had shot his bolt. It had missed the mark. There was nothing more that he could do. The Venetians had forced him to realize that the Middle Ages were over. The wrath of the Church which had brought Barbarossa to kiss the Papal toe in St Mark's and compelled another emperor to wait in the snow for Hildebrand's pardon at Canossa no longer had the power to make Christians tremble and fear for their salvation. The sword of St Peter had broken in his hand.

But it would seem that Pope Paul was a realist: he began to put out peace feelers. France was only too ready to mediate; and so another wrangle began in which the Pope's plenipotentiary, Cardinal de Joyeuse, tried to impose all the old conditions and the Venetian *Signoria* showed themselves as adamant as ever. They received the Papal envoy seated and without uncovering, and it was only after long negotiations that a compromise was reached, both satisfactory for the Venetians and face-saving for the Pope. It was agreed that the *Signoria's* edict against the excommunication should be revoked and that the Jesuits and other expelled orders should be allowed to return to Venice. But the Venetians refused to alter any of their laws, although, for the sake of peace, they agreed that on this one occasion, but never again, the new Patriarch should go to Rome and have his appointment confirmed by the Pope. As for the two erring priests, they should be delivered, not to the Holy Office, but to the King of France for judgement.

And so the ban of the Church was lifted from that sturdy and stiff-necked race of men who, although religious, had never hesitated to subordinate Catholicism to the welfare of the Republic and who had aptly described themselves as Venetians first and Christians afterwards. Fra Paolo Sarpi, whose courage and cleverness had been the very spirit of the Resistance, was summoned to Rome to give an account of himself but very wisely refused to go. So the Holy Inquisition was powerless. The Republic rewarded this great patriot by making him state councillor in jurisprudence, and Fra Paolo Sarpi returned to the convent of the Servants of Mary.

Already political or private enemies had made several attempts to murder Fra Paolo. So far these had been unsuccessful, but at last one nearly succeeded. On the evening of October 25, 1607, he was waylaid on the bridge of Santa Fosca, not far from the convent of the Servites. The bravos stabbed him three times and then fled for refuge to the house of the Papal Nuncio at San Francesco della Vigna, where they remained until such time as they could escape by sea. Fra Paolo had been left for dead, but miraculously he survived and lived very happily—and very well guarded—for another sixteen years. When he was picked up on that October evening, one dagger was still embedded in him. It had gone in through his ear and come out through his cheekbone, a circumstance which gave rise to a famous pun. Whenever he was asked who had attacked him, he would point to the stiletto and say: "*Agnosco stylum Curiar Romanae.*" ("I recognize the Roman style.")

Whether Fra Paolo's hint was justified can never be proved. It is unthinkable that Pope Paul, a truly saintly man, would have stooped to hire assassins—but it is equally safe to assume that some of his agents would not have hesitated to do so. That Venice had enemies who would stop at nothing was proved by the abortive Bedmar Conspiracy of 1618. At that time there was peace between the Serene Republic and the Holy See, but the enmity of the Spaniards still smouldered and was fanned into flame when Venice gave help to the Duke of Mantua and prevented the marquisate of Montferrat from falling into Spanish hands. And there was anger in the Escurial when the Republic took precautions to ensure her own safety by concluding an alliance with France, the Netherlands, and certain of the Swiss cantons. Steps were taken to exact vengeance, but to what extent this plot had official backing in Spain has never been decided.

The Bedmar Conspiracy is another of those historical puzzles which all through the ages have burgeoned in the Venetian air. Three powerful nobles were involved: the Duke of Ossuna, Viceroy of Naples; the Duke of Toledo, Governor of Milan; and the Marquis of Bedmar, Spanish Ambassador to the Republic of Venice. Their scheme was simple but ambitious: the seizure of the Lido by a fleet from Naples and Sicily; the landing of a Spanish army on the Piazzetta; the destruction of the Doge's Palace, the Arsenal and the Mint; and the wholesale massacre of all who dared to oppose the Spanish rule. To help them, they had bought the services of several French corsairs, of whom the most reliable were two ruffians named Jacques Pierre and Antoine Jaffier. One of their tasks was to enlist all the toughs and bad characters they could find and infiltrate them into Venice. It is said that at one time there were scores of them waiting for the word to rise.

But the Ten were watching.

In 1618 the reigning Doge was Antonio Priuli, rich, generous and renowned for his oratory. But it is only charitable to assume that he was also lacking in observation, for if this honest man had seen what was going on right under his nose, surely he would never have tolerated the shameless rigging of elections. Morals were slackening, rights were abused, and disgraceful irregularities had found their way into the voting procedure. When a seat in the Senate or on one of the councils had to be filled by ballot, it had long been the custom for each voter to drop a ball into a vase. Over the years, the system had become unnecessarily complicated, but it broke down completely when some unscrupulous persons had more than one voting ball in their possession. It was symptomatic of the corruption which was seeping in everywhere, and it was by this trick that a traitor bearing the honoured name of Bragadin gained a seat in the Senate and access to secret information of value to the Spanish Ambassador.

The coup was to take place on Ascension Day, when the Doge and his councillors would be out in the *Bucintoro* at the ceremony of *La Sensa*. But things began to go wrong. The Duke of Ossuna proved to be dilatory and inefficient, and there were too many in on the secret. It has been said that one of the French corsairs sold information to the Ten, but it is unlikely that he would have known more than his own small part in the project. Incredible as it may seem, the fault was undoubtedly Bedmar's, for he made the idiotic mistake of allowing his contact with Bragadin to follow a regular pattern which never varied and which was calculated to arouse the suspicions of the most amateur investigator.

But the Ten were watching and they were no amateurs,

Yet still the Marquis of Bedmar blundered on. No change of procedure, no alteration of time or place to fox his enemies. If ever conspirators deserved to fail it was those Spanish hidalgos and their confederates. Their creature Bragadin frequently visited the church of the Frari. He always knelt by the same faldstool, and always, as soon as he had ended his devotions, his place was taken by another man— who later turned out to be Bedmar's secretary. They appeared to be very devout. Perhaps they overdid it. Perhaps, like so many beginners, they allowed themselves to look furtive. At any rate, some nameless friar, walking or praying in the shadows, became curious about those strange worshippers. Always the same two men, one after the other, kneeling by the same stool. It was certainly odd. So one day, immediately after Bragadin had left the church, the friar examined the stool and found a paper hidden in a slit. The friar, a loyal Venetian, carried it straight to the Doge.

There followed a meeting of the Senate, and at the meeting a trap was set. It was quite a simple little trap but Bragadin fell into it. Casually, he was asked to write some notes. When he had written them, he was shown his report to Bedmar and the handwriting was compared. There was the proof of his guilt in black and white, for this most inept intriguer had made no attempt to disguise his hand; he had used no cryptogram or cypher. In all the long story of secret service was there ever such bungling? No defence was possible. The traitor broke down and confessed everything, declaring that he deserved nothing but death. And death was the penalty he paid. Guards removed him from the Senate Chamber to a dungeon; and there, without further delay, he was strangled by the executioner.

That night the Ten struck.

They had all the information they needed and their *sbirri* went into action. No one knows how many arrests were made, but the next morning the Venetians were horrified to find a row of corpses, each hanging by one leg from a gallows erected between the two columns, on the very spot where the invading Spanish army was to have landed. There are grisly stories of other bodies found floating in the canals—some have said as many as 160, though that is difficult to believe. Yet it is doubtful if many of those involved in this plot to overthrow the Republic escaped the invisible net of the Ten and their inner circle, the Council of Three.

The rest is anticlimax. The Marquis of Bedmar found it advisable to leave Venice in rather a hurry. But there was never any official explanation of why so many men, all strangers in Venice, had been found done to death. There was no public announcement, no Note of remonstrance to the Escurial. Nothing. The secret tribunals preferred to maintain their policy of silence—that terrifying silence, the most powerful weapon in their armoury. It was not until 1674 that the

Abbé de Saint-Réal wrote his classic *Conjuration que les Espagnols formerent en 1618 contre Venise,* and eight years later Otway in his tragedy *Venice Preserved* gave to the world a highly romanticized version of the story. But to the Venetians who lived at the time of the plot it remained a mystery—which was precisely what the Council of Ten and the State Inquisitors intended.

In taking such drastic measures the Ten ran the risk of overplaying their hand, and it was not long before they found themselves in danger of being abolished. As long as this tribunal was believed to be just and impartial, it was tolerated; but it should be remembered that tight as was its grip on the Venetians, it could always be done away with by a vote of the Great Council. A flagrant miscarriage of justice, for instance, might well end its dictatorship.

Such a case occurred in 1622, while people were still shaken by the horrors of the Bedmar affair. The victim was Antonio Foscarini, a patrician who had served his country well as Venetian Ambassador in Paris and London. Somewhat stiff and formal in manner, yet ingratiating enough when he chose, he had won the high regard and friendship of the Queen of England. Unfortunately for him, however, he had also made an implacable enemy of his own secretary, a young man named Guilio Muscorno, who supplemented his income by working as a double agent for Venice and Spain. Whether the Ambassador suspected these activities we are not told, but for some reason he refused to give Muscorno certain references. At the same time, Muscorno became involved in a quarrel with Foscarini's Fool, a halfwitted Scot who had bought two daggers and who threatened to kill him. All things considered, Signor Muscorno decided to return to Venice where he brought the most outrageous charges against his master, accusing him of immorality and of gross disrespect towards the English Queen. These accusations were not upheld by reports from the agents of the Ten; nevertheless, Foscarini was recalled and placed on trial—an investigation which dragged on for three years. At the end of that time he was released, while Muscorno, who had been completely discredited, was sentenced to two years' confinement in a fortress. But Signor Muscorno had sworn to be avenged on his enemy, and somehow, even from prison, he contrived to carry on his vendetta.

Events played into his hands. While he was in England at the court of James I, Foscarini had made the acquaintance of Alethea, wife of Thomas Howard, Earl of Arundel and Surrey. The Howards, now one of the great Roman Catholic families of England, had always had strong inclinations towards Rome; and soon after Foscarini's release, the Countess came to stay in Venice in order to make arrangements for the education of her sons in a country where they would be taught by Catholics. Naturally, Foscarini paid his respects, and it is hardly surprising that at her house he met the Spanish Ambassador.

Foscarini and the Countess were very good friends and soon his visits became more frequent. Moreover, as was not unusual at this time, he went masked. But the eyes and ears of the tribunals were everywhere and the inevitable followed. To Girolamo Vano, a paid spy of the Ten, was given the task of keeping Foscarini under observation. Whether he was also being paid by Muscorno it is impossible to say, but his reports were damning. Accordingly, one April evening in 1622, as Foscarini was leaving the Senate Chamber, a cloak was whipped over his head and he was spirited away to a dungeon. No time was wasted. At a secret trial he was accused of going in disguise to meet the minister of a foreign power and of selling the secrets of the Republic to Spain. He was condemned at once, strangled in prison, and, as a sign that he had died a traitor, he was strung up by one leg from dawn to dusk between the columns on the Piazzetta.

And all the time the man was innocent. He was not the only one to suffer. Returning in her coach from Padua, the Countess of Arundel was met by the news that Foscarini was dead and that she herself was to be asked to leave Venice within three days. This last was a rumour and completely false, but anything more damaging to a lady's reputation it would be difficult to imagine. Fortunately the Countess had courage. She also found another good friend in the English Ambassador, Sir Henry Wotton, who, when he heard her story, accompanied her to the Doge. All possible steps were taken to scotch the rumour, and a written exoneration signed by Doge Priuli was despatched to London. Both King James and the Earl of Arundel later expressed their appreciation of His Serenity's courtesy and kindness.

Four months later, suspicion began to fall on the spy, Girolamo Vano. Whether or not he was given a turn of the rack to help his memory is not recorded, but it was revealed that his evidence had been a tissue of lies. He in his turn was strangled, as he deserved; and, to do them justice, the Ten made full confession of their tragic mistake. The innocence of Antonio Foscarini was proclaimed; he was given a public funeral, and all the honours forfeited at his death were restored to his family.

It was one of the very few occasions on which the Ten lifted the veil of secrecy which shrouded their actions. Why they should have done so is still uncertain—perhaps they realized that the confidence of the people had been shaken and that their very existence rested on a single vote. Once suspicions were aroused, it was logical that other misdemeanours of the tribunal would come to light; and soon the inevitable reformer arose in the person of Reniero Zeno, a fearless and dedicated councillor who had already held several important posts in the service of the Republic.

At this time there was a new Doge, Giovanni Cornaro, a man, like so many of his associates, already corrupt and, in particular, tainted with the vice of nepotism. It was forbidden for a Doge's relatives to benefit financially from his high office, but the favours which Cornaro obtained for his family soon became a public scandal. To mention only three of the most flagrant offences: his brother, Dean of St Mark's, when travelling to Rome was allowed a cardinal's expenses; one of his sons was given a cardinal's hat, which was absolutely against the law; and another son, Giorgio, illegally imported cattle from Zara, a very profitable racket to which the Venetian authorities shut their eyes.

It was against such irregularities as these, as well as against the secret tribunals, that Reniero Zeno waged war for several years. By doing so he made the Cornari his enemies and was banished from the city. But in 1627 a public outcry hastened his return, and probably to his own surprise he found that he had actually been elected a member of the Council of Ten. Perhaps the other members considered this an effective way of muzzling him. But if so they were wrong, for he promptly used his new position to continue his fight against corruption. He was a born iconoclast, blunt, proud, outspoken and no respecter of persons. There were stormy scenes in the Hall of the Great Council, during which the Doge was discomfited and had to give way.

But this was seventeenth-century Italy and Zeno should have

foreseen the next move. One evening as he was leaving the Doge's Palace, five assassins attacked him under the Porta della Carta. Perhaps they did their work badly or they may have been disturbed. In any case, though badly wounded, Reniero Zeno escaped with his life and managed to stagger or crawl to one of the gondolas on the Molo. The bravos, of course, remained "unknown," but the fact that Giorgio Cornaro fled from Venice that night was regarded by some as significant.

As soon as he had recovered, Zeno renewed his attack on corruption and, even when ordered to do so by the Ten, refused to pledge himself to keep their secrets. There were more incredible scenes in the Great Council, with everybody shouting at once and councillors banging the benches to make themselves heard above the pandemonium. The Ten passed another sentence on Zeno—banishment for ten years to the fortress of Cattaro—but this aroused so much indignation that it was hastily dropped and all records of the sentence were ordered to be destroyed.

The Ten must have known that their very existence as a tribunal was threatened, for Zeno had turned the majority of the Great Council against them and a hostile vote could mean abolition. But they were clever. They bowed before the storm and made several minor concessions, while a committee which had been formed to reduce their power did nothing but foolishly abolish the *Zonta*—that body of co-opted members which for so many years had ensured a fair trial for the accused in difficult or unusual cases.

So the Ten won. By yielding a little they regained the support of the majority, and all Zeno's work had been for nothing. He had hoped to return to the Great Council the power now held by the secret tribunals. But when it came to a showdown, those supine Venetian politicians lacked the spirit to loosen their chains. They had grown used to them. Freedom no longer seemed so desirable. Therefore the Council of Ten survived and everything went on as before.

And then fate struck another blow. Venice suffered the loss of Crete—or Candia, as not only the principal city but the whole island was called in those days. The Candiot War dragged on for over twenty years and drained the Republic of blood and treasure, but it kindled another of those temporary revivals of her old fighting spirit.

Indeed, so many valiant feats of arms were performed by land and sea that some thought to see Venice regain her lost place among the nations.

Once again the Republic found herself at war with her old enemies the Ottomans—a war forced upon her by an aggressor and which no statecraft could have averted. A Turkish fleet carrying pilgrims to Mecca was destroyed by some ships from Malta which afterwards sought shelter in the Venetian port of Canea on the northwest coast of Crete. This gave the Sultan Ibrahim just the excuse he needed to launch an attack on the island and annex it to the Turkish Empire. But he went about it with great cunning. He could not conceal from Venetian agents that he was fitting out a fleet, but he let it be known that he sought to avenge himself on the Knights of Malta. He reproached Venice for allowing enemies to take shelter in her harbours; then, while negotiations were still in progress and without any declaration of war, he struck. On the thirtieth of April, 1645, a Turkish squadron cast anchor outside Canea. Realizing that resistance would be useless, the Venetian commander fired the magazine of the citadel, blowing up himself and the garrison—and the Turks had a foothold on the island. But the conquest was to occupy them for nearly a quarter of a century, thus tying their hands and weakening them in other spheres of action. If it had not been for the running sore of Crete, John Sobieski might not have been able to drive them from the walls of Vienna.

The Republic rose to meet the challenge. The Lido fortifications were strengthened; troops were rushed to Dalmatia and Istria; and Venetian warships scoured the seas for Barbary corsairs in almost her old style. But certain other measures were taken which did not redound to her credit. The State, being in desperate need of money, required every citizen to hand in three-quarters of his gold and silver plate; and high office and rank were quite shamelessly put up for sale. Those who wished to become members of the nobility were merely asked to prove that they were legitimate and that neither they nor their fathers or grandfathers had been what Shakespeare called "rude mechanicals." Honour thus satisfied and a handsome donation paid into the coffers, the happy aspirants were duly proclaimed patricians of Venice. A few fortunate foreigners were also admitted—

at a slightly higher fee. So seed was planted which a hundred years later was to bear bitter fruit.

This time Italian help was forthcoming, though it was feeble and ineffective. The Pope and the rulers of Naples and Tuscany each sent five galleys to take part in this new crusade against the infidel. But the ships never reached Crete and their commanders did not show the slightest inclination for action.

The main theatre of war stretched from the Adriatic to Constantinople, though there must have been many engagements between Venetians and the North African corsairs—nameless encounters which left no record but floating bodies and gutted ships. All the fighting, however, centred on Candia, the Cretan capital. It was one of the great sieges of history, with the garrison hopelessly outnumbered but holding on grimly, and even the women hurling stones at the swarming hordes of Janissaries and bashi-bazouks. Drums and cymbals sounded relentlessly, day after day, week after week. The Turkish artillery, which included the largest gun yet seen, reduced strong ramparts to rubble. Breaches had to be repaired and held. Once the Turks occupied a bastion looking straight down into the Piazza. People lived in pits—we would call them dugouts now—and beneath the defences there was a network of mines and countermines. As a result, ferocious fights took place underground when the dividing wall of earth caved in and the rival sappers met face to face with knives and picks and shovels.

There was some slight hope that the siege might end when news came from Constantinople that the Sultan Ibrahim had been murdered in his own seraglio; and the Venetians, thinking to take advantage of the changed situation, sent the usual envoys to congratulate his successor and explore the possibilities of peace. But the new Sultan, Mohammed IV, would not even listen. When he heard that Candia refused to surrender, he ordered the interpreter to be strangled out of hand and the Christian envoys dagged though the steets in chains.

In 1651 the Venetians, heavily outnumbered as usual, won a sea battle near the island of Paros. Francesco Morosini was made commander in chief, but in Venice rivals intrigued against him and he was recalled to face a court-martial. He was honourably acquitted; and then, in 1667, he was sent to relieve Candia. His task was hopeless and he must have known it. No building in the city, which was constantly rocked by explosions, remained intact; and there was little relief from bombardment and hand-to-hand fighting on the walls. Between the months of May and November no fewer than 618 mines were sprung, 32 major assaults were repulsed, and there were 17 sorties. All of which meant loss of men.

It is true that reinforcements, some of them volunteers, were able to make their way into the city, but many of them were more of a hindrance than a help. It had become fashionable for the young bloods of Europe to serve a term in Candia—which usually meant displays of bravado, madcap sallies against the Turkish lines, and a waste of good soldiers trying to save fools from the consequences of their own folly. France had been generous in her help, but a strong force under the Duc de Beaufort contained too many daredevils. What was needed was stubborn endurance and unspectacular defensive tactics; but *Toujours l'attaque!* seems to have been the gallant Frenchmen's motto; and, against the commander in chief's express wishes, they hurled themselves at the enemy. The result was two hundred heads (incluuding de Beaufort's) on spears, paraded before the Turkish Vizier, Achmet Kiupergli.

Fortunately for his surviving men, Morosini understood that this was no time for heroics. In courage he was second to none; but he could see that further resistance was useless and he was not prepared to hand over men, women and children to torture and slavery. Accordingly, after holding a council of war and asking the opinion of his officers, he opened negotiations with Achmet and obtained reasonable terms. The city had to be surrendered, of course, but the Vizier was a man of honour and kept his word. Both soldiers and civilians were given safe-conduct through the Turkish lines; and then, on September 27, 1669, Francesco Morosini delivered up the keys of Candia. The siege had ended in the destruction of the city and a loss to the Republic of 30,000 killed and wounded.

There can be no doubt that in capitulating without orders from his superiors, Morosini risked being court-martialled for the second time and sentenced to death. Legally he had put himself in the wrong; but although the Venetians were not noted for leniency towards unsuccessful commanders, they recognized that the circumstances were exceptional. The Captain-General was made to stand trial—his enemies saw to that!—but he was triumphantly acquitted again, and as a reward for his courage and patriotism, he was made a Procurator of St Mark. All Europe applauded.

Twice more was this future Doge to draw his sword against the Ottomans. In 1684, after a brilliant campaign, he reconquered the Morea and liberated Athens; and the enemy so dreaded the sound of his name that a Turkish fleet in the Archipelago retreated at the approach of his ships, refusing to give battle. Considering the fanatical heroism of the Turks, that was perhaps the finest compliment that Morosini was ever paid.

17. An Englishman Abroad

John Evelyn
Sightseeing
Night Life in Venice
Carnival

The noble church of Santa Maria della Salute was slowly rising. Except for that, Venice in the mid-seventeenth century looked almost as she does today, though people of quality were wearing their clothes with that elegant air of unbuttoned ease which has become familiar to us through the paintings of Van Dyck. Many of the patricians favoured their own distinctive costumes, but there were visitors from every country in Europe: ringleted ladies in full-sleeved satin gowns with collars and cuffs of the famous Venetian lace, and long-haired gentlemen in buff bucket-boots and wide cavalier hats with sweeping plumes. There could be no better guide to the pleasure-loving Venice of that time than an Englishman abroad, Mr John Evelyn of Wotton House, near Dorking in the county of Surrey, whose diary is one of the delights of English literature.

In 1642, three years before the Turks attacked Candia, civil war had broken out in England. John Evelyn was loyal to King Charles, but after one brief appearance on the battlefield (a trifle late), he decided that martial glory was not for him. As he put it: "12th November was the battle of Brentwood surprisingly fought. . . . I came in with my horse and arms just at the retreat; but was not permitted to stay longer than the 15th by reason of the army marching to Gloucester; which would have left both me and my brothers exposed to ruin, without any advantage to His Majesty . . . and on the 10th (of December) returned to Wotton, nobody knowing of my having been with His Majesty's army."

To have remained in England would have meant declaring himself Cavalier or Roundhead, so, having obtained the King's permission to travel abroad in 1643, Mr Evelyn made a leisurely progress through Holland, France and Italy—and so to Venice, where he arrived in the month of June 1645 and took up comfortable lodgings at the inn of the Black Eagle, near the Rialto Bridge. "The next morning," he reports, "finding myself extremely weary and beaten with my journey, I went to one of their bagnios, where you are treated after the Eastern manner, washing with hot and cold water, with oils, and being rubbed with a kind of strigil of seal's-skin, put on the operator's hand like a glove. This bath did so open my pores that it cost me one of the worst colds I ever had in my life."

Evelyn and his companions had hurried from Rome so as to be in Venice on Ascension Day, when the Doge rowed out in the *Bucintoro* for his *Spozalizio del Mare*. He tells us of his first experience of a gondola: "Two days after, taking a gondola, which is their water-coach (for land ones, there are many old men in this city who never saw one, or rarely a horse) we rowed up and down the channels which answer to our streets. These vessels are built very long and narrow, having necks and tails of steel, somewhat spreading at the beak like a fish's tail, and kept so exceedingly polished as to give a great lustre; some are adorned with carving, others lined with velvet (commonly black), with curtains and tassels, and seats like couches, to lie stretched on, while he who rows stands upright on the very edge of the boat, and, with one oar bending forward as if he would fall into the sea, rows and turns with incredible dexterity, thus passing from channel to channel, landing his fare or patron at what house he pleases."

He was much impressed by the Rialto Bridge with its one great arch and "pretty shops." He continues: "It was evening and the Canal where the Noblesse go to take the air . . . was full of ladies and gentlemen. There are many times dangerous stops by reason of the multitude of gondolas ready to sink one another; and indeed they affect to lean them on one side, that one who is not accustomed to it would be afraid of over-setting. Here they were singing, playing on harpsichords, and other music, and serenading their mistresses; in another place racing and other pastimes upon the water, it being now exceeding hot.

"Next day I went to their exchange, a place like ours frequented by merchants, but nothing so magnificent: from thence my guide led me to the Fondigo di Todeschi, which is their magazine, and here many of the merchants, especially Germans, have their lodging and diet, as in a college. The outside of this stately fabric is painted by Giorgione de Castelfranco, and Titian himself.

"Hence I passed through the Merceria, which is one of the most delicious streets in the world for the sweetness of it, and is all the way on both sides tapestried as it were with cloth of gold, rich damasks and other silks, which the shops expose and hang before their houses from the first floor, and with that variety that for nearly half the year spent chiefly in this city, I hardly remember to have seen the same piece twice exposed; to this add the perfumes, apothecaries' shops, and the innumerable cages of nightingales which they keep, which entertain you with their melody from shop to shop, so that shutting your eyes you would imagine yourself in the country, when indeed you are in the midst of the sea. It is almost as silent as the middle of a field, there being neither rattling of coaches nor trampling of horses. This street, paved with brick and exceedingly clean, brought us through an arch into the famous piazza of St Mark.

"Over this porch stands that admirable clock, celebrated next to that of Strasburg for its many movements; amongst which, about twelve and six, which are their hours for Ave Maria, when all the town are on their knees, come forth the three Kings led by a star, and passing by the image of Christ in His Mother's arms, do their reverence, and enter into the clock by another door. At the top of this turret another automaton strikes the quarters; and an honest merchant told me that one day walking in the Piazza, he saw the fellow who kept the clock struck with this hammer so forcibly, as he was stooping his head near the bell to mend something amiss at the instant of striking, that being stunned, he reeled over the battlements and broke his neck.

"And so we entered into St Mark's Church, before which stand two brass pedestals exquisitely cast and figured, which bear as many tall masts painted red, on which, upon great festivals they hang flags and streamers."

It would seem that John Evelyn made one slight mistake here, for he mentioned only two of Leopardi's pedestals. The pedestals were cast in 1505 for the flags of Crete, Cyprus and the Morea, and all three were certainly there a hundred years after Evelyn's visit, for they were painted by Canaletto. What is more, they are made of bronze, not brass. But why quibble about the little slips of a man who has given us this unforgettable description of the Basilica:

"The church is . . . Gothic; yet for the preciousness of the materials being of several rich marbles, abundance of porphyry, serpentine etc., far exceeding any in Rome, St Peter's hardly excepted. I much admired the splendid history of our blessed Saviour, composed all of mosaic over the *facciata,* below which and over the chief gate are four horses cast in copper as big as the life, the same that formerly were transported from Rome by Constantine to Byzantium, and thence by the Venetians hither. They are supported by eight porphyry columns of very great size and value. Being come into the church, you see nothing and tread on nothing, but what is precious. The floor is all inlaid with agates, lazulis, calcedons, jaspers, porphyries and other rich marbles, admirable also for the work; the walls sumptuously encrusted and presenting to the imagination the shapes of men, birds, houses, flowers, and a thousand varieties. The roof is of most excellent mosaic; but what most persons admire is the new work of the emblematic tree at the other passage out of the church. In the midst of this rich volto rise five cupolas, the middle very large and sustained by thirty-six marble columns, eight of which are of precious marbles: under these cupolas is the high altar, on which is a reliquary of several sorts of jewels, engraved with figures after the Greek manner and set together with plates of pure gold. The altar is covered with a canopy of ophite, on which is sculptured the story of the Bible, and so on the pillars, which are of Parian marble, that support it. Behind these are four other columns of transparent and true Oriental alabaster, brought hither out of the mines of Solomon's Temple as they report."

In John Evelyn's description of St Mark's we find mention of several objects of sacred or historical interest which we have en-

countered before. He goes on: "There are many chapels and notable
monuments of illustrious persons, dukes, cardinals, etc., as Zeno,
J. Soranzi, and others: there is likewise a vast baptistery of copper.
Among other venerable relics is a stone on which they say our Blessed
Lord stood preaching to those of Tyre and Sidon, and near the door
is an image of Christ, much adorned, esteeming it very sacred, for
that a rude fellow striking it, they say there gushed out a torrent of
blood. . . . Going out of the church they showed us the stone where
Alexander III trod on the neck of the Emperor Barbarossa."

After a detailed account of the fabulously rich contents of the
Treasury, and one criticism—that, in his opinion, St Mark's was
"much too dark and dismal, and of heavy work"—Mr Evelyn reverts
to secular matters. "A French gentleman and myself went to the
Courts of Justice, the Senate-house and Ducal Palace. The first court
near this church is almost wholly built of several coloured sorts of
marble, like chequer-work on the outside; this is sustained by vast
pillars, not very shapely, but observable for their capitals, and that out
of thirty-three no two are alike. Under this fabric is the cloister
where merchants meet morning and evening, as also the grave senators and gentlemen, to confer of state affairs in their gowns and caps,
like so many philosophers; 'tis a very noble and solemn spectacle. In
another quadrangle stood two square columns of white marble,
carved, which they said had been erected to hang one of their Dukes
on who designed to make himself Sovereign. Going through a stately
arch there were standing in divers niches statues of great value,
among which is the so celebrated *Eve*, esteemed worth its weight in
gold; it is just opposite to the stairs where are *Colossuses of Mars* and
Neptune by Sansovino. We went up into a corridor built with several
Tribunals and Courts of Justice; and by a well-contrived staircase
were landed in the Senate-hall, which appears to be one of the most
noble and spacious rooms in Europe, being seventy-six paces long
and thirty-two in breadth. At the upper end are the Tribunals of the
Doge, Council of Ten, and Assistants; in the body of the hall are
lower ranks of seats capable of containing 1500 Senators, for they
consist of no fewer on grand debates. Over the Duke's throne are the
paintings of the *Final Judgement* by Tintoretto, esteemed among the
best pieces in Europe. On the roof are the famous *Acts of the Republic*, painted by several excellent masters, especially Bassano; next

to them are the effigies of the several Dukes, with their Elogies. Then, we turned into a great Court painted with the *Battle of Lepanto,* an excellent piece; afterwards, into the Chamber of the Council of Ten, painted by the most celebrated masters. From hence, by the special favour of an *Illustrissimo,* we were carried to see the private Armoury of the Palace, and so to the same court we first entered, nobly built of polished white marble, part of which is the Duke's Court *pro tempore;* there are two walls adorned with excellent work in copper. This led us to the seaside, where stand those two columns of ophite stone in the entire piece, of a great height, one bearing St Mark's Lion, the other St Theodorus: these pillars were brought from Greece, and set up by Nicholas Baraterius, the architect; between them public executions are performed.

"Having fed our eyes with the noble prospect of the Island of St George, the galleys, gondolas, and other vessels passing to and fro, we walked under the cloister on the other side of this goodly piazza, being a most magnificent building, the design of Sansovino. Here we went into the *Zecca* or Mint; at the entrance stand two prodigious giants, or Hercules, of white marble: we saw them melt, beat, and coin silver, gold and copper. We then went up to the Procuratory, and a library of excellent MSS and books belonging to it and the public. After this, we climbed up the Tower of St Mark, which we might have done on horseback, as it is said one of the French Kings did; there being no stairs, or steps, but returns that take up an entire square on the arches forty feet, broad enough for a coach. This steeple stands by itself without any church near it, and is rather a watch tower in the corner of the great Piazza, 230 feet in height [most authorities give the height as 325 feet], the foundation exceeding deep; on the top is an angel, that turns with the wind; and from hence is a prospect down the Adriatic, as far as Istria and the Dalmatian side, with the surprising sight of this miraculous city, lying on the bosom of the sea, in the shape of a lute, the numberless islands tacked together by no fewer than 450 bridges. At the foot of this tower is a public tribunal of excellent work in white marble polished, adorned with several brass statues and figures of stone and mezzo-relievo, the performance of some rare artist.

"It was now Ascension-Week and the great mart or fair of the whole year was kept, every body at liberty and jolly; the noblemen stalking with their ladies on *choppines*. These are high-heeled shoes, particularly affected by these proud dames, or, as some say, invented to keep them at home, it being very difficult to walk with them; whence, one being asked how he liked the Venetian dames, replied that they were *mezzo carne, mezzo ligno* (half flesh, half wood) and he would have none of them. The truth is, their garb is very odd, as seeming always in masquerade; their other habits are also totally different from all nations. They wear very long crisp hair, of several streaks and colours which they make so by a wash, dishevelling it on the brims of a broad hat that has no crown, but a hole to put out their heads by; they dry them in the sun, as one may see them at their windows. In their tire they set silk flowers and sparkling stones, their petticoats coming from their very arm-pits, so that they are near three quarters and a half apron; their sleeves are made exceedingly wide, under which their shift sleeves as wide, and commonly tucked up to the shoulder, showing their naked arms, through false sleeves of tiffany, girt with a bracelet or two, with knots of point richly tagged about their shoulders and other places of their body, which they usually cover with a kind of yellow veil, of lawn, very transparent. Thus attired, they set their hands on the heads of two matron-like servants, or old women, to support them, who are mumbling their beads. It is ridiculous to see how these ladies crawl in and out of their gondolas, by reason of their *choppines;* and what dwarfs they appear, when taken down from their wooden scaffolds, of these I saw near thirty together, stalking half as high again as the rest of the world. For courtesans or the citizens may not wear *choppines*, but cover their bodies and faces with a veil of a certain glittering taffeta, or lustree, out of which they now and then dart a glance of their eye, the whole face being otherwise entirely hid with it; nor may the common misses take this habit, but go abroad barefaced. To the corners of these virgin-veils hang broad but flat tassels of curious Point de Venice. The married women go in black veils. The nobility wear the same colour, but a fine cloth lined with taffeta, in summer, with fur of the bellies of squirrels, in the winter, which all put on at a certain day, girt with a girdle embossed with silver; the vest not being much different from what our Bachelors of Art wear in Oxford, and a hood of cloth, made like a sack, cast over their left shoulder, and a round cloth black cap fringed with wool, which is not so comely; they also wear their collar open, to show the diamond buckle of the stock of their shirt. I have never seen pearl for colour and bigness comparable to what the ladies wear, most of the noble families being very rich in jewels, especially pearls, which are always left to the son or brother who is destined to marry; which the eldest seldom do. The Doge's vest is of crimson velvet, the Procurator's etc. of damask, very stately. Nor was I less surprised with the strange variety of the several nations seen every day in the streets and piazzas: Jews, Turks, Armenians, Persians, Moors, Greeks, Sclavonians, some with their targets and bucklers, and all in their native fashions, negotiating in this famous Emporium, which is always crowded with strangers. . . .

"This night, having with my Lord Bruce taken our places before, we went to the Opera, where comedies and other plays are represented in recitative music, by the most excellent musicians, vocal and instrumental, with variety of scenes painted and contrived with no less art of perspective, and machines for flying in the air, and other wonderful notions; taken together, it is one of the most magnificent and expensive diversions the wit of man can invent. The history was, *Hercules in Lydia;* the scenes changed thirteen times. The famous voices, Anna Rencia, a Roman, and reputed the best treble of women; but there was an eunuch who, in my opinion surpassed her, also a Genoese that sung an incomparable bass. This held us by the eyes and ears till two in the morning, when we went to the Chetto de San Felice, to see the noblemen and their ladies play at Basset, a game of cards which is much used; but they play not in public, and all that have inclination to it are in masquerade, without speaking one word, and so they come in, play, lose or gain, and go away as they please. This time of licence is only in Carnival and this Ascension-Week; neither are their theatres open for that other magnificence, or for ordinary comedians, save on these solemnities, they being a frugal and wise people, and exact observers of all sumptuary laws."

Hearing that there was a ship about to sail for the Holy Land, Evelyn decided to see Jerusalem, Syria, Egypt and Turkey. He even laid in a stock of provisions—including two sheep—and a medicine chest in case of illness. Then, at the last minute, he was disappointed. ". . . our vessel (whereof Captain Powell was master) happened to be pressed for the service of the State, to carry provisions to Candia, now newly attacked by the Turks; which altogether frustrated my design, to my great mortification." So he paid the first of several visits to Padua instead, and on his return was taken over the great Arsenal of Venice. This enormous shipyard was one of the wonders of Europe, but clearly his guide exaggerated. Galleasses with twenty-eight banks of oars and stands of arms for 800,000 men are hardly credible. He goes on:

"The arsenal is thought to be one of the best furnished in the world. We entered by a strong port, always guarded, and, ascending by a spacious gallery, saw arms of back, breast and head, for many thousands; in another were saddles; over them, ensigns taken from the Turks. Another hall is for the meeting of the Senate; passing a graff [a trench or moat] are the smith's forges, where they are continually employed on anchors and iron work. Near it is a well of fresh water, which they impute to two rhinoceros's horns which they say lie in it, and will preserve it from ever being empoisoned. Then we came to where the carpenters were building their magazines of oars, masts, etc., for an hundred galleys and ships, which have all their apparel and furniture near them. Then the foundry, where they cast ordnance; the forge is 450 paces long, and one of them has thirteen furnaces. There is one cannon weighing 16,573 lbs., cast while Henry the Third dined, and put into a galley, built, rigged, and fitted for launching within that time. They have also arms for twelve galleasses, which are vessels to row, of almost 150 feet long, and thirty wide, not counting prow or poop, and contain twenty-eight banks of oars, each seven men, and to carry 1300 men with three masts. In another, a magazine for fifty galleys, and a place for some hundreds more. Here stands the *Bucentaur*, with an ample deck and so contrived that the slaves are not seen, having on the poop a throne for the Doge to sit, when he goes in triumph to espouse the Adriatic. Here is also a gallery of 200 yards long for cables, and above that a magazine for hemp. Opposite these are the saltpetre houses, and a large row of cells or houses to protect their galleys from the weather. Over the gate, as we go out, is a room full of great and small guns, some of which discharge six times at once. Then there is a court full of cannon, bullets, chains, grapples, grenadoes, etc., and over that arms for 800,000 men, and by themselves arms for 400, taken from some that were in a plot against the State; together with weapons of offence and defence for sixty-two ships; thirty-two pieces of ordnance, on carriages taken from the Turks, and one prodigious mortar-piece. In a word, it is not to be reckoned up what this large place contains of this sort. There are now twenty-three galleys and four galley-grossi of 100 oars of a side. The whole arsenal is walled about, and may be in compass about three miles, with twelve towers for the watch, besides that the sea environs it. The workmen, who are ordinarily 500, march out in military order, and every evening receive their pay through a small hole in the gate where the governor lives.

"The next day I saw a wretch executed, who had murdered his master, for which he had his head chopped off by an axe that slid down a frame of timber, between the two tall columns in St Mark's piazza, at the seabrink; the executioner striking on the axe with a beetle; and so the head fell off the block."

By San Zanipolo Evelyn admired Verrocchio's statue of Colleoni. He also visited a number of churches, including San Giorgio dei Greci, where he had an argument with a Candiot Greek about a religious procession. There followed another short visit to Padua and its famous university.

"Three days after, I returned to Venice, and passed over to Murano, famous for the best glasses in the world, where having viewed their furnaces, and seen their work, I made a collection of diverse curiosities and glasses, which I sent for England by long sea. It is the white flints they have from Pavia, which they pound and sift exceedingly small, and mix with ashes made of a sea-weed out of Syria, and a white sand, that causes this manufacture to excel. The town is a Podestaria by itself, at some miles distant on the sea from Venice, and like it built upon several small islands. In this place are excellent oysters, small and well-tasted like our Colchester, and they were the first, as I remember, that I could eat; for I had naturally an aversion to them.

"At our return to Venice, we met several gondolas full of Venetian ladies, who come thus far in fine weather to take the air, with music and other refreshments."

There followed two more journeys to Padua—the first to decline the very great privilege of becoming *Syndicus Artistarum* at the University. Evelyn's decision did not please certain Englishmen who had worked hard for his election, but it was a wise one, for it could have proved an expensive honour and it would most certainly have impeded the progress of his tour.

The second visit was even less enjoyable, for the streets of Padua had become extremely dangerous after dark. The city was infested with soldiers on the loose and those perennial pests, the student-hooligans. "Many houses were broken open in the night, some murders committed, and the nuns next our lodging disturbed, so as we were forced to be on our guard with pistols and other fire-arms to defend our doors."

Then, to crown it all, Evelyn was taken ill, through drinking wine cooled with snow and ice, though by Christmas he had recovered sufficiently to join with his friends in inviting all the English and Scots in Padua to a feast, "which sunk our excellent wine considerably."

Sometime after the first of the year Evelyn returned to Venice. His diary records: "1646. In January, Signor Molino was chosen Doge of Venice, but the extreme snow that fell, and the cold, hindered my going to see the solemnity, so I stirred not from Padua till Shrovetide, when all the world repairs to Venice, to see the folly and madness of the Carnival; the men, women, and persons of all conditions disguising themselves in antique dresses, with extravagant music and a thousand gambols, traversing the streets from house to house, all place being then accessible and free to enter. Abroad, they fling eggs filled with sweet water, but sometimes not over-sweet. They also have a barbarous custom of hunting bulls about the streets and piazzas, which is very dangerous, the passages being generally narrow. The youth of the several wards and parishes contend in other masteries and pastimes, so that it is impossible to recount the universal madness of this place during this time of license. The great banks are set up for those who will play at basset; the comedians have liberty, and the operas are open; witty pasquils are thrown about, and the mountebanks have their stages at every corner. The diversion which chiefly took me up was three noble operas, where there were excellent voices and music, the most celebrated of which was the famous Anna Rencia, whom we invited to a fish-dinner after four days in Lent, when they had given over at the theatre. Accompanied with an eunuch whom she brought with her, she entertained us with rare music, both of them singing to a harpsichord. It growing late, a gentleman of Venice came for her, to show her the galleys, now ready to sail for Candia. This entertainment produced a second, given to us by the English consul of the merchants, inviting us to his house, where he had the

Genoese, the most celebrated bass in Italy, who was one of the late opera-band. This diversion held us so late at night, that, conveying a gentlewoman who had supped with us to her gondola at the usual place of landing, we were shot at by two carbines from another gondola, in which were a noble Venetian and his courtesan unwilling to be disturbed, which made us run in and fetch other weapons, not knowing what the matter was, till we were informed of the danger we might incur by pursuing it farther. Three days after this, I took my leave of Venice."

And so, after one brief return to the city to say goodbye to his friends, this most curious and observant traveller began his homeward journey across the Plain of Lombardy and the Alps. He was one of a party which, to his intense disgust, included another gentleman who was as staunch a Roundhead as he was a Royalist. There can be no doubt that the dislike was mutual; but, being two Englishmen abroad, there can also be no doubt that they were both too reserved and polite to say so.

In Paris John Evelyn married and then returned to England. He refused employment under Oliver Cromwell, and all through the Protectorate, at some risk, he carried on a correspondence in cipher with the exiled Charles II.

After the Restoration he enjoyed court favour until the end of his long and happy life. He was never appointed to high office, but he held several minor posts under Charles II, James II and William III. Like his friend Samuel Pepys and, indeed, King Charles himself, he remained at his post during the plague; but the dissolute court of Whitehall, that haunt of rakes and harlots, disgusted him as it disgusted all decent men. He strongly opposed James II's attempts to force the Roman Catholic religion on his unwilling country, and courageously refused to license Papist literature attacking the Church of England. In 1706 he died at the age of eighty-five.

John Evelyn of Wotton was no genius, but he was a scholar blessed with interest in everything about him and the ability to communicate his enthusiasm. We can read his account of the Venice of his time and say confidently, as he would have said himself: "Thus it was."

18. The City of Masks

The Triumph of the Three
The Playground of Europe
The Credit Side
The Final Phase

Francesco Morosini was the last Doge to command the forces of the Republic in action; and for five years after his death in 1694, the Venetians had to face the Turks without his inspired leadership. They lost battle after battle, and the signing of the peace treaty of Carlowitz left the once mighty Serenissima shorn of all her overseas possessions except the Morea, the island of Corfu, and some isolated towns in Greece and Dalmatia.

War-weary and weakened, Venice played no part in the war of the Spanish Succession—and paid the price of neutrality by finding herself almost friendless when the Ottomans attacked the Morea again in 1714. It is true that she received some help from the Pope, the Grand Duke of Tuscany, and the Knights of Malta, but never enough to be effective. Such territory as remained from the conquests of Morosini was stripped from her, piece by piece; and she was only saved from further humiliations by the brilliant victories of Prince Eugene in Austria and the Balkans, culminating in the capture of Belgrade. Realizing that in the Imperial armies they had met their match, the Turks sullenly withdrew from the Greek Archipelago to lick their wounds and regroup their forces in the face of this new threat. But when they had gone and another peace treaty was signed,

Venice was treated as of no account and was forced to relinquish the Morea. Verona, Padua, Vicenza and other towns on the mainland were still hers, but outside Italy only Corfu remained.

So from this time until almost the end of the eighteenth century, the story of the Venetian Republic becomes a social rather than a political history, for although she maintained a facade of greatness, in reality she had abandoned all thought of power and, for the second time in nine hundred years, had retreated to Rialto. From now on she confined her dominions to the capital itself, the adjacent islands, the cities of the Veneto, and Corfu. Wisely she had renounced conquest and was enlightened enough to discard war as an instrument of policy. Her one aim now was peace. But unfortunately it was not the peace of the Strong Man Armed who seeks no quarrel with his neighbour: this was to be peace at any price, for her leaders, it would seem, believed that if she was helpless she might be left alone.

She cut the Lion's claws and clipped his wings. There were still ships in the yards of the Arsenal, but many of them were without crews and quite unfit to put to sea. As for her army of mercenaries—that was disbanded except for a regiment or two to keep law and order; and before the end of the century it was said, only half jokingly, that most of her small stock of gunpowder had been used for fireworks. But her chief lack was moral fibre, especially among her rulers. Defeat by the Turks and a long period of enervating ease and self-indulgence had sapped her spirit and her will to resist. The Bride of the Sea was going the same way as Byzantium.

Impotent abroad, and at home helpless in the grip of tyranny the more shameful because it was self-imposed: that was the plight in which the Republic found herself in her pitiful old age. The eighteenth century was the Age of Reason; and the new intellectuals, many of them atheists and rebels, stirred restlessly under the iron rule of the Inquisitors of State. For the Council of Three, gradually usurping more and more power, had become a law unto itself and committed various despotic acts which were anathema to advanced thinkers. But the rebellious intellectuals had their remedy—or thought they had. The Three, it will be remembered, were also members of the Council of Ten and were answerable to the larger tribunal which, in its turn—in theory, at least—received its orders from the Great Council. So an enquiry was ordered and five *Correttori* or investigators were appointed to examine all allegations of abuses by the Three. In due course their findings were published, and they were not unanimous. The *Correttori* were two against three. The minority were for curbing or even abolishing the State Inquisitors, a move which, their opponents suggested, would later be followed by the suppression of the Council of Ten. But the majority, arguing that the autocratic behaviour of the Three had been exaggerated, favored preserving the status quo, except that they wished the State Inquisitors to be independent of the Ten. Marco Foscarini, a Procurator, soon to be Doge, came down heavily on their side; and what was to become, to all intents and purposes, absolute rule by the Three was confirmed by a small majority in the Great Council.

The victory of the State Inquisitors was greeted with enthusiasm by both the patricians and the people, for both parties fondly imagined that it would be to their advantage to have unseen but strong hands on the reins. Each class wished to see the other restrained, and the method did not trouble them, for they had grown used to dictatorship and forgotten the very smell of freedom. Foscarini and the three *Correttori* who had been in the majority were feted with serenades and fireworks, while the unfortunate investigators who had struck this last blow for liberty were in danger of having their houses burned down by the mob and, ironically, were only saved by the servants of those very Inquisitors whom they had tried to suppress. So, just as in 1627 the Council of Ten had won a new lease on life, the far more tyrannical Three weathered the storm and, backed by the support of the new Doge, Marco Foscarini, clamped down on Venice with a grip that was never loosened while the Republic lived. Except for one unsuccessful revolt, the dissentients gave up the struggle. They knew that they were beaten and that a new era had begun when their old masters reimposed their will with the help of Messer Grande—the name by which the chief of the secret police was always known. The Three were seldom mentioned but never forgotten: two men in black robes and one in red, who ruled the Republic from that little room on the second floor of the Doge's Palace.

Soon they had spun a web which reached into every corner of Venice. And yet they themselves might well have said that they asked very little—merely a show of conformity in religion and noninterference in affairs of State. Venetians and visitors were to amuse themselves and cease to bother their heads about serious matters; and to make sure that they did so, the agents of the Three were increased in number until they had become an invisible army. It would be difficult to overestimate their number or their omniscience. It can confidently be stated that in every great noble's palace there was at least one informer, and no man in his senses would have talked politics in front of a waiter or a servant. Pretended priests, your trusted retainer, your own familiar friend: they could all be paid spies. In fact, so thorough was the surveillance that it has even been said that in certain cases gondoliers were ordered to report each night on the conversation of their fares. It was a sinister system but there is no denying its efficiency. The foreign spy, the assassin, the sorcerer, the conspirator: they all came within the jurisdiction of the secret tribunal. And there was no safety in flight. If a suspect escaped from Venice (and if he was worth the trouble) the agents of the Three would follow him—all over Europe, if necessary—until he was haled back to the dungeons or left lying in some dark alley with a stiletto between his shoulder blades. In fairness it should be added that imprisonment was rare, for the Three, flowing with the tide, winked at offences which did not affect Church or State unless they became so flagrant that they could no longer be tolerated. But for certain crimes—including that of making a powerful enemy—one could still endure all the horrors of the *Piombi* and the *Pozzi*.

Eighteenth-century Venice was the complete permissive society; and, looking back over two hundred years, it is interesting to study its effects—and its end. In this playground of Europe the visitor found all the signs of absolute freedom. Even the women were no longer segregated, a revolutionary change for people who lived on the edge of the East. As Lady Mary Wortley Montagu wrote in 1739: "It is the fashion of the greatest ladies to walk the streets, which are admirably paved; and a mask, price sixpence, with a little cloak and the head of a domino, the genteel dress to carry you everywhere."

Every legitimate amusement and every vice was catered for, and the beautiful city drew the travellers of the time like a magnet. A symphony in coral, rose and amber—palaces, domes and *campanili* bathed in a blue translucence: a place, it would seem, designed for love and laughter, for music, roses and wine. It must be admitted that society was somewhat mixed. There were young gentlemen on the Grand Tour, wicked old gentlemen hoping to renew their misspent youth, rakes, sharpers, dilettanti, virtuous ladies who could not see evil beyond the ends of their noses, and other ladies whose virtue had become slightly tarnished. Powdered and patched in the latest mode, they all came crowding into Venice to dance and flirt and play Faro, to eat ices at Florian's on the Piazza and whisper scandal while the great bell boomed in the Campanile and the pigeons rose in a whirring cloud above the grey-green domes of St Mark's.

Frivolity and dissipation were the order of the day and night. The poet Gozzi returned home one night to find all the lights blazing and somebody else giving a magnificent party in his house: he had the novel experience of being shown round by a strange majordomo. There was even a club of fools called the Casino degli Asini, to join which the aspirant must have performed in public some notable act of foolery, preferably vulgar. There were seven theatres at which could be seen plays by Goldoni and other authors, or the witty improvisations of the commedia dell' arte, while for the more sober there was the Opera, where glorious arias by Galuppi, Paisiello and Piccini were sung (though not in Venice alone) by the castrated *soprani* in whom even the worthy John Evelyn had seen nothing strange.

Sometimes it is difficult to realize that this was the same city which had bred men like Doge Ziani and Carlo Zeno. The rot had begun at the top, among the "new" patricians who had bought their nobility for hard cash at the time of the Candiot War; and like a plague it had spread downwards until it infected all ranks of society. Lacking tradition and despising trade—that firm foundation on which the Republic had risen—the new men had no wish to emulate the deeds of those who had fought and died to save their city from Turk and Genoese. Instead, they had embarked on an orgy of lust and frivolity such as had seldom been seen in Europe since the fall of Constantinople.

The Serenissima was slowly dying. The Exchequer was emptying. Exports were dwindling. In the sixteenth century Venice had produced 28,000 pieces of woollen material each year: in the eighteenth century it had sunk to 700. She had had it too good for too long; and, in spite of her increasing lack of resources, the taste for extravagance had grown until it had become almost a mania. Entertainments, both public and private, became more and more magnificent. The festivities which marked the election of Doge Ruzzini in 1732 cost 34,473 Venetian lire: at the installation of Lodovico Manin in 1789 they cost 189,192. Yet arms were rusting in the Arsenal and there was mounting unemployment.

Men no longer aspired to serve the State: they preferred to serve themselves. Gaiety was their god. They laughed at everything, and for many even their religion had become a mockery. There were so-called nuns who wore pearls and immoderately low-cut "habits"; the inmates of three convents quarrelled bitterly over which of them should provide a mistress for the Papal Nuncio; and historian Philippe Monnier tells of two abbesses who fought a duel with daggers for the love of the Abbé Pomponne. And when men and women no longer worship God, they too often turn to the Devil. Hence every now and then, as through a gap in a curtain, we glimpse that dangerous dabbling with the occult which in a sophisticated society is a sure sign of decadence.

Yet this is the Venice, deceptively beautiful as a rotten apple, which has always attracted the poets and the romantic novelists. It lives again in Casanova's memoirs and in the evocative canvases of Guardi, Longhi and Canaletto: the soft serenade from some dark rio; Harlequin and Scaramouche; a capering line of masqueraders casting long shadows in the moonlight; or lovers stealing down to their gondola, cloaked to the chin and made ghastly by long-nosed white satin masks.

An almost incredible place, but it really did exist, that City of Masks. On the subject of the famous Carnival of Venice, Philippe Monnier wrote: "Six months of the year it lasts, from October to Christmas, from Twelfth Night to Lent; on Ascension Day it starts again for two weeks, and again upon St Mark's Day, and whenever a doge is elected, whenever a procurator is chosen, on the least occasion always, on the slightest pretext. . . . In masks men and women do business and buy fish, write their letters, pay their visits, and plead their causes in the courts. With a mask on his face a man may say or do as he pleases."

They even wore masks when they played cards, for mystery was in the very air they breathed. Gambling was the fashionable vice of the eighteenth century, but nowhere was it carried to such inordinate lengths as in Venice. More than once men are known to have hazarded their wives on the turn of a card, and it was far from unusual for gamesters—like the Abbé Grioni in 1762—to stake their clothes and go home naked.

The real temple of chance was the notorious Ridotto, a huge building not far from the church of San Moise. Late in the century it was suppressed by the authorities, but it had a good run of over a hundred years. The fashionable games were faro and basset, and the bankers were always nobles. It was their exclusive privilege, dressed in their robes of State but unmasked, to preside at the tables —between sixty and eighty of them. Historians differ as to whether or not they were allowed to gamble on their own account, but they certainly played on behalf of various companies and syndicates which paid them a regular salary. The other gamesters (except ladies of the nobility) were all masked, and, just as in Mr Evelyn's time, they were not allowed to speak. Play was high, thousands of sequins changing hands every night in dead silence by faceless gamblers.

It need hardly be said that among such people marital fidelity had become a joke. Every wealthy patrician who wished to be thought a Man of Pleasure had his own little *casino* in the city itself or on one of the islands of the lagoon. In one of these elegantly furnished retreats, all gilt girandoles, candelabra and mirrors, Murano glass and Dresden china, the owner and his lady of the moment could enjoy a delicious supper, followed by frolics which are best left to the imagination.

Then too there was that extraordinary creature, the *cicisbeo,* the recognized companion of a married woman and a familiar figure in the Venice of that time. He was neither a gigolo nor a hired escort. Nor was he necessarily a lover. This *cavaliere serviente* received no pay, and in many cases it would be unfair to brand the husband as a cuckold. But quite understandably, Lord Coke, on a visit to Venice, was scandalized. In his bluff British way, he wrote:

"How shall I spell, how shall I paint, how shall I describe the animal known by the name of *chichisbee* (*cicisbeo*)? He is an appendix to matrimony. Within a week of her nuptials a young lady makes choice of her *chichisbee.* From that moment she never appears in public with her husband, nor is ever imprudent enough to be seen without her *chichisbee*. He is her guardian, her friend, her gentleman usher. He attends her in the morning as soon as she is awake; he presents to her chocolate before she rises; he sets her slippers; and as soon as his morning visit is over withdraws where he pleases. The lady admits him not to dinner; the husband only has that honour. In the afternoon he returns to attend her in her visits. When she sees company at home, he is to hand her from one end of the room to the other, from chair to chair, and from side to side. If she enters into a particular discourse with another person, the *chichisbee* retires into a corner with the lap-dog, or sits in the window teaching the macaw to speak Italian. If the lady sits down to play, it is the duty of the *chichisbee* to sort her cards. The husband (believe me, I entreat you, if you can) beholds these familiarities not only contentedly but with pleasure. He himself has the honourable employment of *chichisbee* in another house; and in both situations, as husband and *chichisbee*, neither gives nor receives the least tinct of jealousy."

Perhaps one explanation of this strange state of affairs may be found in the fact that the lady's husband was her parents' choice; the *cicisbeo*, her own. Human nature being what it is, there must have been times when the affair became far from platonic, and no doubt more than one *cicisbeo* went floating out to sea in a sack. But on rare occasions the custom could be rather charming. Another eighteenth-century visitor, Lady Miller, had this to say:

"I felt a shock at first sight of a tottering old pair I saw entering a coffee-house the other evening. They were both shaking with the palsy, leant upon each other, and supported themselves with a crutch-stick. They were both bent almost double with the weight of years and infirmities. . . . I inquired who the venerable couple were, and learned that the old gentleman had been the faithful *cavaliere* of the same lady above forty years; that they regularly visited the Place St Mark, and the coffee-houses, and, with the most steady constancy, had loved each other, till age and disease were conducting them, hand in hand, together to the grave."

And now, on the credit side, what have we? What names deserve honourable mention? The total of those in the first rank is not impressive: a few composers and writers; a handful of genre painters and miniaturists; and one very great artist—Tiepolo. Then we have one solitary admiral who upheld the honour of St Mark, and the engineers who carried out the Republic's last great adventure in building.

Among the painters, Longhi, Guardi and Canaletto attempted no large-scale works on religious or historical subjects. They were content to give us the Venice that lay all around them—preserved forever by their skill. In a different way, too, the delicate art of Rosalba Carriera most effectively reflects the spirit of that effete society. Her pale pastels, lovely and unsubstantial as the bloom on a peach, and those exquisitely finished little portraits on tiny ovals of ivory, are a perfect expression of the frivolous, glittering Venice of the masks. In contrast, as one can see in many a church, Giambattista Tiepolo returned to the Grand Manner, and it would not be incorrect to describe him as a painter born out of his time. Inspired by the genius of Veronese, his works are wild, passionate, turbulent. He revelled in violent movement, in flying hair and draperies, in foreshortened limbs that seem to be reaching out of the canvas, but, above all, in light—the opal distances and marvellous, sea-reflecting light of Venice.

The pen is best represented by two contrasting playwrights: the incomparable Goldoni, with his well observed, matter-of-fact comedies of Venetian life; and Carlo Gozzi, the conservative, melancholy poet and satirist who sought refuge from a society that he despised in fantastic plays and fairy tales, the most famous of which, translated by Schiller, was *Turandot.*

Of the musicians, Baldassare Galuppi is the name which first springs to mind. He must have been one of the most prolific composers who ever lived, for he could write the scores of five operas in a year, and some of his best were for libretti by Carlo Goldoni. In 1741 he visited England and composed a *pasticcio* for the Haymarket Theatre; twenty years later he was Master of the Music at St Mark's; and in 1766 he visited Russia at the invitation of the Empress Catherine II.

The engineers' skill was outstanding, and one can still see their work in the wonderful *Murazzi* or sea walls, 6,000 yards long, which form a strong rampart along the line of the Lido, breaking the force of the Adriatic waves in their everlasting onslaught. To the poet Goethe, this splendid masterpiece, worthy of a more virile age, was a work of art.

The admiral was Angelo Emo. In 1784, at a time when the European powers and the United States were still paying protection money to the Dey of Algiers, the Bey of Tunis, and the Rulers of Tripoli and Sallee, Venice roused herself from her torpor, made one great effort, and reluctantly fitted out a fleet. Under the command of Admiral Emo, her ships answered the challenge of Barbary and, when the demand for money became exorbitant, sought out and fought the corsairs wherever they were to be found. For a time the Mediterranean was purged of this menace to her shipping. The war lasted for three years and Emo's success should have been followed up. But the exertion had proved too much. No reinforcements were sent. Nothing was done. It was left to others—notably Commodore Decatur of the United States Navy and, later, combined British and Dutch squadrons commanded by Lord Exmouth—to continue the good work in the years preceding the French Conquest of Algiers. But to Angelo Emo belongs the honour of winning the last victory of the Venetian Republic.

As the Serenissima passed through the final phase of her self-destruction, the new nobility thought of nothing but their own ease and pleasure; and, like the common people, they were helpless in the hands of the Three. So, for that matter, were the old nobility, the most ancient aristocracy in Europe, the descendants of those patrician families who had served the Republic so well and whose names run like golden threads through the tapestry of Venetian history. It might be thought that they could have matched the hour with the man. Yet it was not so. A fortunate few carried on in the old style, with fifty or sixty liveried servants and half a dozen private gondolas at their mooring posts. But for the majority times were hard, and many an *illustrissimo* drifted into the ranks of the *Barnabotti*, a strange fraternity of noble mendicants who were nearly all housed near the church of San Barnaba—hence the name. Being patricians, it was unthinkable that they should degrade themselves by working. In order, therefore, that they should not starve, the State allowed them a pittance, which they supplemented by cadging on their friends for gifts of money euphemistically called loans.

A horde of parasites, they were still noblemen whose names were inscribed in *Il Libro d'Oro*. As such they retained their ancient right to seats on the Great Council and, simply by accident of birth, could exercise an influence on affairs denied to the ordinary citizen who was not above soiling his hands with an honest day's labour. Furthermore, by acting together, these blue-blooded beggars could occasionally elect one of their number to high office.

One such gentleman, Giorgio Pisani, was actually made a procurator; ironically enough, it was he, in consort with a Contarini and some other decadent patricians, who showed his gratitude by organizing the one conspiracy of the century! A passing reference has already been made to this fiasco, which took place in 1780. The plan was to overthrow the government—indeed, all recognized forms of government—and exalt Pisani and his friends to leadership of the Republic. It was a futile little plot which aroused more contempt than fear, and of course it failed. The Three knew all about it, and the rebels did not even have the satisfaction of being taken seriously. They were not flung into the Wells or executed as traitors. They were dismissed with light sentences of exile and presumably were also deprived of their dole. One should not condemn all the *Barnabotti*. There were too many cases of genuine hardship, too many real tragedies. But the very existence of this fraternity of subsidized drones was another sign of the decadence which pervaded Venetian society.

Yet, with a childish refusal to face facts, the Serene Republic still pretended to be a great power. People spoke and behaved as if their city still ruled the Mediterranean, when in truth she was no longer capable of defending the Basin of St Mark. But the facts were ignored. It will be remembered that to commemorate Orseolo's victory over the Narentine pirates, the beautifully simple ceremony of *La Sensa* had been instituted, and that gradually, as the Republic became more powerful and rich, the impressive ritual of prayer and libation had been elaborated and vulgarized into the *Sposalizio del Mare*, which drew tourists and sightseers from all over Europe.

Now, in the eighteenth century, it had reached the peak of its rather trumpery splendour. On Ascension Day the reigning Doge, attended by a crowd of dignatories, walked in state to the Piazzetta to board the great crimson-and-gold *Bucintoro*, its forty-eight oars manned by *Arsenalotti* to whom this somewhat laborious task was a jealously guarded privilege. In this floating palace, red velvet and lace, gilt, gold fringe and tassels were everywhere. There was an elaborate chair for the Doge, and others nearly as grand for the

Patriarch, bishops, councillors, ambassadors and other notables who were to witness the espousal. They were surrounded by gilt cherubs, figures of Prudence, Strength, Apollo, the Muses, the Sciences and the Arts; and as they were slowly rowed across the lagoon to the Porto di Lido, they were followed at a respectful distance by a swarm of smaller craft, many painted and gilded until they savoured more of the fairground than the shipyard.

After the usual prayers and litanies and the sweet singing of the choir, the marriage was consummated by the Doge casting a ring out of a special little window in the stern of the *Bucintoro*. But by now the whole show had become a mockery; Venice was no longer the Bride of the Sea but only a raddled old trollop—a travesty of the lovely virgin for whom Orseolo had drawn the sword.

With love and laughter the Venetians frittered away the eighteenth century, while all the time the velocity of their headlong descent increased. One might gloss over the truth with a charming picture of periwigged senators in their robes, of gentlemen with muffs and masks, of laughing girls dancing a furlana to the thud and jingle of tambourines, and of exquisite ladies in hooped skirts, with tiny three-cornered hats perched rakishly over their black silk *zendaletti*. But prettifying the sordid is like painting the face of a corpse. Behind the dominoes and the painted fans, Venice was a little hell: the poor *Barnabotti* in their torn lace and patched brocade; the miles of festering alleys; the stench of the side canals in summer; and under all the hectic gaiety, the invisible machinery of tyranny.

To their credit, some might say, the Venetians went to the Devil laughing. At least there was no dissimulation. In France, in England, at the courts of a dozen little German electors, vice was rampant: but only in Venice was there no attempt to hide it. Alone among the nations she openly flaunted her degradation. A century later, Robert Browning had the last word on the subject:

> *As for Venice and its people, merely born*
>   *to bloom and drop,*
> *Here on earth they bore their fruitage, mirth*
>   *and folly were the crop.*
> *What of soul was left, I wonder, when the*
>   *kissing had to stop?*

19. Casanova in Venice

Rake's Progress
The Piombi
Escape
The Wasted Years

Two hours after sunset on a cold November evening in the year 1753, a tall, bold-eyed young man was waiting by the statue of Colleoni in the Campo dei SS Giovanni e Paolo. His name was Giovanni Jacopo Casanova de Seingalt, but he is known to fame—or infamy—simply as Casanova.

Presently, as he records it, a gondola drew in and a slim figure in a mask alighted. Seeing that the newcomer was dressed as a man, he wished that he had brought his pistols; but soon his fears were dispelled, for the "mask" came hurrying towards him with outstretched hands and he recognized the lady whom, in his memoirs, he refers to as M**** M****. For all her rose velvet coat and black satin breeches, she was a beautiful nun who had become his mistress and who seems to have had little difficulty in taking French leave from her convent.

Casanova, whose father, a man of good family, had turned actor and made a runaway match with a shoemaker's daughter, was one of the most remarkable characters in the eighteenth or any other century. He was also the author of one of the most salacious but lively autobiographies ever written—the notorious memoirs which recount the highlights of his long career as a libertine. The book also brings vividly to life the declining days of the Republic, and the land and peoples of other European countries as well, for he was a much travelled man. But Venice was his birthplace and his spirit haunts her still. The story of that city without Casanova would be *Hamlet* without the Prince.

He was an adventurer born—cynical, audacious, amoral, inordinately vain, with a useful gift for self-deception which served him instead of a conscience. He had a talent for landing on his feet and a habit of spoiling his own chances, for the story is always the same: instant success, the favour of the highest—and then some treachery or mean little swindle, followed by a hurried departure for some new hunting ground where (as he said of his skill as a card cheat) he could correct the mistakes and tricks of fortune. But his real object in life was pleasure, and to Casanova that meant *amore*. He had a superabundant zest for life and he was certainly attractive to women: according to his own account, they went down before him like skittles.

He was a man who was seldom at a loss. If one thing failed, he tried something else with unabated self-confidence. In this winter of 1753 he was only twenty-eight years of age, yet already he had been an abbé, secretary to Cardinal Acquaviva, ensign in the army, professional violinist, cardsharp, charlatan and exponent of the Black Art. He had also won three thousand ducats in a lottery and served a short term of imprisonment in the fortress of Sant' Andrea.

He was educated at Padua and then sent to study for the priesthood at a Roman Catholic seminary in Venice. After being finally persuaded that there was no future in the Church for a neophyte guilty of gross immorality and of falling down drunk in the pulpit, he held a military commission which took him as far afield as Corfu and Constantinople. But nothing lasted long with Casanova and soon he was back in Venice, living by his wits and by playing the violin in the orchestra of the San Samuele Theatre. And then his luck turned.

Leaving the Palazzo Soranzo one morning, after a professional engagement as a musician, he had the good fortune to see a Senator named Bragadin drop a letter. In an instant Casanova had whipped it up and returned it with a low bow; and when the Senator got into his waiting gondola, Casanova got in too. It was a triumph of brazen impudence and it reaped its reward. On his way home, the unfortunate

Senator had a fit of apoplexy. Casanova was there to render first aid, and this happy accident gave him his entrée into the Palazzo Bragadin, where not only did he oust the real doctor, but he became a fixture, with his own valet, his own gondola, and ten sequins a month for pocket money.

How did he do it? One can only conclude that it was by sheer charm. But he never missed an opportunity; and perceiving that Bragadin and two of his friends were interested in the occult, on the spur of the moment he spun a convincing yarn about an imaginary hermit in the mountains who had bestowed upon him the secret of the Clavicle of Solomon or Cabala, as it is called in Hebrew Theosophy. This was not the first time that, for profit, Casanova had practised the forbidden arts: in fact, his memoirs show that he half believed in them himself. There were even occasions when he was frightened by his own antics. Once, dressed in a white robe, a sceptre in one hand, a supposedly sacred sword in the other, he performed some mumbo jumbo at midnight in a Venetian garden while two awe-struck spectators looked down upon him from a balcony. In a circle of paper inscribed with magical symbols, he was declaiming some gibberish when suddenly a storm broke. In *My Life and Adventures*, this is what he had to say about it:

"Such a storm was a very natural occurrence, and I had no reason to be astonished at it, but, somehow, fear was beginning to creep into me and I wished myself in my room. My fright soon increased at the sight of the lightning, and on hearing the claps of thunder which succeeded each other with frightful rapidity, and seemed to roar over my very head. I then realized what extraordinary effect fear can have on the mind, for I fancied that, if I was not annihilated by the fires of heaven which were flashing over me, it was only because they could not enter my magic ring. Thus I was admiring my own deceitful work! That foolish reason alone prevented me from leaving the circle in spite of the fear that caused me to shudder. If it had not been for that belief, the result of a cowardly fright, I would not have remained one moment where I was, and my hurried flight would no doubt have opened the eyes of my two dupes, who could not have failed to see that, far from being a magician, I was only a poltroon. . . . My system, which I thought proof against every accident, had vanished: I acknowledged an avenging God."

The affair with the beautiful nun was quite a long one—for

Casanova. They could pass the time very pleasantly, for he had the use of an elegant little casino on the island of Murano which had once been the property of the English Ambassador. Secure in their masks, they went to the Opera and to the Ridotto, where on one occasion M**** M**** broke the bank—an unusual experience for one who had taken a vow of holy poverty. But her superiors knew nothing about it; and hers must have been a very lax nunnery, even for those days. The grating which separated the inmates from visitors was provided with a secret spring by which it could be opened wider; and sometimes, when the Carnival was at its height, life for the cloistered ladies was enlivened by a ball. Outside, the Piazza and the banks of the Grand Canal were in pandemonium—a riot of clowns, giants, Turks and demons, Scaramouche in his cock's feather and the sinister Polichinello. The air was full of confetti. The night was rent by laughter, screams and the lilt of music, while even in the nunnery there was an echo of the gaiety. As Casanova puts it:

"In Venice, during the Carnival, that innocent pleasure is allowed in convents. The guests dance in the parlour, and the sisters remain behind the grating, enjoying the sight of the ball which is over by sunset. Then all the guests retire and the poor nuns are for a long time happy in the recollection of the pleasure enjoyed by their eyes. The ball was to take place in the afternoon of the day appointed for my meeting with M**** M**** in the evening at the casino of Murano, but that could not prevent me from going to it. . . .

"I went at once to the convent; the parlour was full; but thanks to my costume of Pierrot, which was seen in Venice but very seldom, everybody made room for me. I walked on, assuming the gait of a booby, the true characteristic of my costume, and I stopped near the dancers. After I had examined the Pantaloons, Punches, Harlequins, and Merry Andrews, I went near the grating, where I saw all the nuns and boarders, some seated, some standing, and without appearing to notice any of them in particular, I remarked my friend very intent upon the dances. I then walked round the room, eyeing everybody from head to foot and drawing the general attention upon myself.

"I chose for my partner in the minuet a pretty girl dressed as a Columbine, and I took her hand in so awkward a manner and with such an air of stupidity that everybody laughed and made room for us. My partner danced very well according to her costume, and I kept my character with such perfection that the laughter was general. After the minuet I danced twelve furlanas with the greatest vigour. Out of breath, I threw myself on a sofa, pretending to go to sleep, and the moment I began to snore, everybody respected the slumbers of Pierrot. The quadrille lasted one hour and I took no part in it; but immediately after it, a Harlequin approached me with the impertinence which belongs to his costume, and flogged me with his wand. In my quality (character) of Pierrot I had no weapons; I seized him round the waist and carried him round the parlour, running all the time, while he kept flogging me. I then put him down. Adroitly snatching the wand out of his hand, I lifted his Columbine on my shoulders and pursued him, striking him with the wand, to the great delight and mirth of the company. The Columbine was screaming because she was afraid of my tumbling down and of showing her centre of gravity to everybody in the fall. She had good reason to fear; for suddenly a foolish Merry Andrew came behind me, tripped me up, and down I tumbled. Everybody hooted Master Punch. I quickly picked myself up, and rather vexed I began a regular fight with the insolent fellow. He was of my size but awkward, and he had nothing but strength; I threw him, and shaking him vigorously on all sides I contrived to deprive him of his hump and false stomach. The nuns, who had never seen such a merry sight, clapped their hands, everybody laughed loudly, and improving my opportunity I ran through the crowd and disappeared."

So Casanova escaped from the convent, to kill time gambling and generally playing the fool at the Ridotto before his appointment that same evening at the casino with M**** M****. He tired of her in the end, of course, as he tired of so many others. But soon he was to be deprived for a time of the women who played such a large part in his life, for, although he did not realize it, the sands were running out. Speaking one time of the State Inquisitors, he said that the only people who could live in peace in Venice were those of whose existence the Tribunal was ignorant. He should have remembered that remark and kept in the background, or even taken a short holiday abroad. Instead, he made himself a public nuisance, and to those who had no taste for diabolism, a dangerous nuisance. In matters of morals the Three were nothing if not tolerant, but sorcery was beyond the pale. Casanova should have remembered, too, that he had enemies, any one of whom might have dropped a denunciation into the Lion's Mouth.

He had his warnings—so many indeed that, bearing in mind the efficiency of the Tribunal's agents, it is difficult to believe that there may not have been deliberate leaks by the Three, who would have much preferred not to have been forced to take extreme measures. Casanova received at least one anonymous letter, which he treated with contempt; a secretary at a foreign embassy told him that he was suspected not only of sorcery but of espionage; even Senator Bragadin, who had himself been an Inquisitor of State, advised him to leave Venice immediately. But Casanova took no notice: as he said himself, he was blinded by folly. So the inevitable happened. At daybreak on the sixteenth of July, 1755, Messer Grande with a strong force of *sbirri* took possession of the house. He was awakened and ordered to answer to his name.

"At my 'Yes, I am Casanova,' he told me to rise, put on my clothes, to give him all the papers and manuscripts in my possession, and to follow him.

" 'On whose authority do you order me to do this?'

" 'By the authority of the Tribunal.' "

Casanova was now in serious trouble. Out of sheer bravado, he dressed in his best suit and a laced shirt—as if, Messer Grande remarked grimly, he were going to a wedding; but bluff would not help him this time. He had been found in possession of forbidden books: *The Zecor-Ben, The Key of Solomon the King,* and other works of magic containing incantations for conjuring up demons.

In the police barge, with four *sbirri* to guard him, he was taken by devious ways to the prison quay—the Riva degli Schiavoni— where he was marched across the covered Bridge of Sighs from the new prisons to the Doge's Palace. There he was handed over to the secretary of the Inquisitors, who briefly ordered the gaoler to take him to a cell in the *Piombi*. No charge was brought against him and there was no mention of a trial.

He was taken upstairs and along corridors to the west side of the palace. Here the windows of the garret, onto which the doors of three cells open, look down into the courtyard. Casanova had a bad fright when he saw a curious machine like a huge iron horseshoe with a

winch, for this was the garotte by means of which condemned prisoners were strangled. But he was not under sentence of death. A low
iron door was opened and he was made to enter a cell. The door
clanged behind him; a key turned; and he heard the retreating foot-
steps of the guards and gaoler. Then, as he frankly confesses, he gave
way to despair:

"Stunned with grief, I leant my elbows on the top of the grating
(in the door). . . . This opening would have lighted my cell, if a square
beam supporting the roof, which joined the wall below the window,
had not intercepted what little light came into that horrid garret.
After making the tour of my sad abode, my head lowered, as the cell
was not more than five and a half feet high, I found by groping that
it formed three quarters of a square of twelve feet. . . . The heat was
great, and my instinct made me go mechanically to the grating, the
only place where I could lean my elbows. I could not see the window
but I saw the light in the garret, and rats of a fearful size which
walked unconcernedly about it. . . . I passed eight hours in silence
and without stirring."

That cell nearly broke Casanova's heart. At first he had to sleep on
straw and there was no furniture except a fixed bench and a bucket.
Those cramped quarters in which, being a tall man, he could not stand
upright were like an oven in summer and ice-cold in winter, when the
cell was in complete darkness for nineteen hours out of the twenty-
four. The rats filled him with revulsion, and myriads of fleas, he says,
gave him spasmodic convulsions and poisoned his blood.

Yet, according to the standards of the eighteenth century, he was
well treated. He was given a small allowance of money; and having,
besides, three sequins in his pocket, he was able to buy clothes, a bed,
a table and books—though those religious works considered suitable
by the Inquisitors did not appeal to the literary taste of Casanova!
On New Year's Day 1756, his good friend Bragadin sent him a
present of a fur-lined dressing gown; and best of all, after a time he
was allowed to walk in the garret each day for half an hour, while his
cell was cleaned.

In those months of adversity, a new Casanova emerged. We have
seen his vanity and his impudence: the other side of the coin was his
indomitable resolution. A not surprising phenomenon, for whatever
the moralists may say, conceit and courage often go together. Night

after night he buoyed himself up with the hope that he would be freed in the morning; then he decided that he would be released on the first of October, when the three newly elected Inquisitors began their term of office; and then at last, when all hope had died, he made up his mind to escape.

One day, during his walk in the garret, he examined a heap of rubbish and found a twenty-inch iron bolt and a small piece of black marble. Using the marble as a whetstone and his saliva for oil, he toiled for eight days sharpening the bolt; by the end of that time he had converted it into a useable spike or crowbar. His plan was to dig through the floor under his bed and make his escape through the Hall of the Three immediately beneath his cell.

He began working feverishly on the first Monday in Lent. But he had many setbacks which taxed his ingenuity. The daily sweeping out of his cell, for example, threatened to expose his digging. This problem he solved by cutting his finger, making his handkerchief bloody, and telling the gaoler that the dust so affected his lungs that he had been spitting blood. The cell was swept no more.

Once, for a time, his work was interrupted while another prisoner shared his quarters; but for all his faults, Casanova had the will to persevere at a task which most men would have thought impossible. By skillful contrivance and a few clever lies to Lorenzo the gaoler, he obtained the materials for an oil lamp, flint and steel. Then, day after day, night after night, week after week, he dug. Stark naked and streaming with sweat, he fought that hard, stubborn timber, happy if by the end of the day he had a handful of chips.

"I lay on my belly, my spike in my hand, with a napkin close by in which to gather the fragments of board as I scooped them out. My task was to destroy the board by driving into it the point of my crowbar. At first the pieces I got away were not much larger than grains of wheat, but they soon increased in size.

"The board was made of deal, and was sixteen inches broad. I began to pierce it at its juncture with another board, and as there were no nails or clamps my work was simple. After six hours' toil, I tied up the napkin, and put it on one side to empty it the following day behind the pile of papers in the garret. The fragments were four or five times larger in bulk than the hole from which they came. I put my bed back in its place, and on emptying the napkin the next morning I took care so to dispose the fragments that they should not be seen.

"Having broken through the first board, which I found to be two inches thick, I was stopped by a second which I judged to be as thick as the first. Tormented by the fear of new visitors, I redoubled my efforts, and in three weeks I had pierced the three boards of which the floor was composed; and then I thought that all was lost, for I found I had to pierce a bed of small pieces of marble known in Venice as *terrazzo marmorin.*"

He pierced the marble. Remembering that Hannibal was said to have softened the rocks of the Alps with vinegar, he obtained a supply of it from Lorenzo by feigning a toothache. Below the pavement was another plank, and this he found difficult to reach, for the hole was now ten inches deep. Then he struck a beam and knew that he would have to enlarge the hole sideways, but first he cautiously made a small peephole. There beneath him was the Hall of the Three.

Casanova fixed his escape for the eve of St. Augustine's feast day, for he knew that on that occasion there would be a meeting of the Great Council. The room below, through which he would have to pass, would therefore be empty. One can imagine the fever of hope which possessed him, the impatience with which he counted off the hours as the great bell boomed from the Campanile. Then, two days before the Feast of St. Augustine, he was told that he was to change his cell.

He nearly went mad. He stormed and raved, and made every excuse for staying where he was. Lorenzo thought that he was demented, for, probably through patrician influence—perhaps that of his friend Bragadin—he was to be transferred to a lighter, more comfortable cell on the east side of the palace, overlooking the Rio di Palazzo and affording a glimpse of the distant Lido. Casanova managed to hide the crowbar in his armchair which was transferred with him; but all those months of labour counted for nothing, and when the hole in the floor was discovered, Lorenzo came bursting into the new cell, almost inarticulate with rage, demanding to know who had supplied him with his hatchet and tools. But by this time Casanova had recovered his nerve. "Why, you did," he replied coolly, "and you took them back again." For all his audacity, he was a worried man, for he thought that his punishment might be perpetual imprisonment in the Wells. But he had sown the seeds of fear in Lorenzo. Afraid for his job, the gaoler decided that it would be safer to fill in the hole and forget it. But he took his revenge by providing his prisoner with putrid veal which stank so appallingly in the August heat that Casanova almost starved until Lorenzo felt that he had evened up the score and stopped the penal treatment.

Months had been wasted but Casanova was not beaten. He knew that in the future his cell would be searched regularly: he would never be given another chance to dig through floor or walls. There remained the ceiling. There were other prisoners on the floor above him, directly under the leaden roof. But how was he to communicate with them?

It was Lorenzo who unwittingly supplied the answer. He had charge of his prisoners' allowances and regarded any surplus cash as his own perquisite. So it paid him to preach economy. When, therefore, Casanova next asked him to buy some books, Lorenzo suggested that one of the prisoners on the floor above might have some he would be willing to lend. He was a monk named Marino Balbi, and he shared a cell with an old patrician named Count Asquino, a lawyer who had been indiscreet enough to defend country folk against the nobility.

Acting on Lorenzo's suggestion, Casanova sent Balbi his copy of Petteau's *Rationarium,* and next morning received in exchange the first volume of Wolff's works, with some epigramatic verses written on a loose leaf. Casanova now split his little-finger nail, which he had purposely been growing long, and using the tiny sliver for a pen with some mulberry juice saved from a meal for ink, he wrote out a list of his books which he concealed in the spine of the next volume which he lent to Balbi. On the fly-leaf he wrote the one word *"Latet"* ("Hidden").

Balbi was weak, irritable and vicious; and, as a punishment for some disgraceful irregularities, he had been sent to the Leads on the recommendation of the superior of his order. Wise in the ways of men, Casanova soon gained ascendancy over this rascal, and having obtained from him pencil and paper (hidden in the spine of a book), he began issuing orders which Balbi was either too weak or too frightened to disobey. The monk was told to cut through his wall into a narrow corridor immediately over Casanova's cell. Once in the corridor, he was to dig through the floor until only a thin layer of boards remained, which could be broken through when Casanova was ready to ascend. His plan was to leave the *Piombi* by way of the roof.

In the meantime, Balbi was to ask Lorenzo to buy him a number of big paper pictures of saints. These would serve admirably to mask the hole in the wall. But how was he to make a hole if he did not possess a tool? Somehow Casanova had to find a way of sending up his crowbar. After much thought, he bought a Bible—a huge folio Vulgate and Septuagint, which had just been published. As usual, the hiding-place was to be in the spine of the book. But the crowbar was two inches too long.

Undaunted, he set his imagination to work to solve this new problem. He told Lorenzo that on St Michael's Day he wanted to repay Balbi's kindness by presenting him with a dish of macaroni and cheese made with his own hands. This was to be no mean gift: so would Lorenzo please lend him the very largest dish that he could find?

The gaoler must have been liberally tipped, for on the great day he brought to the cell not only an enormous dish and a saucepan of hot macaroni, but all the necessary utensils and ingredients. Casanova made the cheese sauce and filled the huge dish to the brim; then, telling Lorenzo that he wished to lend Balbi his new Bible, he suggested that the gaoler should take them both at the same time. Placing the dish on the Bible, where it effectively hid the end of the crowbar, he handed them both to Lorenzo, being careful to keep the back of the book towards the bearer and warning him not to spill any grease on the beautiful new Bible. The slow witted gaoler was suitably impressed. With his eyes firmly fixed on the swimming sauce, he made his way up the stairs and, suspecting nothing, delivered Bible, macaroni and crowbar to Balbi.

Casanova had now been a prisoner in the *Piombi* for fifteen months. He had timed his escape for October 31, when the State Inquisitors and their secretary were always on the mainland and when, consequently, Lorenzo always took the opportunity to get drunk. The difficulties mounted, but Casanova with his quick wits and courage overcame them all. Soon after Balbi had given the three knocks which were the signal that he was ready to break through the ceiling, Casanova was unpleasantly surprised by the arrival of a new cell mate, an ex-barber named Soradaci, who, as a secret agent of the

Ten, had been foolish enough to accept a bribe. This little wretch was a religious fanatic whose piety was tinged with superstition verging on mania. But the opportunity to escape was too good to be missed, so Casanova feigned even deeper devotion, playing on Soradaci's gullibility. The experienced student of human nature had taken the measure of his man; and very quickly Casanova was able to make his dupe believe almost anything he pleased. Solemnly he told Soradaci how he had learned in a dream that an angel was coming down to deliver them from captivity; and Soradaci, overcome by the revelation, spent many hours on his knees, weeping and praying, though the most impassioned prayer came from the shameless Casanova.

When at last the "angel" came down through the ceiling, Soradaci was taken aback by Balbi's disreputable appearance and obvious signs of exhaustion, but Casanova explained blandly that when angels take on the guise of mortals they become subject to human limitations. Soradaci was no longer fooled, but he was too frightened to say so. Instead, he meekly trimmed their beards with a pair of scissors which somehow Balbi had hidden in his cell.

Equipped with a length of rope made of their sheets and anything else which could be torn up and knotted, Casanova climbed up into the little corridor and Balbi's cell. The roof timbers were so rotten that they presented no difficulty, and with his crowbar he managed to lever up one of the leaden plates of the roof. Balbi's cell mate, Count Asquino, was too fat for the climb and accepted the fact like a gentleman, while Soradaci, who had acquired a wholesome fear of Casanova, begged to be left behind. Casanova was delighted; and, with characteristic impudence, he gave Soradaci a note for the Inquisitors in which he explained politely that as he had been detained under the Leads without being consulted, they could hardly blame him if he departed without consulting them.

Then came the most perilous part of his adventure: long hours spent clambering in the dark over the sloping roofs of the Doge's Palace. They were wet and slippery in the sea mist, and one false move would have meant death, either on the pavement or in the shallow canal. Balbi proved to be utterly useless. Groaning and grumbling, he had to be cajoled, dragged or pushed over every yard. Casanova admits that at one time he was sorely tempted to rid himself of this encumbrance with one good kick, and it says much for his patience and self-control that he refrained from doing so.

In the faint moonlight, as he explored, he could see the dim shapes of the domes of St Mark's looming out of the shadows beside him. Presently, in the other direction and about two-thirds of the way down the slope of the roof, he spied a dormer window by means of which it might be possible to reenter the palace with the aid of his rope and a long ladder which workmen had conveniently left on a little platform or terrace. After breaking the window and helping the shivering Balbi to safety by sitting astride the dormer and lowering him into the room with the rope, Casanova decided that his only chance of following him was by making use of his ladder. Clinging on as best he could above that awful gulf of darkness, he would have to manoeuvre the first few rungs in through the window and then somehow tilt up the other end of the ladder until it swung down to the floor. He did it, but it nearly cost him his life. He says:

"I slid down beside the ladder to the parapet, which held up the points of my feet, as I was lying on my belly. In this position I pushed the ladder forward, and was able to get it into the window to the length of a foot, and that diminished by a good deal its weight. I now only had to push it in another two feet, as I was sure that I could get it in altogether by means of the rope from the roof of the window. To impel the ladder to the extent required I got on my knees, and in an instant I was over the parapet as far as my chest, sustained only by my elbows.

"I shudder still when I think of this awful moment, which cannot be conceived in all its horror. My natural instinct made me almost unconsciously strain every nerve to regain the parapet, and—I had almost said miraculously—I succeeded. Taking care not to let myself slip back an inch, I struggled upwards with my hands and arms, until my belly was resting on the edge of the parapet. Fortunately the ladder was safe, for with that unlucky effort which had nearly cost me so dearly I had pushed it in more than three feet, and there it remained."

Once inside the palace, the two men made their way down to the lower floors. At one point, Casanova had to smash a door panel with his crowbar. Fortunately no one heard the noise. Climbing through the jagged hole they were both badly cut, but at least they found themselves on the other side. It was· different when they came to the main door of the palace, above the Giants' Staircase. Here they would have needed a battering ram to force their way through. All they could do was to sit down and wait for daybreak. Ragged, blood-stained and filthy, they looked like a pair of brigands, so they employed the time in making themselves as presentable as possible. At last dawn came; the door opened; and before an astonished porter even realized what had happened, they had pushed past him, run down the stairs, through the Porta della Carta, and out on to the Piazzetta. Casanova pushed Balbi into the nearest gondola and—loudly, so as to be overheard—told the boatman to call another gondolier and take them to Fusina—fast.

The gondola slid away from the Molo, past the Customs House, and down the broad Guidecca Canal. Presently Casanova casually asked one of the gondoliers if they would reach Mestre in an hour.

"But you said Fusina."

"No, Mestre."

Having carefully laid a false scent to put pursuers off the trail, there was now nothing more that Casanova could do. He lay back in his seat and soon they were out on the open lagoon. Behind them, rising out of the sea, glittered churches, palaces and towers—rose, amethyst and silver in the pearly light of early morning; while ahead, far away across the flats, they could see the jagged snow peaks of the Alps. That way lay freedom.

Casanova had one more shock. Safe, as he thought, on the mainland, he went into a church to give thanks for his deliverance, and found himself face to face with one of the three State Inquisitors. Recognized, he kept his head and coolly bluffed his way out, but after that he lost no time in getting clear of Venetian territory.

We are only concerned with Casanova in Venice; but his subsequent career, to summarize it briefly, was only what one might expect of a man with his gifts and his failings. In Switzerland he met Voltaire and a fellow charlatan, "Count" Cagliostro. He was expelled from Florence. He was expelled from Madrid. In Rome the Pope created him a Knight of the Golden Spur. In Berlin he refused a post offered to him by Frederick the Great. In Paris he became a director of the State lotteries, made the acquaintance of Madame de Pompadour, and left in a hurry when he heard that he was to be imprisoned under a *lettre de cachet.* In Poland he was kindly received by the King, fought a duel with General Count Branicki—and fired before the signal was given. Another hurried departure.

He was charmed to meet a son whose existence he had not even suspected; while in Holland he was horrified to recognize in a low prostitute a once young and innocent girl whom, years before, he had turned into a wanton. It says something for Casanova that he had the grace to be ashamed. But it was England that finished him. There, with no knowledge of the language, he soon found himself in the wrong company. In Denmark Street, Soho, he became the dupe of a London whore and her terrible crew—characters straight out of Hogarth. They ruined him and forced him to flee the country: he was never quite the same again. He returned to Venice, was forgiven, and became—of all things—a spy for the Three. Then at last, in 1798, all but forgotten, he died peacefully at the Count von Waldstein's castle in Bohemia, where he had acted as librarian and written his famous book.

The life story of Casanova can be summed up in one word: waste. Here was a man of amazing strength and vitality, endowed with one of the most brilliant intellects of his time: an iron will, a cool head, and the ability to charm nearly everybody he met. He might have scaled the heights, but he deliberately chose to squander a long life in selfish indulgence and petty trickery. When the end came, what had he achieved? He was the hero of one of the most daring escapes ever recorded; he had written a book which might well have been called *The Confessions of a Hedonist;* and he had bequeathed a new word to the English language.

20. Full Circle

General Bonaparte
The Last Doge
Peace with Dishonour
The Reckoning

And so the wheel turned full circle. If ever there was a case of history repeating itself, it is to be found in the linked destinies of Venice and Byzantium. So let us look back across the centuries and recapitulate. We see a relentless progression, step by step, from cause to effect. Venice sowed the seeds of her own ruin long before she rose to greatness. She did so when "blind old Dandolo," at the head of a young and vigorous republic, diverted the Fourth Crusade and brought about the sack of Constantinople. The Imperial City, which for centuries had held the Asian hordes in check, never rose again to power, though her walls continued to enclose a sanctuary of ignoble ease. Her population, softened by luxury, neglected their defences. They had peace of a sort, it is true. But at what a price! For when the time came Constantinople fell like an overripe plum. It had been forgotten that the price of security is eternal vigilance.

So the gates of Europe were left unguarded.

And now followed, belatedly, the sequel, which might be called just retribution. The Turkish conquests, for which Venice must bear a large share of the blame, closed the Levantine ports and most of the trade of the Orient to her merchants. Together with the League of Cambrai and the discovery of the new sea routes which left her high and dry, this disaster was the direct cause of her own descent from world power—slow at first, but increasing in velocity until it became a headlong plunge to destruction. She too, like Byzantium, weakened herself by pleasure and indulgence. Nothing mattered except the gaiety of an everlasting masquerade. Her heroes were Pierrot and Harlequin; her national anthem, a serenade. The very thought of war, or indeed, of anything serious, was avoided—for several days Doge Renier's death was kept secret for fear that news of tragedy might spoil the Shrovetide Carnival. In the shelter of her lagoons Venice laughed at life, the clown among the nations, until at last a new Young Republic rose in its strength to destroy her.

In 1796 Revolutionary France had thrown back the enemy from her frontiers and, turning from self-defence to conquest, had let loose a flood of war which was to engulf Europe for twenty years. And out of the maelstrom of battle and civil strife she had thrown up a military genius, a leader such as the world had not known since the days of Alexander. The Man of Destiny! The Little Corporal! He was not Napoleon yet; he was General Bonaparte, the lean, youthful Bonaparte with the sallow face, and long lank hair, and the burning fanatical eyes. In his cocked hat and tricolour sash he had burst on the world like a tornado. He knew what he wanted to do and he did it. He would tolerate no opposition. When told that the Alps would bar his progress, he declared harshly, "There shall be no Alps!"—and built a road across the Simplon through country thought to be inaccessible.

Having taken the mountains in his stride, he won victory after victory. He had brought with him into Italy 80,000 of some of the finest troops in the world: tough, hardbitten little bluecoats, trudging along, mile after mile, to the husky rattle of the drums. They were dusty, bedraggled, bandaged, bloody, in shabby uniforms, some of them shoeless, with only their muskets and sabres bright. Yet give them a crust and a mouthful of brandy and they would march or fight all day.

And they had allies. By their side was the Cisalpine Legion of Italian revolutionaries marching under the green-white-and-red which one day would become the colours of United Italy. French conscripts, Italian volunteers: together they were irresistible. Already they had routed the Austrians at Montenotte, Millesimo and Lodi. And now, bestriding the Plain of Lombardy, Bonaparte cast hostile eyes on the decrepit Venetian Republic which, in this campaign against the Austrians, might conceivably menace his line of retreat. The man had no pity—only will-power and an utter contempt for weakness. He despised this so-called Serenissima, this servile, senile state which had so obligingly softened itself up for destruction. In his view, Venice was an anachronism: her day was done. He had no use for the "Pantaloons," as he called them: pampered senators, blue-blooded decadents and secret tribunals. "A feeble-minded, mean-spirited people, unfit for liberty," Philippe Monnier tells us was Napoleon's verdict. It was time for these *aristos* to be swept away by the strong arm of the Sacred People.

It would seem that at first Bonaparte's idea was merely to make Venice pay the expenses of his Italian campaign, but very soon he must have realized that the city would make a rich prize and that it was his for the taking. There were fine buildings, ships, an arsenal, art treasures—and Bonaparte was a great lover of art treasures, especially those belonging to other people. Moreover, the pitiful remains of the Venetian Empire might prove a useful bargaining counter when the time came to make peace with Austria. They might even be offered in exchange for the Rhenish provinces which France coveted.

To find an excuse for the "liberation" of Venice would not be difficult. Had she not given shelter to the Comte de Lille, brother of the murdered King of France? Had she not permitted the passage of Austrian troops through her territory and allowed them to occupy the fortress of Peschiera? Every French sentry shot, every straggler killed by the angry peasants, could be blown up into an "incident"—an insufferable act of provocation.

But at this time, in the spring of 1797, it suited Bonaparte to hold his fire and send the Venetians a half-contemptuous offer of alliance. Everything was going his way. Already, in the previous year, most of the mainland cities, including Bergamo and Brescia, had seceded from their allegiance to Venice, and even Verona had been forced to submit to occupation by the French. Now, with nearly all the Veneto firmly under his heel, he had just won two more brilliant victories, at Arcola and Rivoli. So General Bonaparte decided to be moderate in his demands on Venice. To begin with, he merely asked for money: a trifle of a million francs monthly. Surely a small sum to pay for peace. The alternative was made very clear.

Venice paid. She could hardly do otherwise. But when it came to the question of alliance, she displayed an understandable hesitation. Her one desire was for peace, and an alliance with Bonaparte's France was a sure way of becoming involved in the war which was ravaging Europe. So she temporized. Others, however, were made of sterner stuff. In the mountainous districts of the Veneto there were pockets of resistance, for the highlanders could not forget their centuries of loyalty to the Republic and they were angered by the rapacity of the occupying army. They rose in revolt and appealed to Venice for arms and aid. No help was forthcoming. The rulers of the city were afraid of offending the French. So the brave but futile little rebellion was easily suppressed.

Bonaparte blamed the Venetians, of course: anything which displeased him was laid to their charge. But not even their failure to help their own people could appease him. He had stopped making requests. He gave orders now, and one of them was that Venice should disperse the men and arms which (so his agents informed him) she had been secretly collecting in case the worse came to the worst. In vain the Venetians protested that they were the friends of France. Their explanations were brusquely brushed aside and Bonaparte increased his demands, bullying, listening to no excuses, tearing up the Serenissima's notes of apology unread. He must have muskets, cannon, food, fodder, two hundred sumpter mules, draught horses, the park of artillery at Legnano. And he must have them now! *At once.* Impossible? He recognized no such word. His most moderate demands must be met immediately. Otherwise—war!

To teach those Pantaloons who was master and to impress on them the folly of inciting mountaineers to rebellion, he sent his aide-de-camp, Junot, hurrying to Venice. Junot reached the city on April 15—Easter Saturday, the day on which, by custom immemorial, no political business of any kind was transacted. But like the armies of Europe, custom must give way to Bonaparte. Was the envoy of France to be kept waiting because it was a public holiday?

The Senators were hastily summoned. Junot, booted and spurred, marched defiantly into the hall and sat himself down, uninvited, in the Nuncio's chair, next to the Ducal throne. When he entered and again when he left, Doge and Senators rose respectfully. How times had changed. An earlier Doge would have sent the uniformed lout to learn his manners in the *Piombi*, but those days were over forever. Poor Ludovico Manin had been cast in a different mould.

During the reign of the Sacred People, diplomatic courtesies were no longer observed. Junot wasted no time on polite preamble. In a loud voice he enumerated the points at issue and accused the Venetian Republic of treachery towards the French Directory and General Bonaparte. He threatened the Senate with direst consequences if they did not comply with his General's demands. Never had that august assembly been so insulted.

The downfall of the Republic was hastened by two events which followed within the next few days.

The first was a rising in Verona on the seventeenth of April. Whether the revolt was organized or whether it was a spontaneous outburst of popular feeling is still uncertain. The Veronese are proud people and hot-blooded, with a tradition of street fighting which goes back to the days of Montague and Capulet, and beyond. For months they had endured insults and indignities at the hands of foreign troops whom they regarded as little better than sansculottes. Then suddenly, on the evening of Easter Monday, they rose against their oppressors. Unfortunately, as so often happens, they spoiled their own case by their excesses. A raging mob surged through the streets, killing every Frenchman they could find, and in their fury they did not even spare the sick and wounded. So terrible was the massacre that afterwards it was compared with that other Easter Monday, five hundred years before, when another outraged people slaughtered the French in what came to be known as the Sicilian Vespers. Order was not restored until a strong French force had been rushed to Verona.

The other incident took place at sea, and there can be no doubt that it was a deliberate act of provocation. As the French knew quite well, it had long been the rule that foreign warships were forbidden to enter the Venetian lagoon without permission. But on the twentieth of April the French frigate *Libérateur d'Italie*, which had been cruising in the Adriatic, came right in under the guns of the Lido forts. It seems almost certain that her commander, Captain Laugier, had his orders, for, disregarding a signal to withdraw, he sailed through the Porto di Lido. Fort Sant' Andrea opened fire, and Laugier and several of his seamen were killed.

The news of Laugier's death and of the Verona rising was brought to Bonaparte at Grätz, where he was negotiating the Treaty of Leoben with the Emperor of Austria. Already, in the preliminary stages of the peace conference, he had secretly proposed a partition of what little Venetian territory remained; now he had the excuse he needed to occupy Venice itself and destroy the ancient republic forever. He refused to listen to the Venetian envoys who came hurrying to wait on him with their apologies and explanations. He flew into one of his notorious rages, blaming them for the massacre at Verona and telling them that their hands were dripping with French blood. He shouted them down, declaring that now there would be no alliance. "I will have no more Inquisitors, I will have no more Senate, I will be an Attila to the State of Venice."

On May 1, 1797, he declared war.

Bonaparte's plans were already drawn up, and he put them into operation with his usual speed and efficiency. General Joubert was ordered to Bassano; Victor held Padua; Masséna occupied Goritz. Baraguey d'Hilliers marched to Mestre, and other generals of division took up their positions at Klagenfurth, Sacile, Laibach and Spilimberg, while two cavalry divisions were stationed at Treviso. Thus Venice was completely cut off from the mainland.

Within the beleaguered city, immediate danger reawakened the old spirit—too late. Crowds of the common people thronged the Piazza, shouting *"Viva San Marco!"* and clamouring for arms. But the leaders who should have inspired and sustained them were panic-stricken. If there had been a strong man who could have taken command, there might have been some hope. But Ludovico Manin was a pitiful creature who, when he was elected Doge, had burst into tears, swooned, refused his dinner, and been carried to bed. There was no evil in him: his rule had been mild and benevolent; he was gentle and deeply religious; it was just his misfortune now to be the wrong man in the wrong place at the wrong time. He simply did not have the strength of character to stand up to a bully, and most of his advisers displayed the same lack of moral fibre. There have been Doges renowned for their great deeds or censured for their sins. Poor Ludovico Manin is remembered for his tears.

Some half-hearted attempts to strengthen the city's defences had been made. Food, water, fuel and ammunition were already in store in case of blockade: the order to lay in supplies had been the last act of the Venetian Senate. There were also a few good regiments still available, including the Schiavoni, who had been hastily summoned from Dalmatia, and the *Arsenalotti*. Backed by a people in arms, they might have put up a formidable defence in one of the most difficult cities in Europe to carry by assault. There were still enough ships to make a sea-borne invasion an extremely hazardous undertaking, and the British commodore in the Adriatic had offered to cover the approaches to the Lido with his fleet. Even now, at the eleventh hour, one rousing speech from such a patriot as brave old Vettore Pisani might have saved the situation. But what hope had the Venetians when their elected leaders could do nothing but cry and bewail their misfortunes? Manin and his friends loved Venice, but they were not prepared to fight for her. With the enemy at the gate and the very existence of the Republic threatened, the only instructions given to Nani, Proveditor General of the Lagoons, were to "maintain intact the tranquility of the State and give ease and happiness to its subjects."* Ease and happiness—with Bonaparte conquering Europe! Carlo Zeno must have turned over in his grave.

Yet still the Great Council was not convened. Instead—and quite illegally—the Doge and his closest advisers met in Manin's private apartments and formed themselves into what they called the Conference of Emergency. They debated far into the night, and, incredible as it may seem, the main question before the meeting was whether they should resist Bonaparte or yield to his demands. Almost equally incredible, the majority were for submission. It is said that Condulmer, Nani's second in command, refused to defend the city, while the Procurator Pesaro (also weeping) spoke quite openly of flight, declaring that every country could be home to a brave man. A year later, under Austrian rule, this same "brave man" turned quisling and,

---

* Quoted in James Morris. *The World of Venice* (London: Faber & Faber, 1960), p. 263.

in the role of commissary, calmly administered the oath of allegiance to his fellow patricians.

But this was in the future. At present, Pesaro was still posing as a patriot—a rather tearful patriot perhaps, but tears were the order of the day. The debate dragged on. Then, while they were arguing and repining, a messenger from the Admiral of the Fleet burst in upon them to say that the French were erecting earthworks and mounting batteries on the shore of the mainland. The Admiral awaited orders. Should he or should he not open fire?

The reaction of the Conference to this message was even greater agitation. Doge Manin paced the room in any agony of indecision and was heard to mutter that they could not even be sure of sleeping safely in their beds that night. Then the sound of distant gunfire told them that the Admiral had found it necessary to act on his own initiative. Yet he was still waiting for an answer, and presently one was sent to him. He was ordered to use force, if necessary, to destroy the enemy's works. But all the sting was taken out of the command by instructing him also to propose terms for an armistice. One can guess how this confession of weakness was received by those rough generals of the Revolution.

At length, on the twelfth of May—and for the last time—the Great Council met. Again the proceedings were contrary to the law, which decreed that no decision was legal unless at least 600 members were present. On this occasion there were only 537, but that was not allowed to stand in the way of the abject surrender which was the wish of the majority. The Doge, in tears again, moved a resolution that the ancient patrician government should be abolished forthwith and that, to comply with Bonaparte's wishes, it should be replaced by a new provisional government of the People.

The resolution was put to the vote. Only twenty councillors were for standing firm; five abstained; 512 voted for surrender. Later, Ludovico Manin was to write in his diary that "at the moment of going to the vote, some shots were heard, which created much timidity." But all was well, for he goes on to say that there was no disorder and that presently the councillors became sufficiently calm to proceed with the voting. And, as it happened, they had nothing to fear. That fusillade was a farewell salute—dare one say derisory?—from the loyal regiment of Schiavoni who, as Bonaparte had commanded, were being shipped back to Dalmatia as hastily as they had been summoned.

When Doge Manin went to bed that night, he removed the white linen cap which was always worn under the ducal *corno* and handed it to his valet, saying sadly, "Take it away. We shall not need it any more." He could not have spoken more truly. It will be remembered that the linen cap was worn so that if, for any reason, a Doge of Venice had to remove his jewelled bonnet, he might not appear uncovered. But that was when the Serenissima still valued her dignity. Now this 120th and last Doge and the majority of the Great Council had not only allowed themselves to be browbeaten by an upstart Revolutionary general, but had displayed an almost indecent haste in obeying his orders. This was a policy of nonresistance carried over the edge of lunacy. To propitiate young Bonaparte the Schiavoni had already been dismissed, and four days after that final meeting of the Great Council it was announced that Venice would now be ruled by a temporary government more in accordance with the new doctrine of Liberty, Equality and Fraternity. The patricians voluntarily renounced their hereditary rights of nobility, and it was decreed that in future all edicts would begin with the words: "In the name of the Sovereign People, the Venetian temporary government—." The Council of Ten was abolished forever; and the three Inquisitors, who had committed no crime against the State, were arrested and sent to gaol. But the *Piombi* and *Pozzi* were thrown open and all prisoners found there—there were very few—were released.

The Venetians may have become a pacific people but there were many who hotly resented this cowardly capitulation. There were angry murmurs and signs of mutiny in the ranks of the *Arsenalotti,* and shots were fired when gondoliers and others rioted in the Piazza. Soon it became evident that Venice could still breed patriots, especially among the working class—the despised rabble. So it was decided that the French must be called in to preserve law and order; the latter graciously consented to cooperate; and—crowning indignity —the Venetians themselves provided transport for their deliverers. At dead of night, as if darkness could hide their shame, they sent forty boats to Mestre, and the 5th and 6th regiments of the Line, under the command of General Baraguey d'Hilliers, were ferried across the lagoon.

At sunrise they landed on the Piazzetta and piled arms in the Square—those raggle-taggle, chattering but indomitable little infantrymen who, Philippe Monnier tells us, exhibited "clamorous and lively delight"—as well they might after this bloodless victory. The Piazza rang with their bugle calls, their revolutionary songs, and rasping orders in French, and then with the steady tramp-tramp of their marching as they debouched from the Square to occupy every key point in the city. At the same time, other units were taking possession of the islands of the lagoon.

To his credit, the pitiful Ludovico Manin refused the presidency of the new municipal government. He retired to a comfortable house which he owned, where he spent the remaining few years of his life in piety and good works and in mourning the fate of the city that he had been too feeble to defend.

Manin was not missed. At a time of violent change, when everything is in the melting pot, collaborators will always be found who see in their country's misfortune a stepping stone to their own advancement. Men of this breed, flaunting the tricoloured cockade in their hats, eagerly seized the reins of power and announced that this was a time for rejoicing.

Accordingly, early in June, there was a festival in the Piazza. In the centre of that vast square which for nearly a thousand years had been the hub of Venetian history, a Tree of Liberty, decked with the red Phrygian cap of the Revolution, was erected; and beneath it, while the troops paraded and the Venetians watched—with laughter, with tears, or in sullen silence, according to their natures—there was a great bonfire. Into the flames went all those things which had no place in the New Order and might remind men of the past: the ducal insignia—mantle, robe, jewelled corno—even *Il Libro d'Oro*. The three red masts which had once borne the banners of Cyprus, Candia and the Morea now flew the red-white-and-blue of Revolutionary France. Placards praising Bonaparte and the French adorned the columns on the Piazzetta, one of which was draped with black as a sign of mourning for Captain Laugier. Thanks were offered to "the glorious French nation and the immortal Bonaparte," and to crown the occasion, a solemn Te Deum was sung in St Mark's.

All coats-of-arms and titles were swept away. And a little later some priceless works of art were swept away too, when a number of pictures, books and manuscripts were transported to Paris. It will be remembered that centuries before, Doria the Genoese had uttered his famous threat that he would bridle the four bronze horses outside the Basilica. Napoleon Bonaparte went one better, for he sent them home to the French capital, where they remained until he himself was bridled after Waterloo. The famous Lion of St Mark from one of the Piazzetta columns accompanied them. But on other representations of the Venetian emblem—at the head of municipal edicts, for example—the words on the open book on which the lion rests his paw were not considered sufficiently democratic. So his *Pax tibi, Marce, Evangelista Meus* was changed to *The Rights of Man and of Citizenship*. . . . "At last," said a gondolier drily, "he has turned over a new leaf."

So there was thanksgiving for subjugation in the Basilica of St Mark, and outside in the crowded Piazza that hollow, organised rejoicing. And on that same unreal but unforgettable day of insincere prayer and forced laughter, the whip was cracked and French troops began to patrol the city. One cannot envy the 5th and 6th of the Line, who were saddled with this duty, or begrudge a certain sympathy to the rank and file of the liberators. For under the surface Venice was seething with shame and anger. Any old soldier who has served in an army of occupation knows what it is to smart under hostile glances: the deceptive smile; the apparently friendly talk; and then, as he turns away, the sudden hardening of the eyes. Night patrols were dangerous, especially in the poorer quarters; and every now and then, at dawn, a dead Frenchman was found in a canal.

The nations of Europe soon took the measure of the situation. In Paris the Venetian Ambassador was handed his passport, for, it was explained, he could hardly represent a country which no longer existed. The other great powers quickly followed suit. Only in Madrid, at the Court of St James and, ironically, by the Sublime Porte at

Constantinople, were her ambassadors retained for a time. But this was only diplomatic courtesy, a polite fiction, and everyone knew it. The Venetian Republic was no more. All her tarnished glory, all that she had fought and striven and sinned for had passed away. And it had all happened in a few days. She had made no struggle for survival, for she was old and sick and rotten through and through.

And so she died.

Epilogue

In October 1797, under the terms of the peace treaty of Campo Formio, Venice was handed over to Austria, together with part of her mainland territory. All that remained of the Veneto after the partition was annexed to the newly formed Cisalpine Republic, a puppet state under the control of France. But during the Napoleonic Wars, Venice was a shuttlecock: French again after the Battle of Austerlitz in 1805; then returned to Austria in 1814 by the Congress of Vienna.

Throughout the long peace which followed Waterloo, the Venetians, hopeless and apathetic, languished under foreign rule. An anonymous Victorian writer tells us that Venice "appeared to have lost all the life and light that had once rendered her so attractive." But at least the hectic gaiety of those nightmare years of the eighteenth century had gone. The clergy and the leading citizens were no longer corrupt, while gradually the men and women of a new generation, free from the vice which in their parents' time had pervaded the whole city, were regaining many of those qualities by which their ancestors had achieved greatness. Above all, they longed for the freedom which they had lost. To do them justice, the Austrians did their best to rule Venice wisely and well. But they met with no response, no cooperation. The Venetians had learned to endure but they were no longer prepared to grovel.

A sad city of memories. Occasionally, it is true, life was enlivened by foreign visitors, of whom, perhaps, the most famous was Lord Byron. A born rebel at odds with the world, one whose death was more glorious than his life, it is strange that he should have been so inordinately sensitive of his crippled foot. The Countess Albrizzi wrote: "Among his peculiar habits was that of never showing himself on foot. He was never seen to walk through the streets of Venice . . . and there are some who assert that he has never seen, excepting from a window, the wonders of the Piazza di San Marco, so powerful in him was the desire not to show himself deformed in any part of his person." On the other hand, he gave full rein to his taste for shocking society and became the hero—or anti-hero—of a whole sheaf of anecdotes, most of which, as it happens, reflect the lighter side of his character: Lord Byron riding on the sandbanks of the Lido with Shelley; Lord Byron spending a whole winter learning Armenian from the monks of San Lazzaro; Lord Byron swimming down the Grand Canal, a valet following with his clothes in a gondola—and swimming across the Grand Canal, fully dressed, merely because he was in a hurry; his lordship in love with Marianna; La Guiccioli in love with his lordship. And then there was that occasion when an infatuated young woman whose advances he had repulsed burst into the Palazzo Mocenigo while he was dining, flourished a table knife and threatened to stab herself if he did not return her passion. Realizing from the calm way in which he went on eating his dinner that he had not the slightest intention of doing so, she very sensibly changed her mind. With a magnificent gesture, she hurled herself from his balcony into the Grand Canal—only to be ignominiously fished out by an astonished gondolier. Everyone said, of course, that the wicked English lord had thrown her in. There was that night, too, when as he was coming out of the Fenice Theatre with yet another lady on his arm, someone was foolish enough to attempt to jostle him. "I was obliged in making way," he wrote, "almost to 'beat a Venetian and traduce the state,' being compelled to regale a person with an English punch in the guts." The great poet's sins blazed to high heaven but he was popular with the Venetians. Perhaps even now, in some forgotten rio, his ghost is chuckling sardonically with the shade of Casanova.

This is the story of the Venetian Republic, which died when it surrendered to Bonaparte. Half a century later there was a valiant attempt to revive it. Venice called herself a republic again, but one cannot breathe life into a corpse. So the attempt was a failure, but it was also remarkable for the fact that at this time, this city of heroes should produce yet another. His name was Daniele Manin and he was a lawyer, the son of a Jew who had been converted to Christianity. There are many great men in the history of Venice, but he was among the noblest of them all, for there are few more inspiring stories of devotion and self-sacrifice. He lived too late. He drew his sword in defence of a state which no longer existed. But, by doing so, he gave the Venetians back their self-respect.

He took his patrician name of Manin from the family which had sponsored him, and in return he gave to the service of Venice everything but his life. Like poor Ludovico, he was a patriot with a deep love for the beautiful city; but, unlike the last of the Doges, whose name he bore, he was ready to suffer for her. In 1848 the Austrians arrested him for treason. But the citizens were behind him and '48 was the Year of Revolutions. With people in half the capitals of Europe manning or storming the barricades, and discontent rife in many parts of the ramshackle empire of the Hapsburgs, the Venetians saw their chance. They rose in revolt, and so effectively that they secured the release of their leader and the expulsion of their oppressors. At once they proclaimed Venice a republic again with Daniele Manin as President, but by the end of the year their enemies had reoccupied the Veneto. Then, in the spring of 1849, the Sardinian Army of Liberation was defeated at Novara, and a strong Austrian force marched on Venice.

Untrained as a soldier, Manin had already raised a Civic Guard; and now, helped by a Neapolitan general, Guglielmo Pepe, this civilian conducted the defence of the city not only with courage and resource, but with such skill as a military organizer that he astonished even his enemies. The provisional government had decided on resistance at all costs, and for seventeen months that army of merchants, shopkeepers and sailors held back all the forces that could be brought against them. A single city defied an empire. This was the great expiation, when the Venetians atoned with their lives for the sins of the eighteenth century and, like their heroic ancestors, won for themselves undying glory.

But the siege of Venice is a tale of endurance and disaster. From the very beginning things went wrong. In May the defenders lost one of their most important outposts. Three years before, the Austrians had constructed the railway causeway which links Venice with the mainland. This had been breached by the Venetians, who had continued to hold a small gun emplacement about 1,500 yards from the shore. But now this fell. And before long they were suffering from food shortage and cholera, while there were traitors in the city who tried to undermine Manin's influence. Then more and heavier guns were brought up and Venice was bombarded from land and sea. She stood alone—against the enemy, against famine and disease. As in the old days, appeals to other countries met with no response, for the nations of Europe no longer regarded Venice as the Serene Republic but as a city in revolt against its rightful sovereign, the Emperor of Austria. Hope faded. Yet still the struggle continued and the *gondolieri* sang as, under heavy fire, they propelled their loads of ammunition up the Grand Canal.

Wordsworth wrote that "no force could violate" Venice, but he was thinking of the great days. For three more weeks the Venetians endured that merciless bombardment; and then, on August 24, 1849, the Austrians granted the garrison an honourable capitulation. There was an amnesty for all except Manin, Pepe and thirty-eight other leaders, and their surrender was accepted by General Gorskowsky. The Austrians reoccupied Venice and a few days later the commander in chief, the redoubtable octogenarian Marshal Radetzky, made his triumphal entry. He found a silent city and an empty Piazza. There was no false rejoicing this time.

Daniele Manin escaped in a French ship. His wife died in Marseilles and he went on alone to lifelong exile in Paris. He had spent all his private fortune on the city he loved so well, and soon he was not only broken in health but almost destitute. Yet still, a leader among the refugees, he continued to work for the unification of Italy. He died in 1857 and was buried in Venice.

After the insurrection the Austrians tightened their grip on the city, and, under the iron rule of Radetzky, hatred was returned for hatred. In the words of a traveller of those days: "The stranger in

Venice finds himself planted between two hostile camps, with merely the choice of sides open to him. Neutrality is solitude in Venice and friendship with neither party: society is exclusive association with the Austrians or with the Italians. The latter do not spare one of their number if he consorts with their masters, and although an alien might expect greater allowance, it is never shown to him. There are all degrees of fineness in Venetian hatred, and after hearing certain persons pour out their gall of bitterness upon the Austrians, you may chance to hear those persons spoken of as tepid in their patriotism by yet more fiery haters."*

In the Risorgimento Venice played no part and gained no imme-diate benefit: that reawakening of the Italian people passed her by. Partly on account of her geographical position and partly because of her success, she had always been a place apart: admired, feared, envied, but never loved by her neighbours. And now she was one of the last to join the new Kingdom of Italy.

In 1859 the King of Sardinia, Vittorio Emanuele II, who for years had been planning and fighting to free the Peninsula from the foreign yoke, allied himself with Napoleon III of France in the struggle for Italian liberty. Together they beat the Austrians in a series of battles, including Magenta and Soferino, while Garibaldi and his Redshirts fought the Neapolitan troops of the House of Bourbon in the South. The Peace of Villafranca brought Lombardy into the new Kingdom of Italy, of which, in 1861, Vittorio Emanuele was proclaimed King, with his capital at Florence. Now only Venice and the Papal States remained outside.

The Venetians, still ruled by Radetzky, had to wait until the summer of 1866, when the Seven Weeks' War broke out between Austria and Prussia. Italy was not slow to ally herself with Bismarck's Prussia and moved her troops into the Veneto. Her army was routed at Custozza, not far from Verona, while in one of the first engage-ments of ironclads the Italian fleet was defeated near Lissa, an island off the coast of Dalmatia. But the Prussians soon brought the war to an end by their overwhelming victory at Sadowa in Bohemia, where the Austrian army was almost annihilated. By the Treaty of Prague,

---

* Quoted in an article in *The National Encyclopaedia.*

Venice became part of the Kingdom of Italy, and in November 1866 King Vittorio Emanuele made his entrance into the city. He received a tumultuous welcome.

The next important event in Venetian history took place on the fourteenth of October, 1902, and it had nothing to do with war or politics. The Campanile fell down. For nearly a thousand years the salt wind from the Adriatic had been steadily wearing away the brickwork, while the timber piles which formed its foundation were rotting in the ooze.

When it was realized that the ancient tower might fall, every possible precaution was taken to prevent loss of life. The midday gun remained silent and no band was allowed to play in the Piazza. But it was taken for granted that some of the loveliest buildings in Venice were doomed. The Campanile was 325 feet high; and well within its range if it fell were the Basilica, the Doge's Palace, the Bridge of Sighs, the Clock Tower, Sansovino's Library of St Mark, and the two columns on the Piazzetta. Everything depended on which way the tower fell.

At dawn on the fourteenth the Piazza was closed, and at five minutes to ten that morning the Campanile collapsed. There was little noise. Very slowly and quietly it telescoped into itself, subsiding almost straight downwards into a huge pile of rubble. A reddish-brown cloud of dust rose high above the rooftops, blotting out everything; but when it cleared, it was discovered that there were no casualties and little damage. The only building destroyed was Sansovino's lovely little Loggetta at the base of the tower, and this has since been replaced by an exact reproduction. Three of the bells were cracked; but the fourth and oldest of them all, the Marangona, which had called the Venetians to work for six hundred years, was found, none the worse for its fall, on top of the mountain of debris. The angel weathervane landed outside the atrium of St Mark's.

A meeting of the city council was called and it was decided that the rubble should be taken out to sea and dumped, and a funeral wreath left floating on the water. But over the Campanile itself there was some difference of opinion. Some councillors flinched from the cost of rebuilding, while there were others who thought that the Piazza looked better without its belfry. But the Mayor of Venice,

Count Grimani, a patrician of the old school, insisted that a new and identical tower must be built. His words are still remembered in the city. *"Com' era, dov' era."* ("As it was and where it was.")

As soon as the decision to rebuild was announced, donations came pouring in from all over the world. The most eminent architects in Italy were engaged; the golden angel's cracked wings were repaired; and His Holiness, Pope Pius X, who had been Patriarch of Venice, had the bells recast at his own expense in the island-foundry of Sant' Elena. Slowly a new Campanile arose, an exact replica of the old one, except that the foundations were considerably stronger. The work took nine years. The original Campanile had been begun on St Mark's Day, April 25, 912. The foundation stone of its successor was laid on St Mark's Day, 1903, and the building was declared complete on St Mark's Day, 1912—exactly one thousand years after the first belfry had begun to rise. To mark the occasion, thousands of pigeons were released to carry the good news to every part of Italy. For the Campanile of St Mark's had always been more than just a belfry. Through good times and bad it had been a watchtower—a guardian— a symbol. It had been an ark which enshrined the very spirit of the Serenissima.

In the First World War 620 bombs were dropped on Venice, but there were hardly any casualties, and although some of her historical monuments were hit, the damage was less than might have been expected. The city was used as a base in the campaign against the Austrians, and at one time it was so near to the front line that observation balloons over the trenches could be seen from the Campanile. October 1917 was the period of greatest danger, for, after the disastrous Austro-German breakthrough at Caporetto, General Cadorna had to face the fact that if the retreat of the Italian Second Army continued westwards as far as the line of the Piave, Venice and much of the Adriatic coast would have to be abandoned.

During Mussolini's dictatorship the outstanding events, so far as Venice was concerned, were the resumption of work (halted by the War) on the new port of Marghera on the mainland and the building of the motorway in 1931. This runs alongside the railway causeway from Mestre until just before it reaches the city. There is a steady double stream of cars to and from the mainland, but for those bound for Venice it is a case of thus far and no farther. It is pleasant to record that at the Piazzale Roma on the edge of the city, all cars are shepherded into an enormous six-storeyed garage, and from there drivers and passengers must travel by water—or walk.

In Daniele Manin's time the Ponte di Rialto was still the only bridge across the Grand Canal; then two iron bridges were constructed: one by the railway station; the other by the Accademia di Belle Arti, at the southern end of the great S-shaped thoroughfare. During the Fascisti regime they were rebuilt in stone and wood respectively, but the Second World War put an end to Italy's era of dictatorship. In May 1945 Benito Mussolini was executed by Italian partisans, and in the same year Venice was occupied by British and New Zealand troops.

Modern Venice, a naval base and one of the principal ports of Italy, is a city of luxury hotels, film and music festivals, and package tours decanting their passengers at the Marco Polo Airport. It is over fifteen hundred years since the forerunners sought sanctuary on the islands of the lagoon, and nearly twelve hundred since they drove the first piles into the mud at Rialto. But never until the present day has Venice been threatened with extinction. We have watched the reduction of her power, the decline of her trade; we have seen her at bay, beset by fire and plague, by internal dissension and foreign enemies. And in all these crises the actual brick and stone and marble have been preserved—sometimes, it would seem, almost miraculously. But now her best friend has turned against her. Her bridegroom has betrayed her at last. For the sea has become her enemy. And the sea has powerful allies.

According to experts, who cannot all be dismissed as alarmists, unless very resolute action is taken over a long period the Venice we know may cease to exist. Such action is already under way. Italia Nostra, a highly efficient organization, not unlike the British National Trust, is doing all it can, together with the regional *Soprintendenza*, the body responsible to the Italian Government for all buildings of historical and artistic importance. But the task to be tackled is gigantic and the funds required make the cost of rebuilding the Campanile look very trivial.

There are several reasons for this tragic state of affairs. One is the abnormally high tides of recent years, with the consequent risk of a serious breach in the Murazzi. There is rising damp. And all the shore of the mainland by Mestre is now one huge industrial complex, belching out chemical fumes which are harmful to the fabric of ancient buildings.

High tides and air pollution: both are contributory causes. But the fact must be faced. Built on rotting piles, Venice is slowly sinking into the mud, and its churches, palaces and houses are disintegrating at an alarming rate. It is thought, too, that the flow of the tides may have been affected by the new deep-water channel for tankers. This has been dredged through the Basin of St Mark to give them a short cut from the open sea to the oil refineries on the mainland. The washes from these tankers and other large vessels pound away at the foundations of this city built for sail and for gondola and *sandolo*. And the big ships are not the only culprits. There are the ferries: the *vaporetti*, which provide a link with the islands, and the useful little water buses which zigzag busily across the Grand Canal. This is the twentieth century. They have their work to do and must be accepted.

The defence of Venice no longer depends on fleets of galleys and men-at-arms. The banner of the Winged Lion no longer rules the Mediterranean. No trumpets sound a farewell fanfare from the Porto di Lido. Yet in one's more romantic moments it is pleasant to imagine that in some office of Italia Nostra, full of files and computers, where a patriot wrestles—not with Turks or Genoese, but with tide tables and statistics—there may, in some unguarded moment, rise in his mind the unspoken thought to which his more naïve ancestors gave vent in a fierce shout: *"Viva San Marco!"*

Bibliography

Bassi, Elean and Trincanato, Egle Renata. *The Palace of the Doges in the History and Art of Venice.* Aldo Martello, Milan, 1961.

Bertarelli, L. V. *Northern Italy from the Alps to Rome.* (The Blue Guides) Macmillan, London, 1927; Rand McNally, New York, 1960.

Bouscaren, T. Lincoln and Ellis, Adam C., S.J. *The Canon Law Digest.* Bruce, Milwaukee, Wisconsin, 1934–1963.

Burckhardt, Jacob. *The Civilization of the Renaissance in Italy.* Allen & Unwin, London, 1928: Harper & Bros., New York, 1958.

Burney, Charles. *Music, Men and Manners in France and Italy—1770.* Folio Society, London, 1969.

Casanova, Giacomo Girolamo de Seingalt. *My Life and Adventures.* Joiner & Steele, London, 1932.

Cellini, Benvenuto. *The Memoirs of Benvenuto Cellini.* (Everyman) Dent, London, 1910; Dutton, New York, 1910.

Clark, Kenneth. *Civilization.* Murray, London, 1969; Harper & Row, New York, 1970.
　　　　　　　　Ruskin Today. Murray, London, 1964.

Colyer, William. *Guide to Venice.* Ward Lock, London. (N.D.)
　　　　　　　Venice, the Lido, and the Islands of the Lagoon. (World Tourist Guide Series) International Publications Service, New York. (N.D.)

Deacon, Richard. *A History of the British Secret Service.* Muller, London, 1969; Taplinger, New York, 1970.

de Sismondi, J. C. L. *A History of the Italian Republics.* (Everyman) Dent, London. (N.D.)

Dick, Stewart. *Master Painters*. Foulis, London and Edinburgh, 1914.

Evelyn, John. *The Diary of John Evelyn*. (Everyman) Dent, London, 1907; Dutton, New York, 1907.

Finlay, George. *History of the Byzantine Empire*. (Everyman) Dent, London, 1913; Dutton, New York, 1906.

Gibbon, Edward. *The Decline and Fall of the Roman Empire*. (Everyman) Dent, London (N.D.); Harcourt, New York, 1960.

Guyard de Berville, Guillaume François. *The Story of the Chevalier Bayard*. Samson Low, London, 1875.

Honour, Hugh. *The Companion Guide to Venice*. (The Companion Guide) Collins, London, 1965.
    Fodor's Venice: A Companion Guide. McKay, New York, 1970.

Hutton, Edward. *The Pageant of Venice*. John Lane, London, 1927.
    Venice and Venetia, 4th ed., rev. Dufour, Chester Springs, Maryland, 1954.

Hyatt, Alfred H. *The Charm of Venice*. Chatto, London, 1924.

Kannik, Preben. *Military Uniforms in Colour*. Blandford, London, 1968; Macmillan, New York, 1968.

Kelly, Francis M. and Schwabe, Randolph. *A Short History of Costume and Armour, Chiefly in England 1066–1800* (2 vols. in 1). Batsford, London, 1925; Blom, New York. (N.D.)

Links, J. G. *Venice for Pleasure*. Bodley Head, London, 1966; Dufour, Chester Springs, Maryland, 1968.

Lucas, E. V. *A Wanderer in Venice*. Methuen, London (N.D.); Macmillan, New York, 1914.

Macaulay, Thomas Babington. *Machiavelli*. (*Essays, Critical and Miscellaneous—The Modern British Essayists*, vol. 1) Carey & Hart, Philadelphia, 1849.

Machiavelli, Niccolo. *Florentine History* (2 vols.). (Everyman) Dent, London, 1905; AMS Press, New York. (N.D.)

Moncrieff, A. R. Hope. *European History*, Vol. II. Gresham, London. (N.D.)

Monnier, Philippe, *Venice in the Eighteenth Century*. Chatto, London, 1910.

Montgomery, Field-Marshal Bernard Law, Viscount of Alamein. *A History of Warfare*. Collins, London, 1968.

Morris, James. *The World of Venice*. Faber, London, 1960; Pantheon, New York, 1960.

Muraro, Michelangelo and Grabar, André. *Treasures of Venice*. (Albert Skira) Times Publications, London (N.D.); World, Cleveland, Ohio, 1963.

Norris, Herbert. *Costumes and Fashion. The Evolution of European Dress through the Earlier Ages*. Dent, London, 1924.

Oliphant, Mrs. (Margaret O.). *The Makers of Venice: Doges, Conquerors, Painters & Men of Letters*. Macmillan, London, 1889; AMS Press, New York. (N.D.)

Oman, C. W. *The Art of War in the Middle Ages.* Cornell University Press, Ithaca, New York, 1960.

        The Byzantine Empire. (The Story of the Nations Series) Fisher Unwin, London, 1892; Putnam's, New York, 1892.

Petrie, Sir Charles Alexander. *Don John of Austria.* Eyre & Spottiswoode, London, 1967.

Polo, Marco. *The Travels of Marco Polo.* Dent, London, 1926; Dutton, New York, 1926.

Power, Eileen. *Mediaeval People.* (University Paperbacks) Methuen, London, 1963; Barnes & Noble, New York, 1963.

Richardson, Mrs. Aubrey (Jerusha D.). *The Doges of Venice.* Methuen, London, 1914.

Robinson, H. Russell, F.S.A. *Oriental Armour.* Herbert Jenkins, London, 1967.

Roscoe, Thomas. *Landscape Annual for 1831: The Tourist in Italy.* Jennings & Chapman, London. (N.D.)

Storti, Amadeo. *A Practical Guide to Venice.*

Symonds, John Addington. *A Venetian Medley.* Oxford University Press, London. (N.D.)

Vasari, Giorgio. *The Lives of the Painters, Sculptors, and Architects* (4 vols.). (Everyman) Dent, London, 1927.

Villehardouin, Geoffroi de and de Joinville, Jean. *Memoirs of the Crusades.* (Everyman) Dent, London, 1955; Dutton, New York, 1955.

von Boehn, Max and Fischel, Oskar. *Modes and Manners* (4 vols. in 2). Harrap, London (N.D.); Blom, New York. (N.D.)

        Vol. I: *From the Decline of the Ancient World to the Renaissance.*
        Vol. II: *The Sixteenth Century.*
        Vol. III: *The Seventeenth Century.*
        Vol. IV: *The Eighteenth Century.*

Wiel, Alethea. *Venice.* (The Story of the Nations Series) Fisher Unwin, London, 1894; Putnam's, New York, 1894.